MILLIONAIRE WOMEN NEXT DOOR

Other Books by Thomas J. Stanley, Ph.D.

Marketing to the Affluent

Selling to the Affluent

Networking with the Affluent and Their Advisors

The Millionaire Next Door (with William D. Danko, Ph.D.)

The Millionaire Mind

MILLIONAIRE *W*OMEN NEXT DOOR

The Many Journeys of
Successful American Businesswomen

THOMAS J. STANLEY, Ph.D.

**Andrews McMeel
Publishing**

Kansas City

05 06 07 08 09 BBG 10 9 8 7 6 5 4 3 2 1

ISBN-13: 978-0-7407-5570-5
ISBN-10: 0-7407-5570-6

Library of Congress Control Number: 2004044873

This publication is designed to provide accurate and authoritative information in regard to the subject matter covered. It is sold with the understanding that neither the author nor the publisher is engaged in rendering legal, investment, accounting, or other professional services. If legal advice or other expert assistance is required, the services of a competent professional person should be sought.

ATTENTION: SCHOOLS AND BUSINESSES
Andrews McMeel books are available at quantity discounts with bulk purchase for educational, business, or sales promotional use. For information, please write to: Special Sales Department, Andrews McMeel Publishing, 4520 Main Street, Kansas City, Missouri 64111.

For Molly, the very best of all best friends

CONTENTS

V.

Part-Time Work, Full-Time Wealth and Satisfaction . . . 225

VI.

Alternate Routes . . . 259

Appendixes . . . 307

TABLES

ACKNOWLEDGMENTS

I am indebted to my wife, Janet, for her guidance, patience, and assistance in helping select concepts and case studies and for her special talent in shaping this manuscript.

I also acknowledge the superb contribution of my children. Dr. Sarah S. Fallaw provided much food for thought regarding life as well as job-related satisfaction measures and concepts. Brad Stanley's inputs about topic selection were invaluable. He also won the "What Title?" contest.

Once again, the Survey Research Center, Institute for Behavioral Research, University of Georgia, did an outstanding job collecting and tabulating the survey data for this book. Special thanks are accorded to Dr. James J. Bason, director of the Survey Research Center; Kathleen J. Shinholser, "key statistician and number cruncher"; Linda J. White; Zelda R. McDowell; Mary Ann Mauney; and Cindy Burroughs.

Acknowledged is the extraordinary effort and brilliant work carried out by Heather Breedlove, CPA, and Teresa Miller, CPA, JD, in crunching numbers.

I am most appreciative and grateful to Frank "Provin" Bulloch and his colleagues at the Edwards Institute for Social Research for designing and developing the content analysis of the factors that account for success.

John Connerat and Tim Fallaw of Connerat and Fallaw did an outstanding job in enhancing the quality control system for this project.

And again, a million thank-yous to Bill Marianes of Troutman Sanders, Atlanta, for his great empathy and expertise in representing me.

I owe a deep debt of gratitude to my editor, Chris Schillig, for her sage editorial comments and superb efforts in molding this manuscript.

Many, many thank-yous are accorded to Tom Thornton, president of Andrews McMeel Publishing, for his continued interest in and support of my work.

Special thanks go out to Teddy "Scoop" Graham, Sharon Weaver, and Kerry Spivey for their help in editing and word processing.

I.

WOMEN IN BUSINESS

CHAPTER 1

An Introduction to Millionaire Women Next Door

Women! . . . Women in business . . . business owners . . .
disastrous. . . . Dangerous for you to excite these people.
Women [as self-employed business owners] have no place in busi-
ness. . . . Personal experience . . . irresponsible for you to glo-
rify these women. . . . The few who succeed are anomalies. . . .
You had better pick another topic. . . . They are only wed to
their businesses. . . . Unmarried. . . . Unkind. . . . Uncaring. . . .
Tyrannical misers. . . . Uncontrollable. . . . Unliked. . . . Unde-
sirable. . . . Unattractive. . . . Unwanted. . . . A bunch of angry,
revenge-seeking workaholics. Women . . . no business being in
business!

*T*he fellow who uttered these words intercepted me shortly
after I made a presentation about the contents of this book. I
refer to him here as Mr. A. Lota-Uns or Al, for short. As he
spoke, I noticed that his face became red while veins bulged from his neck
and temples. Apparently, the content of my presentation angered him.

While Al was lecturing me, I asked myself how it was possible that
everything he had personally experienced regarding "women in business"
was at odds with the empirical data I had collected, which serves as the
basis for this book.[1] Could it be that a few bitter experiences had clouded
his perception? My research indicates that he is dead wrong. How did

---

[1] For information about sources of data and sampling methods, see the Technical Appendix, page 309.

successful self-made businesswomen achieve their wealth? Not one of the women studied mentioned motivations of anger, revenge, resentment, or bitterness. Many discussed forgiving those who had harmed them and forgetting the past. Most receive considerable satisfaction from helping others. They are living proof that accumulating wealth and providing financial assistance to others are not mutually exclusive.

Why did these women provide so much detailed and candid information for this book? Note that not one of them asked that their real names be used. Most participated because they wanted to share their insights, not for glory. They did it to help others who wish to become independent. Of course, the benefit of responding anonymously may have also encouraged many of these women to be very frank about their journeys to success.

It did not concern me that Al's beliefs were at odds with my own findings. But what if young, impressionable women are indoctrinated into believing such things? What if they are taught that women who succeed in business are destined to become the miserable people Al described? These young women will be very reluctant to venture into the world of the self-employed. Imagine what it's like to be the daughter of an Al or others like him. What chance will these women have to succeed on their own in the economic arena?

Most of the women profiled herein report that their parents had a different mind-set than the Als of this world. When asked about their family life growing up, they revealed that their parents encouraged them to take the initiative, to seek out leadership roles. These parents also taught their daughters to have empathy for the needs of others, and they had the utmost respect for their children. Successful women whose parents provided them with such a nurturing environment (Alpha women) outnumber the other type (Beta women) by a ratio of nearly four to one. This is detailed in chapter 4, "The Parents of Successful Businesswomen"; chapter 5, "Beta Women: Beating the Odds Against Succeeding"; and chapter 6, "Alpha Women vs. Beta Women."

Two of Al's derogatory adjectives were of particular interest to me: *unkind* and *uncaring*. High-income-producing women, particularly those who are business owners, give significantly more money to noble causes than do their male counterparts (see chapter 3). Their high propensity for giving generously to charitable organizations is not only confirmed by my own survey but also well documented in the Internal Revenue Service's data. Furthermore, it is not the only form of kindness where women outpace men. Self-made millionaire women who are business owners give more than three times the percentage of their incomes to their relatives than do men (see chapter 9).

Al also claims that businesswomen are misers, but there is nothing miserly about their eleemosynary habits. However, I have found that within the same age and income cohorts, those who are frugal with regard to consumption give a higher percentage of their income to noble causes. It seems that giving and wealth building are not mutually exclusive among those who are best at accumulating wealth and have more to give than hyperconsumers. These findings are detailed in chapter 7, "Generous *and* Wealthy?" and chapter 8, "Learning to Give."

My data show that self-made millionaire women succeeded in business because they worked hard and they worked smarter. It is indeed unfortunate that we do not have enough of them in our economy; only about one in ten businesses with annual revenues of $1 million or more in America are owned and managed by women. This ratio excludes all those women who inherited a business from their relatives or husbands. It also excludes those businesses owned by women in name only that are in reality run by their husbands. Yet things are changing in the right direction. More and more parents now hold the sorts of beliefs about their daughters that the parents of most of the women profiled in this book did. But still the beliefs of the A. Lota-Uns type die hard. Hopefully, my work will help eradicate such primitive ideas.

BUT WHAT IF?

Some women have asked me, "But what if I have no interest in owning a business in the context of a full-time job?" In response, I profiled two business owners who work part-time, rarely more than twenty hours a week (chapters 13 and 14). Both own income-producing real estate.

I also added a chapter on the sales profession (chapter 15). The field of commission sales often provides a more level playing ground for women who wish to be judged purely on productivity. In addition, chapter 16 profiles several wealthy educators. Yes, teachers and professors. They are a frugal segment of the population, more prone to investing than shopping. They tend to support noble causes generously. Educators, especially women educators, have a higher than average propensity to accumulate wealth. There is also a chapter about those women who manage the "family office." Some call them housewives because they don't work outside the home, but they are the ones responsible for their household being positioned far above the norm in terms of wealth than for those in their income and age cohort. In essence, these women are self-employed as scholars of budget planning, accounting, and investing for their families (chapter 17).

THE MEANING OF BEING RICH

You may have a different mind-set from the self-made millionaire businesswomen I have studied. People often ask me, "Why accumulate wealth and then not spend it on oneself?" Hyperspending is at odds with the goals and motives of these women. If you want to become wealthy to consume, you are unlikely to ever be rich. Nearly all of the self-made millionaire women I have interviewed became financially successful because they fervently wanted to be independent. They were never hyperconsumers, nor did they ever feel deprived because they didn't own expensive cars or clothes. In fact, one of their goals is not to reveal that they are rich: never to drive rich, dress rich, or behave in any manner that would reveal their true wealth. Even after accumulating millions of dollars, they are still rather frugal regarding consumer spending. So what do they plan to do with their wealth? Chapter 2, "What Does It Mean to Be Rich?" answers this and many other related questions. Most of these women have absolutely no interest in joining a top-notch country club. The small minority who do are outnumbered by those who do not by a ratio of better than thirteen to one. In sharp contrast, for every 100 of the self-made millionaire women who indicated that making significant contributions to charities and noble causes is an unimportant use of their money, an estimated 750 felt that such a goal is important. If you don't agree with these women, you may wish to reassess the odds that you could become a millionaire.

BE WARY

Before you sign that "unwritten contract of a lifetime" to be a housewife, read chapter 10, "The High Price of Being Controlled." Just because your husband's parents own a family business do not assume that you and their son will one day take over its ownership. Even mature businesses can and often do fail. What if twenty years from now your in-laws are reluctant to transfer ownership to the next generation? Perhaps they will want to sell the business to strangers. If they do, how are you and your husband going to earn a living? Be sure to read "The Case of Fay J. Naivete." Fay and her husband, Rodney, worked for his parents' business for almost twenty years, and it was promised to them. Now ask Fay about promises never kept. Her case is must-reading for women contemplating giving up their economic independence. You should learn never to be fully dependent on others, no matter how sincere their promises. Too many women have paid the high price of being controlled.

Show Me the Objective Data

What if your daughter, Sally, is considering opening an antiques store or some other "trendy" type of retail operation? Before she does, I strongly urge her to review the profitability data for small businesses contained in chapter 12, "Choosing a Business: Opting for Self-Employment." There are more than 100,000 antiques stores, including used-furniture outlets, in this country. The average annual net income generated is only $1,162. Of the 153 categories of businesses profiled, antiques stores ranked 143 in regard to this profitability measure. Far too often inexperienced women open antiques stores because they love antiques, but business ownership and hobbies don't always make good partners.

Perhaps your Sally should become a veterinarian. Why not use some of that money your dad left her for vet school tuition? This type of small business ranks fifth out of the 153 profiled. Then, when you are looking for the ideal graduation gift for Sally, you may want to read chapter 11, "The Gift of Gifts: Demonstrating Empathy for the Real Needs of People."

Shame on You

There is no good reason for you to think that you are "not cut out to be a business owner." Some fear is understandable, but you don't necessarily have to give up your current job to be a business owner. It is not an either-or thing. The characters in chapter 13, "Brian's Journey: From Hunter-Gatherer to Cultivator of Wealth," and chapter 14, "Ann Lawton Hills," became wealthy operating their real estate businesses on a part-time basis. You can do what they did and still work your own day job, but it's much easier if you enjoy the business called income-producing real estate.

And please don't tell me again that you lack the background to succeed in that field. Brian started out at economic ground zero, and Ann Hills began her real estate business when she was in her mid-forties. Neither one ever spent a day in business school. Aren't you growing tired of being among the ranks of hunter-gatherers? Brian and Ann are cultivators of wealth. Do you enjoy your hyperconsumption lifestyle so much that you must fly out of town every week to earn a paycheck to pay your bills? You are not too young to begin making the transformation to a cultivator of wealth. Both Brian and Ann earn money from their rental properties even when they are at home sleeping! Think about that the next time you are ten thousand miles from home, surrounded by strangers, and flying in dreadful weather.

It is up to you. Do you want to spend your life as a hunter and gatherer of income, earning a million mileage points? Or do you want to join the ranks of those financially independent folks? They make their own decisions about their next destination. Right now, you and your career are essentially corporate property. Neither one of you has the luxury of self-determination.

A PORTRAIT OF
SELF-EMPLOYED MILLIONAIRE BUSINESSWOMEN

- We are forty-nine years old[2] (median, defined as 50th percentile), wives, and mothers.[3]
- Typically, we wake up at 5:58 A.M. (median) and retire for the evening at 10:32 P.M. About one in four of us wakes up before 5:45 A.M.; one in twenty rises after 7:25 A.M. One in ten of us retires for

---

[2] The average age for this millionaire group is fifty-two.
[3] Eight in ten (81 percent) are mothers.

the evening later than midnight. Typically, we sleep for just under seven and a half hours per night.

- We usually work forty-nine hours and eighteen minutes a week (median). Only one in ten of us works more than sixty-nine hours per week.
- Typically, we exercise for about three and a half hours (median) per week.
- Our households' total annual realized (taxable) income is $240,217 (median),[4] while our average income is $413,960. Note that those of us with incomes of $500,000 to $999,000 (14 percent) and $1,000,000 or more (11 percent) skew the average upward.
- On average, we earn 71 percent of our households' income.
- We have a household net worth of just under $2.9 million (median), or about forty times the median net worth of the typical American household. On average, our net worth is $4.75 million. About one in twelve (approximately 8 percent) of us has a net worth in excess of $10 million. These decamillionaires skew our average net worth figure upward.
- Only one in twenty of us has never been married. Nearly one in five (18 percent) of us is currently divorced. Of those of us who are currently married, fully one-half have been divorced at least once. Many of us report that our former husbands were exploitive and narcissistic.
- Most of us (60.3 percent) are college graduates. A quarter of us (25.9 percent) hold advanced degrees. About one in four (26.3 percent) attended college but never completed our studies. Just over one-half (51 percent) who completed college paid 100 percent of our own tuition and fees.
- Fewer than one in five (19 percent) of us ever attended a private school of any type, but 54 percent of us have paid the private school tuition for our grandchildren.
- Nearly all (98 percent) of us are home owners. About one in three (34 percent) has a zero mortgage balance on her home; one in five has a balance under $100,000; and only 4 percent have a balance of $500,000 or more.

---

[4] That is more than five times the median income for all households in this country.

- We are significantly more likely than our male counterparts to: develop a detailed accounting system for tracking all household expenditures; research more thoroughly the stocks we are considering as additions to our portfolios; hold stocks longer; use the services of investment counselors, especially those affiliated with trust or commercial investment companies and fee-based financial planners; have a well-defined set of both short- and long-term investment-return goals.

- For those of us who are currently married, only one in twenty reports that her husband has the main responsibility for making financial decisions concerning household budgeting, financial planning, investing, selection of financial advisers, and the like. But 46 percent report that these decisions are made jointly.

- We are supporters of noble causes. On average we donate nearly 7 percent of our annual incomes. That is nearly 3 ½ times the average (about 2 percent) for all households in America.

- We are frugal. The most we've ever spent on a suit for ourselves or anyone else in our families was $400 (median); the figure is $139 for a pair of shoes. More than four in five of us (81 percent) develop a detailed shopping list before grocery shopping.

- In terms of most measures of frugality, we are more frugal than men. For example, we are twice as likely (56 percent versus 26 percent) to have spent time searching for a foreclosed property as a "new home" for our families. And we are significantly more likely (58 percent versus 48 percent) to have our furniture reupholstered or refinished instead of buying new. We have switched long-distance telephone companies more often (61 percent versus 51 percent) to save money. We are significantly more likely to have clothing mended or altered instead of buying new (52 percent versus 37 percent).

- Most of us (56 percent) are not members of a country club, nor is anyone else in our households.

- Nearly seven in ten (69 percent) of us took on leadership roles before becoming teenagers.

- We have disciplined ourselves to look forward to the future, but almost all of us have had some adversity and reversals in life. However, only one in five of us ever spends time thinking about how things could have been.

- We are goal oriented. We persevere. As one successful self-employed woman noted:

  Always kept my eyes on the goal. . . . If you look to the side, that's where you're going. . . . I constantly enhance the belief in my personal ability. . . . Many concerns when I first went solo [opted for self-employment] . . . but ever since, I walk to work every day saying over and over, "I can do whatever I want to do. . . . I can be whatever I want to be. The power and the strength are within me." . . . Trust, always trust, your own intuition, your inner guide.

THE NEED

Why write another book that profiles millionaires? Why shouldn't you just read *The Millionaire Next Door?* The millionaires in that book were studied in detail, but the majority (92 percent) were men, and two-thirds were self-employed. So I felt that it was indeed time for successful businesswomen of the self-made variety to be heard.

For comparative purposes, I have incorporated data and a few case studies about successful men because I felt these were especially informative. All the millionaires profiled herein, women and men, have a household net worth of between $1 million and $25 million. More than 90 percent of the millionaires in America today are within this interval.

Why is the focus of this book on women who are self-made business owners? Of all the high-income vocations in America, self-employed business owners have the highest probability of becoming financially independent. In fact, according to government statistics, those who are self-employed have about five times as much accumulated net worth as those who work for others.

The choice to own and manage your own business is not all about income and wealth. It also involves the desire for independence, satisfaction, and self-actualization. The single most important reason that these women opted for self-employment is that they believed it would allow them to utilize their skills and aptitudes freely to achieve their goals.

Fully 95 percent of these women report that their chosen vocation provides them with a great deal of satisfaction—a satisfaction that is, in fact, related to their consumption habits. Those with the highest levels of satisfaction in their lives tend to spend the smallest percentage of their incomes on consumer goods and services, especially credit services.

The majority of the women profiled are wealth accumulators; they are cultivators of wealth, or Balance Sheet Affluent. In objective terms, people in this category have at least twice the level of net worth (household) than would be expected according to the wealth equation:[5]

Expected net worth = 1/10 (age) x annual realized income

Most Americans are different. They are Income Statement Affluent, hunters and gatherers rather than cultivators. They have one-half or less of the level of wealth predicted by the equation. They have to go to work, day after day, hunting and gathering income, because they have not accumulated enough wealth to do otherwise. In sharp contrast, most of the women profiled in this book do not have to work. They do so because they enjoy their work, but they have the freedom to determine how to allocate both their time and their money. Unfortunately, most Americans will never achieve this level of freedom.

Are we really in the land of the free? Not if most Americans do not have enough wealth accumulated independent of the equity in their homes and automobiles to stop hunting and gathering for just one year. I estimate that the median net worth of the typical American household is $72,000. If you subtract the equity in their homes and automobiles, there's little left. How long could your household survive with just over $20,000 stored up?

Most Americans are not free. They are chained to paychecks, dependent on the income that they think will regularly appear. But what happens when the checks vanish? Then these hunter-gatherers must go into survival mode and find a new source of sustenance, a new hunting ground. In most cases, they will be hunting and gathering for a lifetime.

The women profiled herein will not tolerate such an existence. They are a different breed. They are free. They are cultivators of wealth and satisfied with life. They are in control of their own destiny. They are leaders, and this nation needs a great many more of them.

---

[5] Expected net worth excludes inheritance. Income refers to one's realized pretax annual household income.

CHAPTER 2

What Does It Mean to Be Rich?

ODE TO JESSIE BRIDGES

Dr. Stanley, this article reads like a page from your book—
which I enjoyed very much!

CHARLOTTE OF KELSO, WASHINGTON

*T*his note on a bright fuchsia Post-it was attached to a news-paper article that profiled an extraordinary woman. The headline read, "Widow Leaves $2M to Local Charities" (Eric Apalategui, *Daily News*, Longview, Washington, January 20, 2001, pp. A1, A4).

The headline by no means told the whole story. If the widow had inherited $10 million from her ancestors or if her late husband was the CEO and a large shareholder of a Fortune 500 company, the $2 million might not be newsworthy. But the donor, Mrs. Jessie Bridges, was a self-made millionaire who spent much of her adult life as a bookkeeper, and she had lived for fifty years in the same nondescript single-story home located in a lower-middle-class neighborhood.

These are just some of the facts about Jessie Bridges, a charter member of the Balance Sheet Affluent Club. Readers of the newspaper article about her, including her friends, had never known that she was a millionaire. One of her closest friends and neighbors was quoted as saying,

Jessie kind of kept to herself somewhat, and [was] on the quiet side. . . . To think that I lived next door to a millionaire—not a whole lot of people can say that.

How is it possible that someone who spent much of her career as a bookkeeper became a multimillionaire? Note that Mrs. Bridges's net worth exceeded $2 million. In addition to the $2 million she gave posthumously to noble causes, she also left considerable sums to her friends.

Jessie Bridges's case is not uncommon among millionaire businesswomen. She always followed a frugal lifestyle. She saved and invested her earnings wisely. Mrs. Bridges had money to invest in publicly traded common stocks because of her frugal consumption habits.

The majority of those in the Balance Sheet Affluent Club share another characteristic with Mrs. Bridges—they are business owners. How did bookkeeper Jessie Bridges make the transition to business owner? She accomplished something that many of these successful respondents have told me about. They assert that in a lifetime, at least two or three "great economic opportunities" will reveal themselves to those who are vigilant. And Mrs. Bridges was indeed vigilant.

This widow was nearly sixty years of age and employed as a bookkeeper before she became a business owner. She and two partners invested their savings in the plumbing and heating contracting business they bought from their employer. After all, who knows more about the profitability of a business than its bookkeeper? Many successful businesswomen used their knowledge of their employers' businesses and invested savings there. Thus, they leveraged these resources into business ownership. When people ask me about the type of business they should consider owning, I often advise them to consider purchasing their employer's business.

Some of you might be thinking, "How did a bookkeeper have enough money to buy a significant portion of a heating and plumbing contracting business?" Jessie was always more than a bookkeeper. She was an outstanding money manager, a superlative budgeter, and an excellent research-oriented investor—an investor and saver in an economy filled with hyperconsumers. But Jessie Bridges never felt deprived. Most people like her are happy because their goal is to be independent, and she more than fulfilled that dream.

According to her friends and neighbors, she was a happy and contented woman. Plus, Jessie was a proud person with high self-esteem. Happiness, pride, and high self-esteem are qualities possessed by the majority of women profiled herein. How did they attain these qualities? They set certain goals for themselves, such as becoming self-reliant and financially independent through owning and operating a business. They achieved these goals, and as a result, they are satisfied, proud, and confident.

Jessie Bridges lived a full and wonderful life. Yes, it is possible to be satisfied with your life without indulging yourself with material artifacts. People like Jessie experience great satisfaction without gorging themselves on expensive homes, custom vehicles, boats, showy jewelry, designer furniture, and other luxuries. People generally allocate their resources in ways that they believe will give them the greatest pleasure. How did Mrs. Bridges spend her income, wealth, and time? She enjoyed her work. Owning and operating a successful business enhanced her self-esteem. In addition, Jessie was a "cheap date." Like most of her cohorts, she derived much happiness from activities that are inexpensive yet enjoyable. She was active in various groups at her church and, like the majority of millionaires, enjoyed gardening. She also took pleasure in walking and sewing. It was often difficult for her to find clothing that perfectly fit her under-five-foot frame, but she had no difficulty tailoring the off-the-rack clothing she purchased.

Of course, Jessie's happiness was derived from more than sewing and gardening. She loved spending time with her many friends, and that's one of several reasons why she never moved to a more exclusive neighborhood. Many of her neighbors were among her very best friends. Jessie valued her friendships so much that she included them in her estate plan. She also included her church as a beneficiary.

Four noble causes received $500,000 each from Mrs. Bridges's estate: the local hospice and college foundations, the Salvation Army, and the YMCA. Jessie also willed $200,000 to a medical center. Her frugal lifestyle directly enhanced the causes of several worthy charities. In this regard, we can call her unselfish and refer to Jessie as kind, considerate, and compassionate. In a nutshell, Mrs. Bridges demonstrated considerable empathy for the needs of other people. There is a highly significant correlation between one's position on the empathy scale and one's level of happiness. People who have great empathy tend to be happy folks.

IT'S BETTER THAT NO ONE KNOWS!

Another reason that Jessie never moved to a more exclusive neighborhood—a reason she shares with other charter members of the Balance Sheet Affluent Club—is that there are great benefits to be achieved when no one knows you are a millionaire. The wealthy women I have interviewed have some strong opinions regarding this question. Many enjoy living in modest, middle-class, or even, as in the case of Mrs. Bridges, working-class neighborhoods. Their neighbors have no idea that the woman next door is a multimillionaire.

Imagine that you are a multimillionaire like Mrs. Bridges. You live in a modest home surrounded by blue-collar and lower- to middle-class neighbors. Many of them are among your very best friends. Then one day you happen to be playing cards with several neighbors and the subject of retirement pops up. You mention that you could retire at any time. Your friends ask innocently, "How is that possible?" Your answer is simple and straightforward, "Because I am frugal, and I invested wisely, so today I'm worth two, three, five, even ten million or more." Before long the entire neighborhood will know via the grapevine that you are a millionaire living among those who have a net worth, on average, of less than $100,000, less than 5 percent of what you are worth. Wouldn't your life in the neighborhood be different then?

Women like Mrs. Bridges never feel a need to brag about their financial success. On the contrary, they deliberately and proactively guard against revealing their economic circumstances. Being wealthy among those with modest means can cause problems. You fear that revealing yourself as a millionaire might conjure up jealousy and resentment from both neighbors and friends. You might have to consider why several neighbors are becoming more and more friendly. Could it be that they want to be included in your estate plan? Is it possible that they are just setting you up for a loan request? When you dine out with a few neighbors, you wonder if they expect you to pick up the entire tab.

Is it any surprise that the Mrs. Bridgeses of the world keep their economic status a secret? It's better to be rich and not act, dress, drive, eat, live, or spend rich. This greatly reduces the probability that jealousy might get between you and your neighbors, friends, or employees.

If those in your circle of friends and acquaintances don't know you're rich, their expectations of you may not be so high. You are not expected to live in a luxury home, wear expensive clothing, donate large sums of money to charity, or buy all of them lunch and dinner.

What is expected of you? You just act like all the other neighbors and friends that make up your world. After all, you are the prototypical balance sheet millionaire. You are the owner and manager of a nondescript business, such as a dirt contractor, an executive-staffing agency, a janitorial service, or a heating and air-conditioning contractor. One of the main reasons you have wealth is that you have low overhead. This applies to running both your household and your business efficiently. What if you were in a different position?

What if you were a senior officer in a large public corporation? You might be expected to live in a home that was bigger, more luxurious, and more costly than that of any of the executives who work for you. Could you imagine this senior executive living in a home similar to Mrs. Bridges's? Just envision a well-paid surgeon, trial lawyer, or movie star living in the one-thousand-square-foot home next to Mrs. Bridges. No, this will not happen. Successful executives, surgeons, attorneys, professional ball players, movie celebrities, and the like are expected to earn big dollars. Thus, they feel that people expect them to demonstrate their success by the size and price of their homes. Their egos often dictate a simple message to their brains over and over: "Big house is required . . . big house is required." Are you really better than your competition? Then prove it by outspending them.

SOME OF THE WAYS OF GIVING

Why do people like Mrs. Bridges tend to donate much more of their resources to local causes than to charities that have national or even international reputations—that is, those that are well capitalized and employ large professional staffs? These women have a very strong sense of community, and they are locally oriented. Also, they see their role as helping certain types of noble causes—those that are understaffed, underfunded, underappreciated, nonelitist, and staffed or supported by women like themselves.

Wealthy women often tell me that some of those well-heeled, prestigious charities are staffed by elitists: "They want my donations, but they don't want me on their boards." Many successful businesswomen are turned off by the images that these so-called elitist causes portray. The philanthropic orientation of Mrs. Bridges and her kind is based purely on their need to help others through acts of kindness. Yet many have told me that too often, noble causes become transformed over time. Charities may begin with the noblest of intentions, to raise funds to help others, but over time, they become a haven for those who wish to enhance their image by being associated with causes that have high visibility. Thus, the organization winds up giving more free publicity to these people than it receives from acts of true kindness.

It is amazing how few of the women profiled herein have ever been asked to serve on the local boards of some of the biggest household names in philanthropy. One woman summed it up this way:

> *Better chance to be on that board? . . . If your folks booked passage on the* Mayflower. . . . *Though you'd get on it if you had a trust fund.*

This is particularly shocking since many of these millionaire business owners are among the very best candidates for such positions, having become millionaires purely by their own intellect and hard work. Almost all did it without an ounce of financial assistance from anyone. They are by definition capable leaders, proven generators of revenue, great money managers, and wise investors. Most importantly, they have great empathy for the needs of other people and have a demonstrated desire to contribute to noble causes.

Women like Mrs. Bridges often bequeath considerable sums of their money to charitable organizations they had little or no contact with during their lives. There are several reasons for this. First, they are very active readers of local newspapers and other locally based print media. Highly credible news stories about the good deeds done by local causes are of particular interest to them, and it's not unusual for them to keep files of newspaper stories about the efforts of these groups.

The impressions made by these news accounts are key. "Good press" explains which organizations will be included in the estate plans of women like Jessie. Since even the most astute fund-raisers would overlook a "Mrs. Bridges," charitable organizations need people who can help them get their good deeds reported in the press. Had they not "gotten good press," Mrs. Bridges would not have been able to identify or appreciate the organizations to which she would bequeath her wealth.

There are two ways to fish for wealthy benefactors. You can "chase the fish" with solicitations, or you can do good public relations and let the fish chase the fishing boat!

There is a reason why some of these women leave money to organizations with which they had little or no contact during their lives. They give money posthumously to organizations that supported their own terminal care.

These women never want to be a burden to others. They want to pay for their own long-term or terminal care and that required for their relatives. Even the thought of being disabled and dependent on the whims of a Medicare-based organization frightens them. Therefore, they fund and plan their own terminal care, and they tend to use their own money, not the government's. That is one major reason why they hold on to their wealth.

There is a final reason for the posthumous generosity of women like Mrs. Bridges. If they donated considerable amounts to dozens of charities while still living, it would greatly increase the probability that "everyone in town would know" that they were multimillionaires. The Mrs. Bridges types never want this to happen, and they have no need for their good deeds to be recognized while they are still living. Their satisfaction comes from giving, not from being praised. They recognize the real value of money, and they are able to leverage their wealth. Their hard work, frugal lifestyle, and investing skills will translate into many future years of helping their relatives and supporting noble causes.

ON THE BENEFITS OF BEING RICH

During a recent seminar, I began the program by describing Jessie Bridges. Immediately a hand was raised. The audience member made a familiar argument:

She was a widow with no close relatives . . . had a bookkeeper's background. She was comfortable living in a blue-collar world.

That's just the introduction to the hypothesis that Jessie Bridges was an outlier in the data, a freak or quirk in a high-consumption society. Then the same audience member added:

Who else was she going to give her money to? . . . [She had] no family. So, she saved a lot of money . . . she was a widow. If I were a widow, I would be careful about spending. What about the other millionaire women? What about the ones that are married? The well educated? The middle-class women? Surely they don't give so much away to charity, right?

Wrong! When it comes to giving, Mrs. Bridges was no outlier in the data pool. She had a lot in common with the other wealthy business owners. Most of the women who are profiled here (95 percent) are married or were married, and most have children. Also, the majority have several close relatives, most attended college, and most are from middle-class backgrounds.

Given that profile, you may be thinking that perhaps the audience member had a point. Unlike Mrs. Bridges, these wealthy women have families. You probably suspect that the women will eventually distribute all their wealth to their sons and daughters, husbands, cousins, and in-laws. If this is your prediction, you are wrong. The other members of her cohort are every bit as charitable as Jessie Bridges.

I asked millionaire businesswomen across America about the benefits of being wealthy. The benefits they describe give important insights into how they think. Virtually all asserted that being wealthy allowed them to distribute their wealth in ways that give them the greatest satisfaction, including generous donations to noble causes and gifts to family and friends. For most millionaire women business owners, empathy for others has a tremendous influence on how they distribute and how they intend to distribute their wealth.

Would you like to determine if your views about the definition and benefits of being wealthy are congruent with those of these millionaire respondents? Then take out paper and pen and write down the minimum level of net worth that you feel would be necessary for you to consider yourself wealthy. Now compare that with the dollar threshold at which these self-made millionaire women considered themselves wealthy. The single most often mentioned threshold figure for these respondents was $5 million. In other words, it would take $5 million in net worth (total current value of all assets less any liabilities) for them to feel that they were wealthy and financially independent. The median dollar threshold was about $4.4 million. Roughly one in ten had a threshold of $15 million or more. Take note that for these millionaire respondents, another benefit of being wealthy is being financially independent. For almost all of these women, becoming financially independent was a major goal. They did not want to be dependent on others for income, and the women in this category are able to live for the rest of their lives without worrying about making ends meet.

But once they reach their goal of being financially independent, then what? These women have very different views from the general population about the benefits of being wealthy. Overall, like Mrs. Bridges, they are not enamored with consuming. In fact, an enhanced-consumption lifestyle is very low on their list of the benefits of becoming wealthy. Yet when I tell my audiences that most self-made wealthy women are not hyperspenders, the response is quite predictable:

What is the use of being rich if you are not going to enjoy it!

Allow me to interpret the meaning of "enjoying it." For most people, "enjoying the money" means spending a lot of it on oneself. It translates into bigger, more expensive homes, luxury automobiles, expensive clothing, and other possessions. But not for most self-made wealthy women. Does this mean that they are unhappy? Unsatisfied? Are they miserable misers who just can't part with their first dollar? In fact, according to my research, the large majority of these women are very satisfied. Most are happy. They are content because they have fulfilled their need to be self-reliant and have become self-made affluent. They have discovered that happiness can be achieved—and, actually, greatly enhanced—without their becoming hyperconsumers. For most of these women, a lot of satisfaction comes from their families, from reaching or exceeding their goals, from helping noble causes, and from their vocations, which have provided a clear path to financial independence. Their success in business also greatly enhanced these women's self-esteem and pride.

What about your number? Is your aim high because you see visions of a BMW 7 Series in your driveway? A membership in the top country club? A multimillion-dollar home? A luxury villa in Europe? Expensive art in your living room? If such factors underlie your threshold, keep in mind what I have learned from more than thirty years of studying self-made millionaires.

First, their superordinate goal relates more to financial independence and the pride of unsubsidized achievements than to owning a gallery of expensive consumer artifacts. Second, most self-made millionaires, especially the women in this category, have another thing in common. They are not driven by a bad case of the me-me-mes. That is, their satisfaction more often comes from leading others, being a mentor to others, giving to others, providing for others, and helping others. Thus, it's not the luxury goods or the me-me-mes that highlight these millionaires' lifestyles. Their focus is much more about the you-you-yous.

Just for a few minutes, assume that you are now financially independent—that is, you are a millionaire worth, say, $5 million. My question is quite simple:

What would you do with $5 million?

You may wish to write down your responses before you read about how self-made millionaires would allocate their wealth. How important would the following consumption-related behaviors be in light of your millionaire status? Would it be very important to:

- Purchase a luxurious home?
- Purchase an exquisite vacation and/or retirement home?
- Join a top-notch country club?
- Acquire high-quality art or antiques?
- Purchase a top-of-the-line automobile?

If your answer to any of these questions was yes, then your desires are at odds with those of most of these self-made affluent women, as outlined in Table 2-1.

Only 20 percent of the wealthy women responded that "purchasing a more luxurious home" was important; 60 percent responded with "unimportant." In other words, there were three millionaires who

TABLE 2-1

THE BENEFITS OF BEING WEALTHY ACCORDING TO MILLIONAIRE BUSINESSWOMEN: FOCUS ON OTHERS VS. FOCUS ON SELF[1]

Benefits of Being Wealthy	% Rating Important[2]	Unimportant	Ratio: Important to Unimportant
I. FOCUS ON OTHERS			
Making significant contributions to charitable or noble causes.	60%	8%	7.5
Funding my grandchildren's private school education.[3]	57%	10%	5.7
Providing financial security for my children or grandchildren.[3]	74%	3%	24.7

Benefits of Being Wealthy	% Rating Important[2]	Unimportant	Ratio: Unimportant to Important
II. FOCUS ON SELF			
Purchasing a more luxurious home.	20%	60%	3.0
Purchasing an exquisite vacation and/or retirement home.	21%	51%	2.4
Joining a top-notch country club.	6%	79%	13.2
Owning high-grade art or antiques.	16%	61%	3.8
Purchasing a top-of-the-line automobile.	26%	49%	1.9

[1] All 233 respondents were selected from a nationwide sample of self-made millionaire women who owned and managed their own businesses.

[2] "Important" refers to the percentage of respondents who rated the benefit as being either very important or important. The percentage of respondents who indicated "somewhat important" are not illustrated.

[3] Includes responses from only those respondents (81 percent) who have at least one child.

responded with "unimportant" for every one who rated luxury-home acquisition as being "important."

Now, you may argue that these self-made wealthy women already live in mansions, so why would they be interested in trading up? Well, the mansions-and-millionaires theory is, in fact, a myth. According to my most recent survey, the typical self-made woman millionaire reported that she had never spent more than $299,990 for a home. Yes, more than 50 percent of these wealthy women surveyed paid $299,990 or less for the most expensive home they ever purchased. Fully 98 percent are home owners, as opposed to renters.

Of course, the other argument "from the audience" is that "perhaps many of these wealthy women were just given homes by their rich parents or grandparents." Actually, in seven out of ten cases, these women never received as much as one dollar toward the purchase of a home. That's right! In 70 percent of the cases, there was no subsidized down payment, no interest-free loan, no forgiveness loan, no help at all. Only 6 percent received any part of the funding or equity in a home from the proceeds of an estate. Most of these women were not coddled financially or otherwise by their parents or grandparents.

Perhaps you are lusting for "an exquisite vacation and/or retirement home." And why not? You are playing the role of an imaginary millionaire. It's imaginary, all right. Only 21 percent of these women millionaires feel that a retirement or second home is a benefit of being wealthy. I'm sorry for all those marketers of luxury vacation homes in Aspen and elsewhere, but this is not the ideal target market. Maybe you are thinking that most of these respondents already own a fabulous vacation home. If that were the case, it would explain why only one in five thinks this is an important benefit of being wealthy. Remember that "What's the most you ever spent for a home?" question? The $299,990 figure applied to all forms of homes—primary, secondary, condos, vacation, and retirement.

Let us consider another artifact of our consumption- and status-driven economy. Surely a successful businesswoman who is a multimillionaire would want to join a "top-notch country club." I'm sorry about that speculation, too. Only 6 percent of these women indicated that this was an important benefit of being wealthy. In other words, for every woman who indicated "important," there were 13.2 who responded that joining a top-notch country club was not an important benefit of their success. Let me anticipate your next question: How many of them or anyone in their households are already members of a country club? A 44 percent minority are club members. Of these, fully 75 percent report spending less than $4,000 per year for all club dues and all other fees and club-related expenses. It is more than likely that even those who are members of clubs are not affiliated with the likes of Pebble Beach or Winged Foot!

These millionaire women are much more likely to focus on the needs of others, and only a small minority are strongly into the me-me-mes. Note that 8 percent of millionaire women indicated "unimportant" regarding the benefit of "making significant contributions to charitable or noble causes." Yet nearly ten times this population (79 percent) indicated that joining a top-notch country club was unimportant. Or look at it another way: fully six in ten (60 percent) rated charitable contributions as important, while only six in one hundred (6 percent) rated "joining a top-notch country club" the same way.

What is wrong with these people? Don't they want to enjoy themselves?

This is another typical response from members of my audiences. These folks fail to appreciate that there are other types of people in this world. The wealthy self-made women certainly have the means to become club members, but that doesn't mean they wish to, or that they have an uncontrollable urge to play golf at any country club, luxury or otherwise.

As the data indicate, for every one woman who stated that "making significant contributions" was an unimportant benefit of being wealthy, there were more than seven who felt that it was important. At this juncture, members of my audiences often ask a logical question:

It's easy to say that one intends on making significant charitable donations, but do they?

As noted previously, these women contribute a significantly higher percentage of their incomes than do others in their income cohort. Nearly all (97 percent) contribute at least $4,000 annually. On average, they contribute fifteen times more money to charitable causes each year than does the average American household. On average, their annual dollar contributions significantly exceed the amount they allocate to motor vehicle purchase or lease expenses, including servicing, fuel, and insurance; clothing; or vacations. Their frugal lifestyle is one of the keys to understanding their proclivity for giving generously. One cannot give if one has nothing left after overconsumption. The millionaire women don't have this problem. They give generously today, and they intend to give substantial sums in the future, as documented in their estate plans. The values they have today are the same they will have tomorrow.

Becoming rich does not change these women—few have any intention of changing their consumption lifestyles or their propensity for giving generously to noble causes.

Millionaire women's desire to give is not limited to eleemosynary organizations. More than half (57 percent) intend to fund the private school educations of their grandchildren. As a side note, it's a bit ironic that only 19 percent of these women ever attended any form of private school.

What other intentions are you likely to find in their estate plans? Most (81 percent) of the women are mothers, and a majority (74 percent) indicated that an important benefit of being rich is the ability to provide financial security for one's children and grandchildren. Many women millionaires have told me that they often play the role of bankers for their relatives. They provide "forgiveness loans" and funding for medical and long-term-care expenses incurred by their relatives who lack financial resources. The loans are intended right from the start to be forgiven, never repaid, but labeling these acts of kindness as loans is important because then the pride of the recipients is maintained. It is not unusual for these millionaire women to pay for the healthcare expenses (not covered by insurance) for several members of their families, including parents and siblings. Yes, everyone has a role in life within a family. These wealthy women see their function as a distributor of wealth to those in need.

IN CONTRAST: THE GENERAL POPULATION

The *Wall Street Journal* conducted a national study of 2,095 adults concerning the perceived benefits of being rich (June Fletcher, "When a Million Isn't Enough," *Wall Street Journal*, March 16, 2001, W1, W14). The results are representative of the opinions of the overall adult population in America. For most nonwealthy Americans, the benefits of being rich differ from the pluses for those who are actually rich. According to the *Wall Street Journal* study, the most important advantages of becoming rich center around having more "free time and less work time, and being able to choose whether or not to work." Specifically, respondents who indicated "can choose whether to work" outpaced those who selected "can give money to causes" by a ratio of more than four to one. The charitable-orientation segment was also outnumbered two to one by those with a high-consumption orientation, who would like to "buy whatever you want."

These responses are very different from those given by the self-employed millionaire women in my studies. Americans in general equate wealth with "working less and spending more," but not these women. Even those who have a net worth of $5 million, $10 million, or more are still working. Given their financial status, they don't have to work, but they do because they enjoy working. It gives them pride, high self-esteem, and much satisfaction. No, it's not the income that motivates them. Even after their level of wealth exceeded the threshold they required to consider themselves rich or financially independent, they still adhered to a frugal lifestyle. As they accumulate more, they allocate more and more dollars to noble causes.

They also give more than money. The typical female millionaire business owner works forty-nine hours (median) per week. In spite of this full-time work requirement, nearly seven in ten (68 percent) are active in raising funds for charity. Also, fully 77 percent are leaders of community activities and civic events. Most have a history of assuming leadership roles, dating back to their early school days.

An interesting side note is mentioned in the *Wall Street Journal* study. Respondents were asked about the material artifacts that a person must have to be considered rich. More than one-third (35 percent) indicated that to qualify as rich, a person must own a motor vehicle that costs $75,000 or more! If this were the case, most of the millionaire businesswomen would fail to qualify, because fully 96 percent never owned or leased a motor vehicle costing that much, nor did anyone else in their households ever shell out $75,000 for personal transportation. However, a good number of Americans seem to think otherwise. They think that expensive, conspicuously displayed status-defining products are complements to wealth. Actually, according to most millionaire businesswomen, purchasing expensive motor vehicles and the like are the antithesis of building and maintaining wealth.

Regrets? Not! Revenge? Not!

Most of these women millionaires are strong-willed, able to blot out painful experiences and mistakes from the past. In fact, most feel that their ability to overcome reversals and adversity is a major reason for their success. These women have learned from the past, but they are not Monday morning quarterbacks. They rarely spend time second-guessing themselves, because that would be futile. Almost all have had painful experiences, but as they often tell their young understudies, "It is difficult to succeed in business if you spend a lot of time living in Regretville." In fact, only about one in five (19 percent) report that they

ever spend time thinking about how things should have been.

Most of us know that history cannot be changed. Winners focus on the future, while losers often spend too much time second-guessing themselves. Mrs. Tiwa Meir never, ever gave up, and today she is a major success. Among her many triumphs in life is her ownership of her own freight-management company. When asked what it takes for people to succeed in life, she replied:

Don't cry over spilled milk. . . . Even if you have failed and failed again in business, learn from the experience. Failure is only one more step toward success. Successful people never give up. Believe in yourself; never say I can't, even if you have stumbled. Don't stop trying. . . . Never be afraid to fail . . . and fail again. . . . Fear never trying. Be afraid of quitting.

Mrs. Meir overcame many obstacles put in her way. She was raised in a home environment that was as nonnurturing as one could imagine, and her first husband was a "very bad choice." The painful experiences that Mrs. Meir encountered as a child and a young adult could fill a book. Her initial experiences in business were anything other than successful, but Mrs. Meir had great discipline. She trained herself never to dwell on the past, to always look forward to her future joys.

Work hard, play hard, and keep life fun! Love yourself, and you will always love others.

Most millionaire women business owners believe that overcoming adversity enhances one's resolve and character. It also makes success taste sweeter when it arrives, and it's nice to prove wrong those who belittled and disrespected you. Yes, these women business owners had their share of detractors, including the minority whose parents regularly told them they would never succeed in life. Many others had at least one husband who told them the same thing, and most reported that lending officers at banks often showed them little respect. The list goes on.

Given those circumstances, one might conclude that revenge or at least the "I'll show them I'm not a loser" motive was a basis for the women's success. In fact, more than three hundred millionaire women business owners have told me that revenge is not ever productive. The detailed content analysis of their responses about how to become a success reveals that most of the women emphasized the importance of perseverance, education and training, goal setting, and similar pursuits. But how many of these successful women mentioned or even hinted at the motive of revenge, getting even, or at least, "I'll show them"? Not one of these extraordinary women was motivated to succeed by revenge. Again, they are oriented toward the future. Hate, anger, and retribution are not, and never were, part of their success formula. So remember, you can use your energy and intellect to hate or to achieve, but probably not to do both.

There is a highly significant connection between having a defined set of goals and not regretting the past. Those who state that they

have a clearly defined set of daily, weekly, monthly, annual, and lifetime goals

are significantly more likely than those who don't to state that they

never spend time thinking about how things could or should have been.

If one looks forward, it is difficult to look back over spilt milk, thus, if one focuses on the pains of the past, it is very difficult to plan a successful future.

ONE REGRET

Only a small minority of the successful women have any regrets. Yet one specific category of regret is noteworthy. Most of those who did not attend college or complete their college education wish they had done so. Take Mrs. Garner, for example. She never completed college, but today she is a self-made decamillionaire. Last year she earned more than 80 percent of her household's annual realized income, in excess of $1 million, while her husband earned less than 20 percent.

Mrs. Garner owns and operates a very successful business that imports and manufactures lighting products. She described herself as "very happy . . . highly satisfied with her life." She only has one regret.

I am a college dropout. In spite of this, I have been fortunate enough to do well in business; however, my greatest regret in life is that I did not complete my studies to receive a degree. It will always be an ache in my bones. I have continued to study and learn, but my advice to everyone is stay in for the long haul. You are not as smart as you think! Attain the highest degree possible, and then make your fortune. No one has any sense until they are thirty-five years old anyway—might as well spend those formative years learning—listening instead of talking!

Mrs. Garner compensated for not completing college by spending much of her time studying the trends in her industry. No matter how well this informal learning translated into business success, she still regrets not being a college graduate.

CHAPTER 3

Millionaires: Women vs. Men

How did these businesswomen become millionaires? Examine the data. They did it by doing more of the key activities and achieving better results than most of their male counterparts.

GOAL ORIENTED

*M*ost millionaire women business owners are goal oriented. For every 100 who answered no, 261 answered yes to the following question:

Do you have a clearly defined set of daily, weekly, monthly, annual, and lifetime goals?

Among those who answered no, more than half had already achieved most of their goals, and most of them were over sixty-five years of age. The others who answered no usually reported having one or two major lifetime goals, and they had a very focused approach to achieving their superordinate goals, such as becoming financially independent before age fifty-five, supporting noble causes, or funding their grandchildren's education. Their activities were directed toward these goals. Most of the millionaire business owners in the "yes" segment, those who are oriented more toward multiple goals, reported that they have always been goal oriented, and they have a history of being able to plan and reach multiple goals, often simultaneously.

Who is more likely to be goal oriented, women or men? Within the same occupational (business owner and manager) and economic (net worth between $1 million and $25 million) cohort, the answer is women. For every 100 men who are not, there are about 174 who are goal oriented. As noted above, the ratio is significantly higher for women (100 to 261).

How do so many men succeed in business without having a strong goal orientation? They have one economic goal. Or as one woman aptly put it:

Men [business owners] are like hounds . . . they are at their best following one scent!

Most male millionaire business owners are very focused on making a success of their business. For them, everything revolves around this super-ordinate goal. Women have a much larger set of aims, and many of those goals are not necessarily congruent or even complementary to building a business. For example, the women profiled throughout this book have much more empathy for the needs of others than do men, and they allocate more time, emotion, and economic resources to noble pursuits.

INTELLECTUALLY GIFTED?

Do millionaire women business owners all believe they are intellectually gifted? No! In fact, fewer than three in ten (27 percent) of these women ever in their lifetimes felt that they possessed superior intellect. Could it be that most of them became successful without having a genius IQ? Yes, that seems to be the case. In fact, in the content analysis of the essays about becoming successful written by the millionaire business-women, not one mentioned "superior or high intellect" or even being bright as a factor underlying their success.

The factor they did mention most often was having perseverance and tenacity. On a scale of intelligence, these women would be classi-fied as bright, but not intellectually superior. No, as a group they are not geniuses, but they are hardworking women with great tenacity, and they recognize that perseverance and hard work are more important than performance on standardized tests like the SAT.

About six in ten (61 percent) of these women graduated from college. More than one in four (26 percent) attended college but did not complete the requirements for a bachelor's degree. Another 26 percent hold advanced degrees.

Note that just over half (51 percent) of the women who attended college never received any funding whatsoever from their parents or any other relatives. They worked and paid their own way. Many of those who dropped out of school had to do so for economic reasons. Even those who did receive some financial support from their parents worked to pay their tuition and have spending money. In fact, these women began earning their own spending money before they were teenagers, and later worked part-time in high school and college. Yet most found time to be quite active in student affairs, school events, and extracurricular activities.

Given the large amount of time devoted to nonacademic activities, it's logical to predict that these women had mediocre grades in both high school and college. Well, once again, so much for logical predictions. Actually, most millionaire women business owners performed well academically, and they did significantly better than their male counterparts.

- More than five of ten (52 percent) of these women reported that the grade they received most frequently in high school was an A. In contrast, 36 percent of the men surveyed were A students.
- Many of these women were outstanding students in college. Nearly four in ten (38 percent) of those who completed college graduated in the top 5 percent of their class. Fewer than one in four (23 percent) of their male counterparts ranked in the top 5 percent.
- On average, the women surveyed had a higher grade point average (GPA) in college than did the men (3.4 versus 2.9).

SAT scores are supposedly predictors of potential GPA in college. In turn, a student's college GPA should be an indicator of his SAT scores. In my studies, I have found that SAT scores explain only about 11 percent of the variance in GPA. This relationship is statistically significant, but it leaves much of the GPA variance unexplained. What if SAT scores were a perfect predictor of grade point average? Then in cases where a man and woman had the same SAT scores, they would be expected to have the same grade point average. Interestingly, millionaire women business owners do have nearly the same SAT scores on average (approximately 1140) as millionaire men (approximately 1135). In statistical terms these groups are nearly identical. Although 1140 is statistically speaking "above the norm," it is not indicative of genius intellect, and most of the millionaire women business owners are not intellectually gifted. Yet nearly half (47 percent) graduated from college with honors. That's nearly twice the percentage of their male counterparts.

How is this possible? The women, on average, earned a GPA in college that was half a letter grade higher (3.4) than that of the men (2.9), although both groups had nearly identical SAT scores. The SAT score may give some indication of college performance potential, but it does not measure a student's determination, perseverance, tenacity, hard work, or discipline. Take Jeri R. as an example. Jeri owns and manages a party supply rentals company. She had nearly an A average in high school and was very active in student government and sports. She took the SAT three times; her best score was 1010. This was a good bit below the norm for those who attended her first-choice college, and she was accepted only after "being on the bubble" for a good while. During her orientation at the college, guess what her adviser told her?

Let's see, a 1010 SAT—you're likely to have a 2.4 or 2.5 GPA if you finish!

Apparently this adviser completely discounted Jeri's high grades in high school, but Jeri didn't. Jeri not only finished, she graduated with honors by earning a 3.7 GPA. Jeri is achievement oriented, like most of the women profiled herein.

More than three in four (77 percent) of these women indicated that their high school and college experiences taught them that hard work was more important than genetic high intellect in achieving.

The myth persists that only those with high genetic intellect can succeed in America, but not according to most of these millionaire women.

There is a positive connection between SAT scores and IQ scores, but what about the connection between SAT scores and economic performance in the real world? Among the population of millionaire women business owners, there is no statistically significant connection between SAT scores (a proxy measure of analytical intelligence) and wealth. Most of these successful women worked hard to earn good grades in college, and then they applied themselves and worked hard building their businesses and net worth. They realize that their customers patronize their businesses because of factors other than the SAT scores or IQs of the proprietors.

Women who are successful business owners today seem to have "gotten more out of school" than did men who are successful business owners. The women are significantly more likely than men to give their high school and college experiences much credit in molding them.

- Four of five (80 percent) of the women, as opposed to 69 percent of the men, indicated that their high school and college experiences had a high degree of influence on them in terms of developing the strong work ethic that they possess today.
- Most (60 percent) of these women and 49 percent of the men reported that their high school and college experiences were very important in "teaching them how to properly allocate their time."
- Nearly four of five women (79 percent)—versus 62 percent of their male counterparts—indicated that the encouragement they received from teachers and professors had a significant influence on their becoming productive adults.

Educators did more than encourage these women to excel. Remember, the average age of these millionaire women business owners is fifty-two, and many attended school thirty, even forty years ago, when women were not expected to have their own successful careers. They certainly were not expected to own and manage successful businesses. Part of the reason they did succeed in business can be traced back to their strong role models: the teachers who often served as their mentors in high school or college.

Most millionaire women, self-employed or not, give much credit for their success to their teachers and other strong, self-supporting female mentors. Carol of Iowa summed it up in a recent letter. Like most economically successful women, Carol gives much credit for her achievements to her education.

Dear Dr. Stanley,

I noticed on your Web site that you are writing a book about women. When my friends read your "Millionaire" books they always say, "Carol, it's you he's writing about." I attended public schools where the teachers were role models and mentors. I have had the benefit of knowing many strong women, some who did well financially. From them, I learned to rely on myself and not wait for "Mr. Right" to support me. I was a scholarship student at a small liberal arts college. I had many mentors whose examples shaped my life.

While my net worth can be attributed to frugality and canny investing, my lifestyle is shaped by an excellent education. I have always tended to wander away from the herd in my thinking, but my education taught me self-discipline, independence of thought, and strong ethics.

Because my mother was mostly at work, I was reared by a committee of her sisters and friends. I am the child of a single mother, and my early years were fraught with financial uncertainty. I learned by watching my mother that women have to work harder and longer to achieve financial success. She told me, "Never let them know you can type," and I have followed her advice.

While I am not as wealthy as most of your subjects, my net worth is above $1 million, and like most of your subjects, I started with nothing more than a college scholarship and a good mother. The thing you may find interesting about me is that I have never earned more than $60,000. I have worked in middle management in state government most of my career, in human services, no less. It was satisfying work, but not lucrative.

I have accumulated most of my net worth by living below my means. I have everything I want, but I have learned not to want too much. Also, I avoid debt. In 1982, my net worth was $125,000. The state government was being downsized, and I was in danger of losing my job. I told myself I wanted to get into a position where I would never again be faced with that uncertainty. First, I stopped giving myself raises. All new money went into investments. Then I paid off my house loan, and the house payments could go into investments. I am fairly conser-

vative in my investing but not afraid of risk. In the past eighteen years, I have averaged 15 percent annual growth on my net worth. Most years, I saved 30 percent of my income, if not more.

My net worth is my own, separate from my husband's, and I manage it myself. Recently I "semiretired" and decided to run for political office in my county. It was satisfying to know I could afford the pay cut. While I have no biological children, I have had many foster children. I notice they have learned from me the ability to manage money well, as I learned from my mother.

Sincerely,
Carol

SENIOR SUPERLATIVES

Most men and women who are successful business owners today were not among the so-called beautiful people in high school. They did not win those beauty contests that took place in high school, and I'm not talking about the homecoming king and queen contest. I mean the contest of "superlatives." How would you answer the question about superlatives I have asked many millionaire women and men?

During your high school years, how do you think your teachers in general judged and evaluated you?

If you responded that your teachers very likely judged you as being the most intellectually gifted, having the highest grade point average, or having the highest level of intelligence, you would be in a minority among the population of millionaire business owners (see Table 3-1). Note that only 20 percent of the millionaire women and 11 percent of the men believe that their teachers very likely judged them as having the highest level of intelligence. About the same proportions felt that their teachers very likely judged them as being most intellectually gifted.

What superlative was most often associated with these women? More than four in ten (41 percent) stated that their high school teachers very likely judged them as being the "most dependable." Nearly three in ten (28 percent) indicated "most likely to succeed." The same percentage stated "most conscientious."

Could it be that dependability, the desire to succeed, and being "most conscientious" are more important qualities in becoming a successful business owner than being intellectually gifted or even having the highest grade point average? The data suggests that this is the case.

TABLE 3-1

MILLIONAIRE BUSINESS OWNERS:
HOW DID YOUR TEACHERS LIKELY EVALUATE YOU?

	Percent Indicating Very Likely	
Evaluations, aka Superlatives	Women	Men
Most Dependable	41%	27%
Most Likely to Succeed	28%	18%
Most Conscientious	28%	15%
Most Industrious	20%	18%
Hardest Worker	20%	16%
Highest Level of Intelligence	20%	11%
Most Intellectually Gifted	20%	9%
Highest Grade Point Average	15%	9%
Most Ambitious	14%	13%
Most Popular	13%	8%

Another important principle can be deduced from these results. Note the percentages regarding the superlatives. For all ten, only a minority of the millionaire respondents believe that their high school teachers would judge them as "most." As individuals, many believe that they were always dependable and had a strong desire to succeed, but they are reluctant to pat themselves on the back by designating themselves as number one on any of these scales. One of these women's most admirable qualities is their humility.

Webster's defines *humility* as "the quality of being humble; the modest opinion or estimate of one's own importance or rank." A modest or humble estimate of their merits is reflected in the consumption behavior of these women: note their modest cars, nondescript homes, and other simple belongings. It is also appreciably more difficult to encourage millionaire women business owners, as opposed to their male counterparts, to detail their own accomplishments.

Most of the millionaire women I have interviewed are not at all arrogant or boastful. No matter that they are 100 percent self-made; no matter if they give generously to noble causes. They do not use superlatives to describe themselves. When confronted with a list of their achievements, more often than not they give a lot of credit to their parents, teachers, husbands, mentors, and those who work for them. Modesty and humility explain much of their business success. Employees appreciate and admire leaders who give credit to the rank and file.

ACCOUNTING AND BUDGETING

Most millionaire women are fastidious budgeters. In order to budget, one must account for expenditures, so two out of three (68 percent) indicated:

I know how much our family spends each year for food, clothing, and shelter.

These millionaire business owners accounted for their expenditures long before they reached millionaire status, yet even after becoming wealthy, they still budget and tally their spending. Part of this behavior is habit, but there is more to it than habit alone. The women report a certain feeling of power, control, confidence, and enhanced self-esteem when they can account for expenditures, and this behavior had its origins during their early personality development.

Significantly fewer men who are millionaire business owners (54 percent) report that there is an accounting system operating within their households. If they do not account for expenditures, how can they develop a budget? And if they do not budget, how can they control spending and facilitate saving and investing? It is possible to become wealthy without accounting and budgeting for each and every item— about one in three millionaire women do not have a detailed accounting system for tracking and planning expenditures or investing. Yet these women became millionaires in one generation. How is this possible?

Men are more likely than women to simplify their accounting and budgeting and, ultimately, their system of accumulating wealth. I explained this issue in an earlier work, examining the topic of millionaires who don't budget.

How did they become millionaires? How do they control spending? They create an artificial economic environment of scarcity for themselves and the other members of their household. Nonbudgeters invest first and spend the balance of their income. Many call this the "pay yourself first" strategy. These people invest a minimum of 15 percent of their annual realized income before they pay the sellers of their food, clothes, homes, credit, and the like. (The Millionaire Next Door, p. 41)

This "artificial economic environment of scarcity" system is not ideal, according to most men and women millionaires. It often leads to disharmony among family members because one person in the family makes a unilateral decision about how much of the household's income will be saved and invested. Typically, it is the male business owner or head of household who takes full control of this "pay yourself first" method. Other family members are rarely consulted about how much of the household's income will be allocated to savings and investments.

Since the "pay yourself first" system is found among significantly greater percentages of millionaire males than among millionaire females, you can predict that when you hear the child of a millionaire say,

"Cheap as hell!"

he or she is usually referring to his or her father. In such cases, youngsters often see their fathers as nonbenevolent despots who have shoved their "pay yourself first" system down everyone else's throats. But as these children mature, they develop a greater understanding and respect for the frugal nature of their fathers.

FRUGAL MEASURES

When it comes to operating a household, who tends to be more frugal? Women business owners are significantly more thrifty than their male counterparts. The measures of frugality used herein concern actions taken to reduce the cost and enhance the productivity of operating a household. Nineteen are given in Table 3-2. Of these measures, one might expect that by chance alone women would rate more frugal than men in terms of perhaps two or three of them. However, women were found to be significantly more frugal in regard to nine of the nineteen, and in nominal terms, fifteen of nineteen overall.

Remember that these measures of frugality are used to contrast the behaviors of women and men in roughly the same cohort. Self-employed male business owners, when compared to the entire U.S. population of high-income earners, are very frugal in relative terms. However, their level of frugality is exceeded by women who are self-employed.

TABLE 3-2

MILLIONAIRE BUSINESS OWNERS:
WHO IS MORE FRUGAL, WOMEN OR MEN?

| | | Percent Taking This Action: | | |
Elements of Frugality	Who Is More Frugal?	Women	Men	Significant Difference[1]
1. EXTENDING THE LIFE CYCLE				
Having shoes resoled or repaired	Women	70%	68%	No
Having furniture reupholstered or refinished instead of buying new	Women	58%	48%	Yes[2]
Having clothes mended or altered instead of buying new	Women	52%	37%	Yes
2. REDUCING THE MONTHLY BURDENS				
Raising the thermostat setting on your air conditioner during summer or daytime	Women	65%	56%	Yes
Switching long-distance telephone companies	Women	61%	51%	Yes[2]
Paying off or paid off home mortgage early	Women	56%	51%	No

TABLE 3-2, CONTINUED

MILLIONAIRE BUSINESS OWNERS:
WHO IS MORE FRUGAL, WOMEN OR MEN?

		Percent Taking This Action		
Elements of Frugality	Who Is More Frugal?	Women	Men	Significant Difference[1]
3. PLANNING PURCHASES				
Never buying via telephone solicitations	Men	72%	73%	No
Developing a shopping list before grocery shopping	Women	81%	69%	Yes
Using discount coupons when buying groceries	Women	58%	49%	No
Purchasing appliances or motor vehicles "top-rated" by *Consumer Reports*	Women	51%	43%	No
Leaving department stores as soon as a purchase is made	Women	41%	38%	No
4. PATRONIZING DISCOUNT INSTITUTIONS				
Buying household supplies in bulk at warehouse stores, i.e., Sam's, Costco	Women	65%	51%	Yes
Doing more and more business with a discount brokerage firm (or firms)	Women	28%	26%	No
5. HOME-BUYING ACTIVITIES				
Purchasing a home that is easily affordable	Women	73%	60%	Yes
Deciding *not* to purchase a more expensive home	Women	44%	32%	Yes
Searching for a home that was foreclosed	Women	56%	26%	Yes
Testing a seller's price sensitivity by making a deeply discounted price offer	Men	43%	45%	No
Asking real estate agent to reduce the sales commission	Men	26%	37%	Yes[2]
Being willing to walk away from any deal at any time	Men	83%	84%	No

[1] Probability at less than 0.05 level.
[2] Probability at less than 0.10 level.

What do these results suggest to women who wish to become financially independent business owners? You must be frugal; you must operate a productive house. You must be even more frugal than your male counterparts who are self-employed business owners. You must be the most thrifty among the thrifty. That is what the data describe about how these women became financially successful in one generation.

"THE MOST EVER SPENT"

I have previously written:

> *The typical American millionaire . . . never spent more than $399 for a suit of clothing for himself or for anyone else. . . . Fifty percent . . . paid $399 or less for the most expensive suit they ever purchased. (The Millionaire Next Door, p. 31)*

Women accounted for only 8 percent of the millionaire sample that was the base for *The Millionaire Next Door*. When I mention this to my audiences, typically someone will speak up:

> *Well, that explains it. It is the men who are frugal. They live well below their means. Women are the big spenders, especially on clothing.*

Such statements reflect a stereotype, a common misconception that women spend money freely. Most of the respondents to the *Millionaire Next Door* survey were self-employed business owners, a group that accounts for less than one in five of the current workforce. Yet they are the dominant segment of the millionaire population, and millionaire business owners, male or female, are a frugal bunch.

The millionaire women business owners are, within the context of many consumption categories, at least as frugal as their male counterparts. A general summary of typical expenditures by the millionaire women profiled herein is included in Table 3-3.

Fully half of the male millionaire business owners profiled in *The Millionaire Next Door* never spent more than $399 (median price) for a suit for themselves or anyone else. With an income of $131,000

TABLE 3-3

PRICES PAID BY WOMEN MILLIONAIRES FOR HOMES, MOTOR VEHICLES, CLOTHING, AND ACCESSORIES

HOME OR CONDO			MOTOR VEHICLE			SUIT OF CLOTHING			PAIR OF SHOES			WRISTWATCH		
Most Ever Spent	% that paid Less	More	Most Ever Spent	% that paid Less	More	Most Ever Spent	% that paid Less	More	Most Ever Spent	% that paid Less	More	Most Ever Spent	% that paid Less	More
$78,680	10	90	$21,250	10	90	$199	10	90	$72	10	90	$43	10	90
$148,424	25	75	$29,122	25	75	$240	25	75	$94	25	75	$123	25	75
$299,990	50	50	$38,315	50	50	$400	50	50	$139	50	50	$475	50	50
$448,947	75	25	$49,811	75	25	$740	75	25	$200	75	25	$1,889	75	25
$775,000	90	10	$67,250	90	10	$1,085	90	10	$296	90	10	$4,632	90	10
$994,737	95	5	$79,900	95	5	$1,915	95	5	$392	95	5	$6,210	95	5
$1,500,000	99	1	$106,000	99	1	$3,500	99	1	$790	99	1	$17,000	99	1

(median), the typical male millionaire reports that for his most expensive suit he allocated the equivalent of $1 for every $328 of income that year, computed by dividing the median price of the suit ($399) into his household's annual income. Put another way, the suit cost him only three-tenths of 1 percent of his income.

What about millionaire women? What is the most they or anyone else in their households ever spent on a suit of clothing? The most reported by the typical millionaire businesswoman was $400 (median price), a figure nearly identical to the median price reported by men. Does this fact indicate that these women are just as frugal as the men?

The figure of $400 came from a national survey of millionaire women who are business owners conducted nearly seven years after the *Millionaire Next Door* survey. It is likely that today's $400 suit, or $399 for that matter, sold for less then. But there is a more compelling contrast to be examined. The median annual realized income generated by households headed by the millionaire women was $240,217, and the ratio of this income to the most spent for a suit ($240,217 divided by $400) is about 601 to 1. In other words, a typical millionaire woman allocated the equivalent of only $1 in $601 of income for her most expensive purchase of a suit of clothing. Contrast this with the ratio for men: $1 for every $328 of income.

What about the frugal character of men versus women in the context of other categories of consumer goods? Consider shoe purchases. The typical millionaire woman never paid more than $139 (median price). For the men of *The Millionaire Next Door*, it was $140 (median price). In terms of the ratio of income to purchase price, however, the typical woman allocated only $1 for every $1,728 of income for the most expensive shoe purchase, but the typical male spent $1 for every $936 of income. Translated, these numbers once again suggest that the women are more frugal than their male counterparts.

How about vacations? The most the typical millionaire woman ever spent was $7,526 (median), or about 3.1 percent of her household annual realized income. The typical millionaire man spent $5,663, less in nominal dollar terms, but representing 4.3 percent of his income. Look at it another way. The typical woman allocated about $1 for her most expensive vacation for every $32 of her income; for the men, the ratio was $1 for a vacation to about $23 of income.

PATRONS OF LUXURY MOTOR VEHICLES? NOT!

Is it true that you are what you drive? Those who feel this way may not be impressed with the motor vehicles driven by millionaire business owners, both men and women. Most do not drive expensive cars. This should not come as a surprise to those who have the facts. Reflect for a moment on the objective numbers concerning the sales figures for those motor vehicles whose sticker prices approach or exceed $100,000.

How sad, how unfortunate. There are just not enough of these expensive motor vehicles to go around. There are more than five million millionaire households in America. Given the recent sales figures, what proportion of the millionaire households will be able to satisfy their craving for a brand-new BMW 7 Series? Only 13,389 (the annual number sold in the United States) or only one lucky millionaire household in 373 will qualify for this "total luxury." How unfair. Even worse, as a millionaire, you have a better chance (one in 3,205 versus one in 4,386) of contracting malaria than qualifying for status in the new Ferrari owners' club. (See the sales figures in *Automotive News*, May 27, 2002, p. 28.)

Most millionaires have never purchased a BMW 7 Series, Infinity Q45, Lexus 430, or Mercedes-Benz SLK. Many can, in fact, afford such acquisitions. Yet most millionaires, both women and men, are frugal when it comes to automobile purchases. The most the typical millionaire man paid was $29,238 (median), or the equivalent of $1 for every $4.48 of income. This represents about 22.3 percent of his income (median) or 1.80 percent of his net worth. The typical millionaire woman allocated only about $1 for every $6.27 of her income for this purchase. This translates into 16.0 percent of her income, or 1.30 percent of her net worth for the most she ever paid for a motor vehicle: $38,315 (median price).

TO TELL TIME OR DENOTE STATUS?

I also asked millionaires about the watches they have purchased. In this regard, millionaire women are not as frugal as men, but neither group is likely to purchase a $10,000 diamond-encrusted Rolex or other expensive timepiece. The typical millionaire man paid only $235 (median price), or about the equivalent of $1 for each $557 of his income for a watch. The typical woman millionaire paid $475 (median price) for the most expensive watch she ever purchased. This translates to $1 per $506 of her income.

Keep something in mind when making these comparisons. The women in these studies are significantly more likely to purchase wristwatches as gifts for their husbands, children, and grandchildren than are the men. They typically spend more for other people's watches than for their own, and they do not usually allocate big bucks even for the watches purchased in recognition of an anniversary, graduation, birthday, or other special event. Millionaires, both men and women, recognize that watches are designed to tell time, not denote socioeconomic superiority. Is it any wonder that Seiko is the most popular watch among the millionaires I have interviewed?

YES, A CHEAP DATE!

As I indicated in an earlier work:

> When people ask me about the lifestyles of millionaires, I have a short answer. The typical millionaire is, in three words: "A cheap date!" (The Millionaire Mind, pp. 364–365)

As you might imagine, there are in fact differing degrees of being a "cheap date," and women are higher on the scale than men. Women seem to have less need to be involved in the accoutrements of higher status and more costly activities than men.

- Only one in three (33 percent) of the millionaire businesswomen regularly sew. Few of them reported shopping for anything, including clothing and related goods, on the Internet. Less than one in five (18 percent) of the women—versus 24 percent of the men—reported shopping on the Internet in the last month.
- Only 44 percent of the millionaire businesswomen (including all members of their households) are members of a country club. However, seven in ten (70 percent) of their male counterparts are club members. In both cases, few spend substantial amounts for country club dues and fees. Among the women, three out of four allocate

1 percent or less of their annual income to dues and fees. Men who are members allocate about 50 percent more of their incomes for club expenses than do women. The women do not feel the need (nor do they believe it productive) to join a country club for the purposes of enhancing their business revenue, but the men feel differently. Of course, millionaire men are nearly twice as likely to indicate that they are golfers (51 percent versus 28 percent).

- Since you are unlikely to find a millionaire woman having lunch at her country club with clients, where will she be? Nearly six in ten (57 percent) of the women reported eating at a McDonald's or Burger King in the past thirty days. Only 44 percent of the millionaire men did likewise.
- Women were more likely than men to report that they attended religious activities during the last thirty days (51 percent versus 44 percent).
- Women were somewhat more likely to have prayed (55 percent versus 47 percent) during the last month.
- Most women (68 percent) and men (58 percent) have helped raise funds for at least one charity during the last year, but a larger proportion of men than women have attended fund-raising balls (58 percent versus 44 percent). Women are more likely, however, to be involved in community or civic volunteer work (77 percent versus 67 percent). Overall, within the same age groups and income cohorts, businesswomen are less likely than their male counterparts to demonstrate patronage habits that advertise their status.

PATRONAGE HABITS

Most millionaire businesswomen have developed rather strong retail patronage habits. They tend to be loyal customers to a variety of retail outlets, especially local, privately owned businesses. Most buy motor vehicles from local dealers whom they have dealt with previously. Nearly three in four (72 percent) believe:

My time is more valuable than shopping automobile dealers for so-called big price discounts.

They tend to repeat business with one or two dealers, and only 18 percent aggressively shop dealers when purchasing an automobile. Thus, the ratio of loyal customer type to shopper type is four to one (72 percent versus 18 percent).

Some of this loyalty to a particular dealer is based on a relationship with one particular sales professional who is employed at the dealership they patronize, usually someone who provides extraordinary services to customers. The millionaire women are able and willing to pay a bit more for a motor vehicle than they would if shopping on the Internet, but they know that they would never get the same set of services they do from their local dealers.

They reason that time is money, and it is much more productive to allocate one's time and energy to operating a business than to comparison shopping. As one respondent asked, "Why become an automobile price expert every three or four years?" Their dealer loyalty extends beyond purchasing automobiles, since most of these women prefer to patronize businesses of the "mom and pop" variety. From dry cleaning to appliance sales and service, most feel that the service is superior when provided by suppliers who are self-employed.

Male millionaire business owners are much more likely than women to price shop aggressively for motor vehicles. For most of these men, car shopping is nearly a blood sport in which they must prove their superior power by squeezing the last surplus dollar out of adversaries such as automobile dealers. In fact, 56 percent of these men designate themselves as aggressive price shoppers. This is more than three times the percentage (18 percent) for women who are millionaire business owners.

Women also tend to be loyal to particular stores when it comes to purchasing clothing. Nearly eight in ten (78 percent) indicate that they purchase apparel at the same stores over and over again. These women are not trendy or slaves to fashion concerning their wardrobes, and they buy their clothing to last.

INVESTING IN COMMON STOCK

Being frugal often generates dollars to invest, which will make those dollars grow many times over. Both millionaire women and millionaire men are frugal and habitual investors, but who is more likely to be labeled a "long-term investor"? Millionaire men and women were asked a simple question:

Once you have purchased a stock, how long do you typically keep it?

The women were significantly more likely to be "buy and hold long-term" investors than their male counterparts. Fully 55 percent of the women, versus 42 percent of the men, hold a stock on average for at least four years. Four out of ten women typically buy and then, on average, hold a stock for six years or more. Only about one in three (31 percent) of the men do likewise. Only 8 percent of the women, in contrast to 16 percent of the men, keep a stock for less than one year.

In another measure of investment habits of millionaires, women and men were asked, "In a typical year, how often do you sell stocks in your portfolio?" On average, women sell stocks from their portfolios (actual sell transactions) much less often than do men. More than four in five (81 percent) of the women sell a stock from their portfolios four or fewer times per year. Only 42 percent of the men trade so infrequently. About three in ten men report selling at least ten times during a typical year, whereas only about eight in one hundred of the women report selling as often. The median number of stocks sold by women in a typical year is only 1.2; for men the number is four times higher: 4.8.

Given the greater frequency with which men trade stocks and the fact that fewer employ investment advisers or financial planners, what would one predict about the comparative amounts of time spent studying investments? It would be logical to assume that men spend significantly more time planning their stock portfolios. In fact, just the opposite is true. Women study and plan more but trade less often. Typically, men allocate significantly fewer hours (6 median hours per month) to planning their investments than do women (10.1 median hours). While 32 percent of the women allocate twenty hours or more per month, only about 8 percent of the men spend this much time or more per month planning their investments. Can this perhaps be explained by the fact that men are more likely to allocate more of their income to professional investment advisers and managers? No; once again, the logical explanation does not apply.

On average, women allocate nearly 2 percent (1.8 percent) of their annual income to professional investment advisers, and men spend less, 1.3 percent. Actually, these results are a bit misleading because within the male population there is a small segment, about 15 percent, who spend more than 5 percent of their income annually on investment advice and management. That skews the average figure.

So women spend more time planning their investments, but at the same time, they allocate more dollars to investment advisers and managers. This is especially interesting given the fact that, on an annual basis, men make three times the number of stock transactions, allocating about three times more money annually for stock transaction costs than do women, who devote more hours to studying "market intelligence information." Women are significantly more likely than men to research a stock "thoroughly" before making it part of their portfolio; they are "in-depth" readers of investment information. Men tend to consume and respond more quickly to headlines and sound bites, including panic calls from brokers and "hot flashes" from economic media sources, about the "direction" of a stock.

The men patronize transaction-type investment organizations as well as "action-oriented" male investment professionals. In other words, they are significantly more likely than women to be "prized" customers of stockbrokers and valuable patrons of stockbrokerage firms.

In contrast, women are more likely than their male counterparts to be patrons of the more conservative, fee-based financial planners and investment organizations that are often part of or affiliated with commercial banks or trust companies. Given their different orientations toward investing and the type of investment organizations and professionals they patronize, it's not surprising that women trade less often.

Other studies have also found that men are more active traders than women (see, for example, Brad Barber and Terrance O'Dean, "Boys Will Be Boys: Gender, Overconfidence and Common Stock Investment," *Quarterly Journal of Economics*, vol. 116 (February 2001): pp. 261–92). The authors studied the trading habits of more than thirty-five thousand households during a six-year period and found that men traded 45 percent more frequently than women. Of course, trading costs money. The active trading by men reduced their annual net return on average by 2.65 percent, as opposed to 1.72 percent for women. The authors conclude that men are more active traders because they are over-confident about their ability to select stocks that will perform well in the future. This is especially interesting given the fact that the research discussed herein indicates that women allocate substantially more time to studying and planning their investments in stocks than do men.

When it comes to investing, men are bolder than women, but being bold does not necessarily translate into being rich. The transaction-related costs of hypertrading, in terms of time and money, can erode the performance of even a "lucky" investor. Men may appear to be higher on the financial risk-taking scale than women because they tend to view risk in the context of holding on to stocks, and women see it differently. On average, women believe that the longer they hold a stock, the greater the chances that it will bear fruit. This is not to suggest that millionaire men are hyperinvestors—on the contrary, fewer than 5 percent make fifty or more trades per year. It is no wonder that so many brokerage firms are now touting asset-management services as opposed to transaction fees for millionaires, since they have determined that so-called active traders are a dying species. Asset management with a fixed fee is like taxing a client's wealth. You must pay a set fee no matter how well or poorly your managed assets perform. It's much better to pay a fee for performance to firms which offer such services.

Most millionaires, both men and women, know that allowing others to manage your financial assets can weaken your intellect regarding investments. These individuals have detailed knowledge about investing, and they continue to enhance this database throughout their lives. It's difficult to become physically (or economically) fit if you allow others to exercise (or invest) for you!

DEALING WITH FEAR

Making critical financial-risk-related decisions about one's business and other investments can conjure up fear and worries. Fear is the cornerstone of panic, and panic is the mother of financial disaster. Most millionaire businesspeople take certain actions to enhance thought processes that reduce or even eliminate these fears and worries. Success in taking economic risk has much to do with how one deals with fear and worry. Analogous to this concept is a Wall Street axiom.

Sheep (timid investors) are the last segment to invest in an up market (thus assuring that they will pay top dollar for stocks). Sheep are by definition panic sellers (thus almost assuring that they will lose money). Sheep allow visions of total financial loss to overwhelm their judgment. Wise investors take risks. They do not panic when the direction of a stock moves south.

How do millionaires deal with the fear that is so often associated with financial decisions? These decisions are not limited to just investing in stocks; they include a broad array of business decisions, including the decision to become self-employed. Why is it that most millionaires never panic when confronted with risk? Millionaire businesswomen and their male counterparts have much in common in this regard. More than four in five report taking the following fear-reducing actions.

- Preparation (95% women versus 93% men). Both groups prepare, but women prepare more, seek more information, study more, and read more.
- Hard work (95% women versus 95% men). These men and women believe you can worry or you can work hard at solving a problem; worry only adds to the problem. Focus your mind on hard work, and you'll find it difficult to simultaneously visualize failure.
- Believing in oneself (99% women versus 96% men). Belief in one's ability starts early in life. It's all about setting goals and then achieving them. Today's achievements give one confidence to achieve more in the future.
- Focusing on key issues (84% women versus 91% men). Men are more comfortable focusing on one major issue, while women tend to spend more time examining several issues and then analyzing the possible consequences of related actions. Women are better able than men to run a business and at the same time head up a noble cause. Men feel that without focus on one key issue, their energy and intellect will be diffused.
- Being well organized to deal with major issues (90% women versus 82% men). Women are significantly more likely to indicate that they have strong organizational skills and that being well organized is a *very important* factor in explaining their economic success (56% women versus 38% men).

- Being decisive (88% women versus 93% men). Men suggest that focusing on one key issue allows them to be decisive. Women often report that they are uncomfortable with making "quick decisions." This is one reason that women spend more time researching and studying before taking economically related risks.
- Planning (90% women versus 86% men). Most women and men enjoy the planning process, especially visualizing the successful outcome of their efforts.

Women and men share common methods for fear reduction, but several significant differences distinguish their techniques. In general, women are more likely than men to reduce worry by consulting with others and sharing their concerns. Women typically take the following actions:

- Sharing concerns with a trusted friend (77% women versus 49% men).
- Seeking advice from outstanding people (75% women versus 59% men).
- Sharing concerns with a spouse (83% women versus 69% men).

Women do not find it ego deflating or a sign of weakness to discuss issues with others, although many men define such behavior as a badge of cowardice; they see it as admitting to others that they are weak. Is it true that the male instinct dictates that real men should bear all their fears and worries on their own shoulders? Men are significantly more likely than women to employ typically macho actions and thought processes, such as:

- Using mental toughness developed in sports (38% women versus 51% men).
- Outworking, outthinking, outtoughing the competition (61% women versus 79% men).

Isn't it clear why men who have lost their way will drive around for hours, loath to ask for directions? Also consider some other, more financially related issues. Women are significantly more likely to take the initiative of thoroughly researching a stock offering prior to initiating contact with their investment advisers for related advice. For most women, asking for advice is anything but ego deflating or a sign of weakness.

Men are significantly more likely to buy stocks in a different manner. Believing that seeking advice is a sign of weakness, they avoid research. Why not wait until the broker calls? He has some red-hot stock picks, the "stock du jour," but he warns that "you must show great courage by purchasing immediately. The window on this investment offering of a lifetime will close quickly." Who is more likely to make a "buy" decision so quickly and without the benefit of thoroughly researching the offering? You know the answer: men. Macho men love to demonstrate what they consider to be courageous behavior, and this need is often exploited by some who sell investments with this theme:

> Only a coward would be sheepish enough, dumb enough, to pass on investing in Ajax Limited. Only a coward would first have to check with his wife. You are not a coward, you are not stupid . . . or are you, Mr. Smith? That's why I know you will want to buy at least one thousand shares.

The response is often predictable. When their manhood is challenged, they must take defensive action, but what protects one's macho self-image is not necessarily a good defense of one's financial well-being.

WHO IS MORE ECONOMICALLY PRODUCTIVE?

Given these differences in orientation regarding investing and consumption-related lifestyles, it would be logical to speculate that women who are millionaires are superior to millionaire men in terms of producing wealth. Are women more economically productive than men in converting income to wealth? There are many factors that account for variations in wealth, and investing and spending habits are not the only significant factors.

To explore the relative abilities of women and men to accumulate wealth, you must first look at the big picture concerning economic productivity. One of the best measures of it is the RON index, which refers to return on net worth. What is your RON, Mrs. Jones? Note that Mrs. Jones is not a millionaire, but she thinks that she has accumulated "much wealth." Let us take her total annual realized income from all sources in her household ($125,000) and then compute her household's net worth (the value of all assets less liabilities). Mrs. Jones's household's net worth is $690,000. Dividing her household's income by its net worth, we arrive at a RON of about 18.1 percent for Mrs. Jones. In other words, her household realizes the equivalent of 18.1 percent of its total net worth annually. Mrs. Jones might feel proud of herself for generating such a high RON, but for those in higher income brackets, the lower the RON, the more economically productive the household is. Mrs. Jones's RON tells her that the equivalent of 18.1 percent of her wealth is being subject to income tax annually.

> *The more [you] realize, the more [you] must allocate for income taxes. So millionaires and those who will likely become affluent in the future adhere to an important rule: To build wealth, minimize your realized (taxable) income and maximize your unrealized income (wealth/capital appreciation without a cash flow). (The Millionaire Next Door, p. 55)*

Before she pats herself on the back, Mrs. Jones should compare her RON with those of the typical millionaire women and men profiled in this book. The typical male millionaire who is a business owner or manager has a RON of just over 8 (median). His female counterpart is not as productive. Women have a median RON of about 8.3. Look at the indices in another way. The typical successful businesswoman (given a RON of 8.3) has just over $12.00 of net worth per dollar of realized annual income. This is computed by taking the RON (8.3) and dividing it into 100, or by dividing median worth by median income. Call this measure the economic productivity index, or EPI. Men, on the other hand, have an EPI of approximately $12.50; i.e., they have $12.50 of net worth (median) for each dollar (median) of annual income their households realize.

Using the EPI measure, just where does Mrs. Jones stand? Recall her household's net worth of $690,000 and its income of $125,000. Mrs. Jones has an EPI of only about $5.50. In other words, her household generates about $5.50 of wealth or net worth for every dollar of its annual realized income. How does her EPI stack up against the typical American household's? The typical American household has a median net worth of approximately $72,000 and a median income of approximately $45,000. Thus, Mr. and Mrs. Typical American Household would have a whopping RON of 62.5 and an EPI of only $1.60! Their annual realized income is nearly two-thirds of their total net worth. How long could they survive if their income stream suddenly stopped? Perhaps a year or a bit longer. Note that the typical American household consumes nearly every dollar of income it generates each year.

Look at this another way. The estimated median age of an adult head of household in America is approximately forty-one, and his median net income is approximately $45,000. How much should the typical household in America be worth? Use the wealth equation:

Expected net worth = 1/10 (age) x annual realized income

The typical household in the United States should have a net worth of $184,500. But at $72,000, or about 39 percent of what the equation predicts, it falls far short of this criterion.

An Income Statement Affluent household, a hunter-gatherer household, is one whose net worth is one-half or less of that expected by the wealth equation. Yes, the typical American household fits this parameter. We are a country of spenders. So Mrs. Jones's household is actually a lot more productive than is typical in America. Given her household's annual realized income ($125,000) and the fact that Mrs. Jones is fifty years old, her expected net worth is $625,000. That is a bit below its actual level of $629,000. Yet Mrs. Jones's household does not qualify for the Balance Sheet Affluent status of cultivators because its actual net worth does not exceed the expected level by a multiple of two or more.

Most of the millionaires profiled herein, whether female or male, are cultivators of wealth, and both are highly productive groups. Yet as pointed out, they are somewhat different in terms of their respective RONs and their EPI figures. Thus, the question of whether men are more economically productive than women is not a simple one. But what if, for example, both groups allocated their income the same way? What if the only difference between them was their choice of stocks and not how much they invested in publicly traded equities? If this were the case, given their respective RON scores, then one could at least speculate that men might in fact be more productive (tend to accumulate more wealth per dollar of income) than women.

In reality, however, women millionaires who are business owners allocate their income differently from their male counterparts even beyond their investing and buying habits. Once we review how these two groups differ with respect to charitable contributions and economic gifts, the question of variations in economic productivity can be addressed once again.

WHO IS MORE GENEROUS?

Women are more generous than men in several ways.

The typical woman who is a millionaire business owner allocates 4.7 percent of her household's annual realized income to her adult children, grandchildren, nieces and nephews, brothers and sisters, and the like. Men who are millionaire business owners allocate far less: 1.5 percent.

Also, as noted previously, during their lifetime millionaire women who own and manage their own businesses tend to donate a larger portion of their income to charitable and other noble causes than do their male counterparts. On average, male respondents contributed 5.34 percent of their households' total annual realized income, while the millionaire women surveyed donated an average of 6.84 percent. Women donated, on average, the equivalent of $1 for every $14.62 of income; for men, it was $1 for every $18.73 of income.

There is another interesting finding. About 80 percent of the millionaire women business owners in this sample are currently married. Nearly nine in ten of their husbands work for a living. Yet in more than eight out of ten cases (82 percent), the millionaire women earn the majority of the household income. What does this have to do with charitable giving?

There is a highly significant correlation between the percentage of household income that is earned by the millionaire women and the percentage of the household's income contributed to noble causes.

THE ECONOMIC PRODUCTIVITY QUESTION, AGAIN

What if we make certain adjustments in our calculations that generate EPI? What if women gave the same level of "economic gifts of kindness" to their relatives as men did? If so, they typically would have more than 3 percent (4.7 percent given by women versus 1.5 percent given by men) of their annual income "back in their pockets." Similarly, what if these women donated the same percentage of their income to noble causes (5.34 percent instead of 6.84 percent)? Add another 1.5 percent of income to their pockets. This additional money, invested each year over ten, twenty, or even more years could translate into considerable increases in wealth. Given these adjustments, the RON and EPI measures would indicate that these women may indeed be more economically productive than men.

II.

EARLY
SOCIALIZATION

CHAPTER 4

The Parents of Successful Businesswomen

*M*ost successful women business owners were raised in a parental environment that was a training ground for success. Their parents were their proactive mentors, positive role models, cheerleaders, and motivators. Only two of the more than four hundred women surveyed reported that they were ever pampered, indulged, or treated as if they were exempt from discipline. None of the others were raised as queens or even princesses.

The successful businesswomen profiled herein have strong images of their parents and the environment in which they were raised. Even today, on average nearly thirty years after the women left home, they have vivid memories of the character of the home environment provided by their parents, and they report that their upbringing was highly conducive to becoming a success in life.

These successful women profiled their parents in regard to twenty characteristics, habits, and behaviors. These influential characteristics were distilled from more than one hundred traits and behaviors mentioned by the women who participated in a series of preliminary personal and focus-group interviews and from letters, e-mails, and telephone conversations. It was determined that five major factors were significant in profiling the "habits of parents" of these successful women. These dimensions were generated from a computer program, a factor analysis that clusters components (in this case, characteristics of parents) according to response patterns. Table 4-1 lists these dimensions along with their underlying characteristics.

TABLE 4-1

PARENTAL HABITS: RAISING THE SUCCESSFUL WOMAN

	Parent Index[1]
1. HARMONY/EMPATHY	
Taught me to have empathy for the needs of others (those less fortunate)[2]	749
Ran a very well organized household	333
Provided a home atmosphere filled with love and harmony	355
Had great respect for each other and their children	306
Regularly attended religious services	230
2. INITIATIVE/LEADERSHIP	
Encouraged me to take the initiative	400
Encouraged me to be a creative thinker	275
Taught me to have empathy for the needs of others	749
Taught me never to follow the crowd	407
Encouraged me to take leadership roles in school	239
3. HAPPINESS/SATISFACTION	
Had a strong love of life	341
Rarely complained	212
Were always optimistic	177
4. INDEPENDENCE	
Gave me much responsibility early in life	770
Encouraged me to earn my own spending money	536
Taught me the importance of saving and investing	257
Were strict disciplinarians	262
5. RESPONSIVENESS	
Always had time to listen to my opinions	204
Always used positive incentives to encourage me to achieve	178
Did not threaten me with harsh punishment if I earned a bad grade	608
Were rarely, if ever, cold and indifferent to me	440

[1] Parent Index: Ratio of % of parents with versus without this quality x 100.

[2] This "empathy" component is a construct of both the harmony/empathy and initiative/leadership dimensions.

From the responses of 439 successful women surveyed, an index for each of these characteristics was developed. For example, note the index of 400 for the item "Encouraged me to take the initiative." The number 400 means that for every 100 successful businesswomen (projected from this sample onto the national population of women who are successful businesswomen) who indicated that their parents did not teach them to take the initiative, there were 400 who indicated that their parents did teach them to do so. In other words, four respondents reported that their parents taught them to take the initiative for every one respondent who indicated that her parents did not.

An index of 100 would indicate that equal portions of these successful women (50 percent versus 50 percent) agree that their parents had or did not have a particular trait. Overall, the responses to each of the twenty items suggest that the majority of the parents of these women did in fact provide their daughters with a nurturing environment.

Note that the "empathy" item is a component of both factor 1, harmony and empathy, and factor 2, leadership. The five domains or categories of responses are as follows:

1. Harmony/Empathy. Most of these women were taught from an early age "how to get along with others." As indicated in Table 4-1, for every 100 who were not raised in an atmosphere filled with love and harmony, there were 355 who were indeed the product of a loving and harmonious environment. Their parents also ran a well-organized household and taught their children to respect others. These tools of management eventually translated into these young women becoming business leaders. Simply stated, their parents were folks whom people would likely want as employers, and today their daughters are the type of employers whom employees praise.

2. Initiative/Leadership. Successful business owners by definition are people who have a history of "taking the initiative," but operating a productive enterprise requires more than initiative. It also helps to be creative when selecting one's product or service offerings. Those who are not creative, who follow the crowd with "me too" offerings, or who are not comfortable taking leadership roles are not likely to succeed in business.

For most of these women, initiative, creative thought, empathy for customer needs, and leadership skills were elements of the environment provided by their parents. Being different and being creative were qualities that were nurtured, not ridiculed. Parents gave these women encouragement, praising their daughters for their unique qualities.

3. Happiness/Satisfaction. Those from happy and satisfied parents tend to be happy and satisfied themselves. If you pictured the ideal boss in your mind, she would love life, rarely complain, and be perpetually optimistic. It's much easier to motivate employees and favorably influence customers if one has a very positive attitude. And optimism is infectious, especially in a business setting. Most of these successful businesswomen share their parents' "strong love of life." It is estimated that for every 100 successful women who report that their parents did not have a strong love of life, 341 report that their parents did in fact love life and counted their blessings each and every day.

4. Independence. Most of the women profiled indicated that their parents encouraged them to be independent, wanting them to be strong, financially secure women, and they succeeded in helping their daughters reach this goal. Most of their daughters can vividly recall their parents praising and encouraging them to earn their own spending money. Projected on a national basis, for every 100 of the successful business owners who report that their parents did not do so, there are an estimated 536 who indicate the opposite. Even those who were not encouraged to earn their own spending money had a multitude of part-time and summer jobs while growing up. One of the most pervasive characteristics of these women is their history of early work experiences. With the exception of two responses, *all* of the women began earning very early in life. More than half of those who attended college paid for all of their tuition, fees, and related expenses not covered by scholarships.

5. Responsiveness. Most of these women indicated that their parents "always had time to listen." The ability to listen to the voices of employees, customers, and suppliers is often a critical dimension that explains the success of a business owner or manager. Only a minority of the women reported that their parents were cold and indifferent, and they were outnumbered by a ratio of better than four to one. For whom would you most enjoy working, supplying, and buying? More often than not, the answer is someone who listens intently and genuinely demonstrates interest and enthusiasm.

Alpha and Beta Parents

About three in four (78 percent) of these women had nurturing parents, as is evident from the responses to each of the twenty parental characteristics in Table 4-1. Women who indicated that their parents possessed the majority of these characteristics were arbitrarily designated Alpha women. What about the other 22 percent, the Beta women? They succeeded in spite of being raised by parents who, in general, did not provide them with the nurturing environment of the Alpha women. This chapter discusses in some detail the concept that "nurturing parents produce Alpha women." But some of the most successful women profiled in this book are Beta women. Their need and resolve to overcome the obstacles of their parental environment emerged when they were quite young, and they are profiled in chapter 5. Whether Alpha or Beta, the environment in which they were raised had a major influence upon these women.

From the People Who Gave Us Plaid

It is interesting to take the issue of parenting a step further back and explore the ancestry of our millionaire businesswomen. Note the wide array of countries of origin among them (see Table 4-2). It is clear that for the majority, their forefathers were not on the *Mayflower* or even on the *Queen Elizabeth*, but this made little difference in the arena of business opportunities. Entrance into the ranks of the self-employed is not restricted by one's ethnic background, and no one group has a monopoly on business ownership.

Table 4-2 indicates that those who designated Scottish as their ethnic origin accounted for only 1.7 percent of all households in America, but 8.5 percent of the population of millionaire businesswomen are of Scottish extraction. In regard to concentration, the Scottish ancestry group is five times (5.00) more likely to contain millionaire businesswomen households than would be expected from its overall portion (1.7 percent) of American households. Along the same lines, those with French ancestry ranked second, followed by those of Russian, Dutch, and then English descent.

Note that in previous studies the Scottish ancestry group was also found to rank high in regard to the percentage of its cohort that are in

TABLE 4-2

THE TOP TEN ANCESTRY GROUPS OF MILLIONAIRE BUSINESSWOMEN IN AMERICA

Ancestry Group of Millionaire Businesswomen	Percent of All U.S. Households	Percent of Millionaire Businesswomen Population	Rank: Percent of Millionaire Businesswomen Population	Concentration Ratio: % of All Millionaire Businesswomen Population/% of All Households	Rank: Concentration Ratio
English	10.3%	18.1%	1st	1.76	5th
German	19.4%	14.9%	2nd	0.77	10th
Irish	9.6%	14.8%	3rd	1.54	6th
Scottish	1.7%	8.5%	4th	5.00	1st
French	2.5%	6.6%	5th	2.64	2nd
Native American	4.9%	6.2%	6th	1.27	7th
Italian	4.8%	5.0%	7th	1.04	8th
Dutch	1.6%	3.3%	8th	2.06	4th
Polish	2.9%	2.7%	9th	0.93	9th
Russian	1.1%	2.6%	10th	2.36	3rd

the millionaire net worth segment. (See, for example, *The Millionaire Next Door*, p. 17.) In those studies, 92 percent of the national sample of millionaires were men and nearly 70 percent were self-employed business owners. It does not seem to matter. Those of Scottish ancestry, whether male or female, are significantly more likely than the norm to be millionaires. What about those of Scottish ancestry who are teachers, professors, physicians, attorneys, engineers, or selling professionals? More often than not, the Scots are found to be Balance Sheet as opposed to Income Statement Affluent.

It is very difficult to build a business and achieve without being frugal, and the Scots are known for their frugal ways. After all, they gave us plaid! It never goes out of style, and it does not show stains and dirt like other designs. Beyond these folk themes, those of Scottish ancestry tend to spend less and save and invest more than the norm. Scottish millionaires are among the most frugal of the frugal, and they have passed on their philosophy of thrift to generation after generation.

ALPHA WOMEN OF ALPHA PARENTS

Here are some of the key issues to be addressed in my profiles of successful millionaire businesswomen who had Alpha parents and became Alpha women.

- What did these women learn from their parents? How were they influenced by them?
- What key elements of the parental environment translated into their success as business leaders?
- What influence, if any, did their upbringing have upon their decision to become self-employed business owners?
- Was their choice of business—i.e., specific types of products or services—somehow related to their parental environment?

Most of the women profiled throughout this book are, in fact, Alpha women, but it is important to note that not all Alpha women reported having parents who were nurturing in regard to all five of the domains cited in Table 4-1. Those who had parents lacking in one or more of these measures still found a way to capitalize on those positive qualities that their parents taught them.

FAWN C.

Fawn's parents provided her with an environment that was highly conducive to her becoming a successful adult. In nineteen of the twenty measures of the parental environment, Fawn's parents were judged by their daughter to have provided a very nurturing household. Fawn is a financial success, and like most of the women profiled herein, reports that she is highly satisfied with her life and her career. Fawn is both financially and psychologically secure, and she has high self-confidence and self-esteem. Acquiring the pseudoartifacts of wealth is not the source of Fawn's satisfaction with life and her self-esteem. And Fawn does not need to display her success through what she wears or what she drives. She learned her consumption behavior and attitudes about life from her parents, who taught her to become a successful leader, an owner and manager of her own business. The lessons they taught her read like a list of ideal traits that employees would like their employer to possess.

People like Fawn who were raised in loving and stable environments are better able to deal with the realities of self-employment. Fawn indicated that her parents did an outstanding job in providing their children with much love and harmony. The children were respected and were never treated as servants. Fawn's parents always seemed to have time to answer her questions, and they took the time to listen to each other and to their children. Tasks and chores were part of Fawn's home life, but both her parents were excellent role models and leaders when it came to directing household activities. Her parents did their share of chores with enthusiasm.

Fawn is stable because her parents were emotionally stable. When changes take place in the business environment, which is often stressful, risky, and uncertain, she adjusts to these and never overreacts. Employees do not enjoy working for an unstable employer, and Fawn is an ideal boss. She was also taught by her parents to respect and trust people and to trust her own instincts. She sees the potential in the people she employs and enhances their confidence and productivity by recognizing their individual qualities.

Like most of the successful women who were interviewed, Fawn indicated that her parents taught her to have empathy for the needs of others. She translated this lesson into an integral part of her management style. As a leader, Fawn believes it is important to:

Always watch for every opportunity to quietly support those around you.

Fawn knows something else about leaders: they should be valued and admired. As her parents taught:

Measure your own value in terms of the security and happiness of those who depend on you. Be responsible for their help . . . you will make a difference in your world.

Do your employees admire you? Do they trust you? Do they believe you are not exploiting them? Do they feel you have their best interests at heart? Fawn's employees tend to answer yes to these questions, but what if she suddenly changed her consumption habits? What if she drove to work each day in an expensive luxury car and wore a $20,000 diamond-encrusted watch? Then her employees might begin to question her motives and suspect that their employer was exploiting them. According to Fawn, success is not indicated by consumption; it is the product of what she learned from her parents: be financially and psychologically independent, achieve, have pride and high self-esteem, and help others achieve their goals.

Like her parents, Fawn believes:

Each day on this earth should be treated as a gift.

Most of the successful Alpha women profiled reported that their parents had a similar passion for life; they were optimistic and rarely complained. They were doers who did not waste time or emotional energy complaining. They directed their energy in ways that enhanced their productivity and satisfaction with life.

How did Fawn's parents define independence? They did so in terms of their daughter becoming self-reliant, financially independent, well educated, and an independent thinker. The foundation for becoming financially independent is developing a frugal consumption lifestyle, and how did Fawn's parents encourage their daughter to believe in that ideal? They told Fawn with words and deeds:

> *Fawn, build your self-esteem, your pride, your independence, with what you know, not with what you own. Avoid debt.*

Fawn's parents taught their daughter to focus on learning and promised that financial success would follow. This was sound advice for a woman who today owns and manages her own market research and consulting business, and who continues to learn and enhance her self-esteem as well as the productivity of her business. In an economy that begs for solutions, Fawn suggests that one should

> *never stop learning. It is a great opportunity and joy, especially today.*

Fawn's current success in business did not just happen. She was raised by parents who encouraged their daughter to become well-rounded not only in the classroom environment but also in the world of commerce. Like nearly all the women profiled herein, Fawn had a variety of work experiences, starting before she was a teenager, for her folks believed that knowledge must be leveraged properly if one is to earn a good living. Fawn did exactly this. She earned very high grades in college, but she also had a significant number of real-world, job-related experiences before she completed college.

Fawn's parents also taught her the value of saving and investing and encouraged her to do her own research in terms of selecting stocks. Fawn is her own investment adviser. Over the years, she has tested the efficacy of her research and stock selection against many so-called professional stockbrokers, and her selections always seem to outperform those of the pros. Fawn enjoys doing investment-related research because selecting the proper investments is part of her lust for learning. Also, her self-esteem is enhanced by her being able to make her own investment decisions.

Fawn's folks encouraged her to be a leader, to take the initiative, and never to follow the crowd. Is it any wonder that she opted to become a self-employed business owner? Some call this the vocation of ultimate independence.

What type of wealth transfers did Fawn's parents give to their daughter? They did help pay for some of her undergraduate college expenses, but again, they always encouraged their daughter to earn her own spending money. Little direct encouragement was needed, since Fawn always enjoyed earning. Fawn's parents also helped finance their daughter's venture into self-employment by providing a loan when she was starting her business. In turn, Fawn recently provided a loan to her oldest child for the same purpose.

Fawn emphasized the meaning of honoring one's ancestors. In her mind, we are obligated to excel, to be productive, and to do noble deeds in life.

Be responsible . . . take the initiative . . . lead. Do it for [and] remember all those who have sustained you [your ancestors] with food for the body, mind, and spirit. Be responsible, for they helped make a difference in your world.

Some of us are able to stand on the shoulders of our ancestors, but Fawn is adamant about the dangers of living vicariously. Those whose ancestors were achievers but who have achieved little or nothing on their own often feel no real need to excel in life. They believe that the successes and in some cases the fame of their forefathers position them in the successful segment of society. They may have inherited millions of dollars, own dozens of portraits of successful ancestors and hundreds of other artifacts from their wealthy ancestors, but it does not matter. Success is not something given. According to Fawn, it is something earned, and those who feel otherwise are deluded. If they focus on their ancestors' achievements instead of their own, they will not likely become productive people.

Not in one instance did Fawn or any of the successful business-women profiled herein refer to the successes of their ancestors. They did often cite what they learned from their parents and grandparents, and they detailed their pride in being business owners and leaders. Their focus is not on the past. These are women who are doers today and will be in the future. Even those millionaire women who are direct descendants of the rich or famous don't focus on the achievements of those who came before them.

TRISH S. WEAR

As Dr. J. P. Conrad tells it, he dated a personable young woman throughout college. The two always seemed to be together, but there was one activity that Dr. Conrad avoided—clothes shopping. His girlfriend was especially irritable when looking for swimwear. This otherwise charming woman became cranky the moment she began shopping for a swimsuit because she could never find a bikini that even came close to fitting her properly. She was, according to Dr. Conrad, "a 34DD top with a 32 bottom!" The only way she could deal with the problem was to buy either two suits of different sizes or a large suit that she could then have altered.

It is unfortunate that Dr. Conrad's girlfriend was never exposed to the bathing suits sold by Trish S. Wear. Trish's company specializes in designing and producing swimwear for just about any figure imaginable. Her sixteen-page color catalog features many women wearing swimsuits, and nearly every one of the models depicted has a different shape or size. Here are Trish's words in the introduction of that catalog:

> *Welcome.*
> *Our goal is to create the "perfect swimsuit" for women of all shapes and sizes. We offer mix-and-match separates, as well as figure-flattering one-pieces, cover-ups, and accessories. We specialize in large cups and full-coverage bottoms. . . . Our goal is for every customer to look and feel fantastic in our suits.*
>
> *Our swimwear and dancewear line has been manufactured and available since 1980. Over the years we have taken great pride in fulfilling our customers' wants and needs. Once you've worn ours, you will never wear another brand.*

Later in the catalog Trish gives more details about her high degree of empathy for women of all sizes:

> *From "AA" to "G" cups, from a size 4 to a size 26, we can give you a perfect fit. On bikinis you can order tops and bottoms separately to get the combination just right for your figure!*
>
> *To ensure proper fit, please use the chart below. If you have any questions, please give us a call. We have customer service specialists standing by to help! Call our 800 number.*

Why did Trish opt to become a self-employed owner and manager of her own business, and why did she decide to design, manufacture, and market custom swimwear? The answer to both of these questions has much to do with her parents. They were profiled by their daughter as Alpha types, but not all Alpha parents are the same. Fawn's parents, for example, put a great deal of emphasis on learning. Her parents had great empathy and sensitivity for Fawn's high analytical intelligence, and they understood her keen interest in academic achievement. Fawn had nearly perfect high school and college grades and extraordinarily high SAT scores. Of course, Fawn's parents helped her understand the importance of bridging intellectual learning with the real-world need for information. Given her interests and attitudes, Fawn was a perfect fit for the market-research industry.

But Trish is a different type of woman. Her parents recognized that not all children are interested in earning straight A's in school; not all have a strong desire to graduate number one in their class. Instead, they encouraged certain key attributes that were the foundation for her success in the swimwear business:

They always encouraged me to be creative. . . . One must dream but also be responsible. . . . [Seek] to do what you love, . . . not to follow but to lead. . . . [My job] enables me to use my best talents.

Too often, parents force their children to study a profession or earn an advanced degree, pushing them in certain directions. Why are there so many lawyers who dislike their jobs? Why do so many women who earn law degrees drop out of their profession? Perhaps the reason is lack of real interest. Too often women become attorneys without having a real knowledge of the day-to-day activities of the legal profession.

Conversely, why do more than 95 percent of the businesswomen surveyed for this book indicate that they receive a great deal of satisfaction from their careers? Being self-employed is a large part of it, but it is also about the other key choice that these women make. Almost all these women report that they love and have great passion for the specific type of business they own and manage.

Trish would not likely be the success she is today if it were not for her parents. They were sensitive to the fact that Trish had high creative intellect, and they saw something in her that others might have overlooked.

Creativity is not measured on aptitude tests. Some students can learn every single thing that textbooks and teachers throw at them, but this does not translate into having a high degree of creativity. How well you learn other people's ideas will only get you so far. The marketplace rewards those who create unique solutions to problems. What did Trish's folks do when they saw their young daughter sketching women's clothing designs and, at an early age, cutting and sewing? What did they do when they noticed that their daughter had leadership qualities, was a very responsible, personable child, and always enjoyed earning her own spending money?

Trish's parents encouraged her to dream and to nurture her dreams. They provided "their creative" Trish with an environment that was indeed ideal for molding a child into becoming a successful entrepreneur.

Parents, do you want your children to succeed in business? Then help them find something, a vocation, a product, or a service that they love. As Trish suggests:

> Ask them, "What is your dream?" Dream! Expose them to many things even in play [as young children]. Let them be children, encourage them, as did my parents, to play . . . have fun. . . . Don't stress out your young children. . . . Don't stress them out about worrying [about] . . . what are they going to do for the rest of their lives. Let your children do what they enjoy [select vocations]. Find a way, encourage them to help people at the same time. . . . [Encourage] kind acts. . . . Give them love and confidence . . . encourage them.

Like other members of her cohort, Trish is a generous person, donating "at least 10 percent of her income to noble causes," but she has never in her life spent more than $100 for a pair of shoes, $300 for a suit, $28,000 for a motor vehicle, or $243,000 for a home. Trish has never been a member of a country club, but she does invest about 10 percent of her income each year. She and her husband are long-term investors, and she indicates that she "only sold a stock once . . . to pay for a new kitchen."

Trish was never indulged by her parents, and they never indiscriminately showered gifts on their daughter. Her parents lived within their means. Hyperconsuming was not part of her upbringing, but the desire to achieve and to be financially and psychologically independent was part of her socialization process.

Trish never keeps a credit card balance that would require interest payments, although she is not adverse to using credit for "things that appreciate," such as her home. At one time Trish did apply and was approved for a more unconventional type of loan: her nurturing parents provided their daughter with a "small" loan to start her business. They bet their time, energy, love, and later money on Trish becoming a success. They bet on the right horse.

AVERY

Avery ranks high on most conventional measures of success, and by all accounts she is an extraordinary woman. Her annual realized income places her in the one-in-one-thousand category—she personally earns over $1 million per year, and her net worth is in the high seven figures. But these economic measures of success don't tell her entire story. Avery takes tremendous pride in the fact that she started from economic ground zero. Her parents were of very modest means, but more importantly, they were of the Alpha variety.

Today Avery owns and manages a highly successful consulting business, which she launched entirely with her own savings. This was not a problem for Avery; she has been working and saving since childhood. Helped by scholarships she earned, Avery alone paid for her undergraduate and graduate fees and expenses. She has never received as much as one dollar of economic assistance from her parents or anyone else, but she often "helps out financially" when it comes to her parents and siblings and their children. Avery's parents gave her much more than money, cars, or expensive clothing. They taught her how to think, how to lead, and, of course, how to succeed.

Avery did not start her working career as a self-employed business owner. After she received her MBA, she accepted a job with a large multinational corporation and worked there for six years. During that time, she received numerous promotions and salary increases.

Avery often interfaced with a variety of "outside" consulting types, who targeted her in several ways. They were constantly debriefing Avery about her views and recommendations for changes in corporate strategy. She spent many evenings and weekends responding to questionnaires from a variety of consulting firms and working on additional assignments from them. Avery provided these consultants with every conceivable piece of information about her employer's corporation, and often spent hours presenting her own strategic recommendations. They asked, "What would you suggest in terms of changes?" Months later, they would present a plan, and Avery read every word contained in these plans. It did not take long before she realized something that changed her life. Most of the recommendations in the plans came from a source other than the consulting firms; much of the content was Avery's. She discovered through her own experience that what her favorite professor in business school had said was true:

> *A consultant is someone who borrows your watch and then charges for telling you what time it is!*

Actually, Avery was never bitter about "doing much of the work . . . [and] receiving little or no credit." It was all part of her learning experience. Another part of her learning experience came from hiring and evaluating consultants, and from approving the payments for fees and expenses submitted by consultants. The size of these fees was often "staggering," especially to a young woman who came from modest means.

Why did her employer always ask Avery for her input on these projects? Why indeed. Quite simply, she always came up with the same answer. It was the same theme that her dad often preached to his children:

> *Always, always remember, you are your own greatest [and] . . . best resource!*

When a father tells his ten-year-old daughter this, she may not get the point. She might not see the light even when she is twenty years old. But Avery did understand the meaning of her dad's wisdom when she was "carrying several consultants" on her back.

If you do not believe that you are your greatest resource, then no one else will believe it either. But if you realize that you are, then ask yourself the same questions that Avery posed:

> *Why sell your greatest resource to others? Who should own and benefit from the goose who produces golden eggs?*

Why should Avery spend upwards of eighty hours per week placing her eggs in other people's nests? Avery opted for self-employment, but not before going through a series of what-ifs. For every one, she had the right answer.

Q: What if she could not put together enough capital to go out on her own? How would it be possible to initially pay for office space, furniture, and supplies?

A: Avery had hundreds of meetings with consultants, but not one took place at their offices. A small yet productive consulting firm can be run out of a telephone booth! Consultants sell information, so there is much less financial burden than is normally associated with selling tangible products. Also, consultants are usually paid a sizable portion of their fee before the project is initiated. Why not fund one's business with other people's money?

Q: Was she good enough, smart enough, ambitious enough, to succeed?

A: Avery had had a lot of on-the-job opportunities to judge her competition. She judged herself to be her own best resource.

Q: How and to whom could she market her offerings?

A: Avery had made many contacts in her industry through her trade-association activities. She could speak well in front of an audience and was an experienced writer of reports and strategic plans. She had written many articles for trade journals. Some bore her name; others were ghost-written for her so-called superiors. Avery also had much experience, dating back to grade school, in leading others.

Q: But what would her peers, her so-called on-the-job mentors, think if she quit her corporate job? Who in their right mind would give up a position as an officer of a Fortune 100 company to become a self-employed management consultant? Why enter a profession that is rated as the most stressful in America?

A: Avery's father had told her countless times: Never worry about what others think; always be a leader. Her dad had also followed his own advice when dealing with emotional stress. He'd instilled his beliefs in Avery by repeating, "Never worry; never get upset about anything," and she'd adopted his philosophy about these issues. According to Avery, her dad always preached that one can either worry about problems or work at solving those problems that can be solved. And problems that cannot be solved should not be worried about.

Avery is well suited to be a management consultant. She is well equipped psychologically and spiritually to deal with stress. Thanks to her Alpha parents, she rarely, if ever, worries about anything. Avery learned from her dad's teachings. Her parents provided their children with a loving, nurturing, and stable environment. Her parents instilled in her a strong religious faith, a sense of what is right, and a need to help others. Their nurturing home helped Avery decide to become self-employed, and it had much to do with her need to achieve, to lead, and to utilize her own best resource to the fullest extent.

MRS. MARION MUDD

Not all the Alpha women profiled reported that their parents were nurturing with regard to all the domains in Table 4-1. Some, like Marion Mudd, related that their folks were not always optimistic, nor were they always willing to spend time listening to the opinions of their children. In fact, her folks were sometimes downright "pushy," sharp-tongued, or sarcastic, but they provided their daughter with a great deal of encouragement in most other respects. They taught Marion to be a leader, to have empathy and respect for all types of people, and to think for herself. She was encouraged to question the conventional wisdom and the fashions of so-called trendsetters as depicted by the media and in advertisements.

Marion was trained to be sensitive to opposing viewpoints and countertrends. Being different in thought and deed was something to be proud of, not condemned. Her folks convinced their daughter that she had the ability and aptitude to excel at any task, at any vocation she set her sights on, and that there was no such thing as women's versus men's work or high-status and therefore desirable versus low-status and therefore undesirable work. One's choice of vocation should be based on the satisfaction, the pride, the self-esteem, and the freedom it could provide.

Only a minority of women opt to become self-employed business owners, and that is due, in part, to how they are raised. Marion's parents encouraged her to lead, not follow, and they never put boundaries in her mind about her choice of vocation. Self-employment was a natural choice for her.

Would it be acceptable to you if your daughter chose self-employment? And if she did decide to join these ranks, what types of businesses would you consider ideal? Perhaps you would not object too much if she owned an automobile dealership that sold new cars or luxury motor vehicles. Would you condone your child's choice to become an antiques dealer? Yes, but only if the antiques she marketed were once owned by kings and queens.

What if your daughter wanted to become a purveyor of dirt, soil, fill, and mulch? What would you and your friends and relatives think about your daughter becoming the "dirt lady"? Neither Marion nor her parents cared much about what other people thought, and that is why, in large part, Marion is a successful person today.

Much of Marion's accomplishments can be traced back directly to the nurturing environment that her parents provided. In many ways, their consumption behavior, as well as their deeds and ideas in general, were of the contrarian variety. It's no wonder that Marion takes pride in being referred to as "different." Is there something wrong with being different? On the contrary. Marion is well above the norm in regard to her net worth, satisfaction with life, and contributions made to noble causes, although she's way below the norm for those in her high-income cohort with respect to the amount of money she allocates for consumer products and services.

You may have heard the expression "dirt cheap." Most people do believe that dirt is cheap, that it has a negative value. We pay to get rid of dirt. Why else would more than eighty million households in this country own at least one washing machine? But some people recognize that large quantities of certain types of dirt can be very valuable.

Perceptive people who see value in such things as dirt, scrap metal, rags, or junked motor vehicles perceive opportunities that most of us ignore. About fourteen million motor vehicles are scrapped each year in America, translating into over forty-five billion pounds of metal to be reprocessed. But how many of us give any consideration to collecting, accumulating, buying, or selling rusty, junked cars? Very few, I suspect. The women profiled in this book have a unique talent for spotting opportunities that most others ignore, because their parents taught them to appreciate the value of rejecting the majority opinions. Many had parents who were contrarians, and their alternative thinking often explains why they are successful in business. They were raised by parents who encouraged them to think differently, to follow their own drummer, never the crowd. So it is with Mrs. Mudd. While in excess of 100 million households in this country hate dirt, Mrs. Mudd embraces it. She sells dirt, she buys dirt, she stores dirt, she grades dirt, and she has an affection for dirt. Mrs. Mudd reads trade journals about dirt, dirt-moving equipment, and those who buy and sell dirt. In essence, Mrs. Mudd is extremely dirt-sensitive.

Most people in my audiences are surprised—some even incredulous—when I tell them that a dirt business made Mrs. Mudd a multimillionaire. They are also surprised when I highlight a recent newspaper story detailing the facts about a contract for the dirt needed to construct a new runway at Hartsfield-Jackson International Airport. (See Richard Whitt, "Fairness in Airport Dirt Rebid Pledged," *Atlanta Journal-Constitution*, November 1, 2001, B1, B3.) How much dirt was required and at what price? An estimated twenty-seven million cubic yards of dirt, costing $350 million (or $13 per cubic yard), will be needed for the runway. The dollar figure includes the cost of the dirt and its placement and compacting, but it all comes under the heading of the business called dirt. Mrs. Mudd did not participate in the airport dirt deal because she specializes in "higher-end dirt." High-grade topsoil and planting soil is a major part of her business, and it sells for many times more per cubic yard than the lower-end dirt used for runways and highways. So even in dirt circles, a social hierarchy exists.

Just what type of status does our society ascribe to people who are in the dirt business? They are not viewed as being high on the occupational prestige scale. That's fine with Mrs. Mudd. Her folks taught her to ignore this social convention, and that has much to do with how Mrs. Mudd became wealthy. Society doesn't expect her and her ilk to be members of exclusive country clubs, and in fact, she isn't. Yet one has to wonder just how many country club members in America are in the same financial league as Mrs. Mudd, with her net worth in excess of $7 million. According to my own surveys of high-income households, most country club members have nowhere near a net worth of $7 million, and most are members of the Income Statement Affluent crowd—with high income and low net worth. The majority of members of country clubs are not millionaires.

There is something rather humorous about discussing the profile of Mrs. Mudd in the context of country clubs. You may never find her playing golf at the Elite Golf and Country Club of Prestige Hills, but if you check out her day planner for the last year or so, you will note that she often made appearances there as well as at many other golf clubs.

She was supervising the delivery and distribution of the rather expensive high-grade dirt that is crucial for top golf course greens and fairways. And don't forget the role that dirt plays in producing all those wonderful flowers and shrubs surrounding the clubhouses.

One consistent finding of my research over the years is the connection between occupational status and wealth. Within each homogeneous age and income cohort, there is a negative relationship between occupational status and net worth because it takes a lot of money to maintain the consumption lifestyle that is compatible with high occupational status. But what does society expect of Mrs. Mudd and the other blue-collar entrepreneurs of America? It is perfectly acceptable if they don't drive a BMW. It's okay if they don't live in luxury homes and wear $2,000 suits. And who would expect Mrs. Mudd to hang out at an exclusive country club? Yes, the views of Mrs. Mudd's parents are manifested today in their daughter's contrarian behavior.

Mrs. Mudd is indeed the product of her parents in both her ideas and her actions. They encouraged her to develop her own means of warding off pressures to spend. Mrs. Mudd was inoculated against needing to display her financial success. So what if members of the country club look at her with disdain? She deflects those demeaning, down-the-nose glances. She is immune to snubs and sneers—it's part of her constitution. Mrs. Mudd is a strong, confident woman possessing high self-esteem. And why not? She is her own person. She could easily provide for herself economically for fifty years without working one more day. But there is more to her high self-esteem than financial independence. She is also a very charitable person. Helping others gives her more pride and satisfaction than living a high-consumption lifestyle.

Mrs. Mudd was kind enough to detail what her parents taught her, as well as some of her own beliefs about money, success, and material wealth:

Success should not be measured by . . . how large the house, how expensive the car. . . . I detest flaunted wealth. Success [should be measured] by what a person does in regard to business practices, ethics, environment, and human kindness. . . . Money should be the pleasant outcome of one's endeavors, not the main goal. . . . Be kind, be honest, stay focused and unafraid to go after your dream. . . . The main lesson in becoming financially successful [is] . . . never spend more than you make [and] . . . always save and invest.

Mrs. Mudd excels in all of these areas. She owns and operates a very productive business, and she is a woman of great religious-based integrity.

MRS. BARBARA GEM . . . BY ANY OTHER NAME

Mrs. Gem paid for her own college expenses, including both undergraduate and graduate school. Even when she was in high school, she earned most of her spending money. She received very little financial support from her parents or anyone else. Yet she gives her parents rave reviews concerning many of the intangibles, the key components of the nurturing environment they provided for their children.

These intangibles are much more important in molding a successful daughter than expensive clothing, automobiles, or other consumer goods. It's why Mrs. Barbara Gem is a major success today. Her mother taught her about the value of money. Her parents were fastidious savers and investors, and they were her mentors and role models in this and related areas. Barbara was also trained to be a leader, to be self-reliant, and to earn her own way, even before she was old enough to vote. She never resented the fact that her folks did not fund her college education. Actually, Barbara preferred to pay her own way. To this day, she still takes great pride in having done so.

Barbara's parents often used many great "homespun" proverbs to instill important values in their children. Barbara claims that much of her success in business can be traced back to her parent's teachings, especially about being frugal. They believed that money should be used wisely, that one should allocate dollars in ways that will enhance one's life, not to display or to augment status.

> *Always differentiate between real "need" as opposed to merely "wants." Value automobiles for what they really are . . . a device to get you from point A to point B.*

Given these views about automobiles, Barbara and her family allocate only about 5 percent of their realized income for automobile transportation. That includes all costs: average purchasing costs, servicing, fuel, insurance, and so on. On average, American households annually spend 9 percent of their income for this category. In her fifty years on this earth, Mrs. Gem has never spent more than $20,000 for a motor vehicle, even though today the average price of a new car is in excess of that amount. Mrs. Gem favors purchasing inexpensive used cars and then "wears them out." But there is nothing average about Mrs. Gem's net worth. Excluding the equity in her business, her net worth exceeds $3 million, or more than four times what is statistically expected given her age and income.

Mrs. Gem is very consistent—some would say well coordinated—in her purchase of consumer artifacts. When she and her family drive to church in their well-used used car, not one passenger is wearing a watch that costs more than $100, a suit that was purchased for more than $250, or a pair of shoes that ran more than $120. All this does fit the profile of a productive household. Even the Gems' home is compatible with their other forms of consumption behavior. They paid $100,000 for their "fixer-upper" years ago, and today, after the fixing is complete, the house is worth more than three times the original price. On average, the American home owner allocates nearly one dollar in five (19.8 percent) of his or her annual realized income to housing costs. The Gems' layout is approximately half that amount.

How is it that Mrs. Gem is so frugal? Again, it's in large part the fault of her parents. They taught her how to build her self-esteem and satisfaction with life without regard to material possessions.

Develop great self-esteem [and] . . . satisfaction by using your aptitudes, your gifts. . . . Set and achieve your goals to improve your weaknesses. . . . Ask those who . . . you trust to advise you about how you can become a better person. Strive for constant improvement and lifelong integrity. . . . Be persistent, grateful, and generous. . . . Love and . . . go after it with gusto!

Mrs. Gem epitomizes the axiom that those who have high self-esteem and are well satisfied with their family lives and careers don't have the same strong motives to spend as those who do not.

Find something [a vocation] in life you are passionate about, and if possible, start a business in this area. Work at something you love, not just for money [to spend]. Marry someone that is positive, supportive, and brings out the best in you. Enjoy all the days of your life. Be passionate, positive, and excited. Allow yourself to make mistakes and learn. Allow all around you to do the same.

What if the passion generated for your family and career is not enough to dampen your consumption habits? You may wish to employ yet another technique that was taught to Mrs. Gem by her parents:

Approach all major purchases in terms of hours. Ask yourself, "Exactly how many hours do I have to work at my present pay rate to be able to buy this?"

This theme and derivatives of it were mentioned by many of the other successful businesswomen who were surveyed. You can use the wisdom of Mrs. Gem and what her parents taught her about money. What if your teenage daughter asks, "Why is it that we don't own a Jet Ski, hot tub, tanning bed, or $20,000 worth of home theater equipment?" Do what Mrs. Gem suggests. The median income of a worker today is approximately $38,000. Even if the typical woman is able to take home 80 percent of what is earned, that is only about $30,000. Assume that this typical woman works forty hours per week for fifty weeks a year. This translates into two thousand hours of work per year, or $15 per hour taken home.

So how many hours will the typical woman have to work in order to pay for those expensive toys her daughter wants? This is a great question to ask while you and your children are seated at the dinner table. Pull out the Sunday newspaper and turn to the classifieds. The game begins. You look down the column that lists Jet Skis. Let's see, listing number thirty-seven—what a great opportunity! Someone is selling a Jet Ski at a large discount, and according to the ad it's only four months old.

Paid over $20,000. Will sell for $14,900 OBO. Call Johnny Anxious.

Assume Johnny paid $20,300 for his water toy. At $15 per hour taken home, Johnny had to work 1,353 hours, or 81,180 minutes, or 4,870,800 seconds to earn his very own Jet Ski! In terms of days on the job, at eight hours per day, this translates into 169 days on the job. But don't forget that it also translates into 169 trips to work and 169 trips from work—and all for the joy of owning a Jet Ski.

Now Johnny wants to share the joy of riding a Jet Ski with some other lucky person, but even if he sells it at the asking price, he stands to lose $5,400 of his "investment." How much joy did Johnny receive during the short four months that he owned his water toy? That isn't clear, but assume that he used it nearly every Saturday and Sunday, or approximately thirty-two days. This in turn translates into $169 for every day it was used, not including any finance charges or interest on a possible loan. It does not include the opportunity lost by not investing the money, nor does it include the cost of fuel or insurance or the price of storage or a trailer. Is it any wonder that Johnny wants to transfer his joy to someone else?

Ah, the wisdom of Mrs. Gem. One could devise a table game in which kids are asked by their parents:

I am reading about a Jet Ski listed in today's newspaper. The owner paid $20,300. Guess how much he is willing to sell it for today, just four months after he bought it?

A reward or small prize is given to the child who comes closest to guessing $14,900. Moms and dads could then ask how many hours it would take the typical worker to earn enough to pay for this Jet Ski.

Mrs. Gem stated that people have real needs, such as food, clothing, and a home. She and her children have a great ability to differentiate between needs and frivolous wants. Mrs. Gem and her husband spend a lot on tuition for educating their children, but they have never spent as much as a dollar on loans to purchase "items that depreciate."

Women like Mrs. Gem know that in order to start one's own business certain things have to be sacrificed. The purchase of a new car might have to be postponed. The purchase of a starter or fixer-upper home might have to be substituted for a more upscale abode. Resoled or repaired shoes might have to do for a few years. The list goes on for many people who want to be successful self-employed business owners. Often they will have to put much of their time, energy, and financial resources into the business, and these inputs into one's business are a substitute for hyperspending on what one wears, drives, and owns. Is this always a painful experience? Not if you were raised in an environment similar to Mrs. Gem's. In fact, many of the women profiled herein made few changes in their income-allocation habits once their businesses began to flourish. They never felt a need to live high on the hog.

CHAPTER 5

Beta Women: Beating the Odds Against Succeeding

Young people have the best chance of succeeding if they are brought up by parents who treat them with kindness and respect. . . . I became successful in spite of my upbringing.
—KARI A., BETA WOMAN AND MILLIONAIRE BUSINESS OWNER

*W*hat about those women like Kari A. who were raised by parents who provided them with anything but a nurturing environment? These are Beta women, a minority within the population of successful businesswomen. They were raised in an environment that was not conducive to achieving success, yet they overcame the odds and succeeded in spite of their upbringing. While the odds of their success may be lower than those of women within the Alpha population, Beta women can still attain their goals and join the ranks of millionaire businesswomen.

The case studies of Beta women are of particular value because not every person in this country was or will be raised by parents who fit the profile reported by the Alphas. As a preview, it is important to note something about the character of Beta women. They indeed overcame long odds. Many of them were raised by parents in name only who provided their children with little or no emotional support. Most gave no encouragement to their children in terms of educational achievement or taking leadership roles, and many had little or no respect for their sons and daughters. Beta parents run the full gamut from being merely dysfunctional and disinterested to abusive. How is it possible that Beta women succeeded given their upbringing? The methods and strategies they used are discussed in the case histories included later in this chapter; but first, a brief discussion of the Beta maple tree is relevant. This tree, given its background and harrowing experiences, should have died years ago. Yet today, like the Beta women profiled herein, it thrives. Following this discussion, an analysis of the meaning of success is provided. It is important to understand the key dimensions that account for the many successes of these women and to compare Beta and Alpha women briefly in terms of what it takes to succeed.

Some of the Beta women suggest that their success was due in part to the fact that they established a strong work ethic when they were young. Most did work many hours even when they were in high school, and some encountered a great mentor, an enlightened boss, or an inspirational teacher who encouraged them. Others were fortunate to find a spouse who nurtured their entrepreneurial tendencies. Some did exceptionally well in school and enhanced their ambition, drive, pride, and self-esteem through that accomplishment. Finally, some give much of the credit for their achievements to "having strong religious faith."

These are just some of the logical and plausible explanations for the Beta women's success, but the majority possessed a particular quality that drove them to succeed: a high degree of perseverance. *Tenacity* may be an even better description. They were born with an iron will to persevere and an unusual ability to overcome being raised by miserable parents.

THE BETA MAPLE

How do we explain the successes of Beta women? Perhaps an analogy about a special type of tree, a red maple, would be of use. It was the end of the fall treeplanting season. You were walking through Kmart just before closing time on a Sunday when you noticed a handwritten sign saying, "Closeout Trees, $9.99." Only one remained; the tag said it was a red maple. It was about five feet tall and one and a half inches in diameter. A few of its leaves remained, but they were all wilting. The soil in its pot was as dry and hard as concrete.

Given these conditions, most people probably would not have purchased this tree, but you said to yourself, "What the heck? For $9.99,

I have nothing to lose." You took the tree home and planted it two days later, way in the back of your large yard where two other species of red maples had died. These were trees cultivated by a professional landscaper who'd charged you ten times more for his red maples than you'd just paid at Kmart. Yet both of the maples he'd planted had died. Thus, you were not at all optimistic about the survival of your new tree, so you planted it without applying any special soil amendments or fertilizer. You did not provide it with a nurturing environment.

Fall ended and winter passed. The winter was unusually harsh, with lots of cold temperatures and ice storms. You said to yourself, "If the Kmart maple was not dead when I planted it, it is dead now after all these ice storms." At the time, you had no idea this was a special tree. It was, in fact, a Beta red maple.

In mid-May, you were shocked. By far the best-looking recently planted tree in your yard was the Beta maple. It had not only survived, it thrived, even though you'd never watered it after the day you'd planted it.

For several years, your Beta maple continued to grow like the proverbial beanstalk. It reached a height of almost twenty feet, with a diameter of seven inches, but then disaster struck.

One morning before dawn, a severe storm hit your area. About thirty minutes into it, you heard a loud crack, followed by a thud that shook your entire home. A huge cottonwood tree over a hundred feet high and twenty inches in diameter had fallen down. In the process, it had sheared the top off the Beta maple. There were hardly any branches attached to the Beta maple's stump, and it now looked like a nine-foot-tall pole sticking out of the ground. All around it were parts of the uprooted cottonwood, and that was a good thing, because if it wasn't for the cottonwood branches all around your Beta maple, you would have immediately taken out your chain saw and cut the stump down to ground level. But you had to cut away and dispose of the hundred feet of cottonwood first, taking an hour or two every other day to saw and chop. It took weeks for you to finally clear away most of the cottonwood. By the time you could get to the Beta maple, guess what had happened? The nine-foot stump had exploded with sprouting branches covered with leaves. You thought that just maybe the Beta maple had a chance, so you cut off the splinters on the top and covered the raw wood with tree salve.

Over the past several years, you have been amazed. Near the top of your Beta maple, two major branches have emerged in a U shape, and they grow taller and taller each year. In terms of leaf count, the Beta maple has more than any other maple within its age cohort. How is it possible that ten years after the cottonwood fell, your Beta maple thrives, its health excelling that of trees with better backgrounds and care? Your Beta maple overcame near death by being cut in half. Could it be that adversity brings out the best in some trees, as well as in some people? It is not supposed to be like this. If you buy a tree from a top nursery and have experts care for it, it is supposed to outperform those bought at discount stores and given little care.

The Beta maple story illustrates the fact that certain species cannot be defeated. In fact, adversity seems to make them stronger. So when you are looking for maple seeds from which to grow new trees, you would be wise to select the seeds from the Beta maple. In my work, the most compelling and enlightening cases are often those of Beta women.

You have no control over who your parents are, and you cannot modify their character. If you look at your background and say, "I had anything but nurturing parents," you may think you have an excuse for not becoming a success, and you don't even have to blame yourself for all your failures. In your mind, self-reliance and taking responsibility for one's actions are only for those who were born and raised in a nurturing environment.

So go ahead and fail, or at least do your very best to underachieve. Continue looking back at all the imperfections in your childhood, remembering every moment when you suffered mistreatment. You might have thousands of reasons to fail. Is that who you are today? If so, you may not want to read the case studies that follow, the cases that document the extraordinary character of Beta women. Given their backgrounds, they would not have been chosen to succeed. Some might call them dark horses. The so-called racing experts say, "Never bet on a dark horse to win," but these women have won more than one race. Most had a series of obstacles to overcome, and they did. They have won, they continue to win today, and they will win tomorrow. Their ability to persevere began when they were youngsters, with parental upbringing that ranged from beatings to "just neglect." They had to overlook, overcome, persevere, keep their pride, and succeed in spite of their parents. And overcoming these obstacles was not the end of their journey—it was just the beginning. Many were exploited by their husbands and had to overcome other obstacles that would have killed the ambition in most people. Yet they persevered. They aspired to overcome. Beta women demonstrate great courage, much strength of character, and lots of tenacity.

ON BECOMING SUCCESSFUL

How can youngsters become successful adults? This question was addressed by 313 financially successful women. Each respondent was selected from a nationwide survey of women who own and manage their own businesses, and the essays they wrote provided an excellent basis for contrasting Alpha and Beta women. The implicit assumption was that each woman would provide suggestions based on her personal experience, and that is what they did. Essentially, they told the story of their own success.

In order to determine the salient attributes (success factors) that underlie these 313 success stories, a content analysis was undertaken. What common suggestions do Alpha and Beta women make? Nearly one-half (48 percent) of the Alpha women alluded to perseverance as a key factor that explains success (see Table 5-1), and a significantly greater proportion of the Beta women (76 percent) also asserted that perseverance was a salient dimension. Perseverance was the single most frequently cited factor for both Alpha and Beta women. A complete listing of all the success factors compiled from the content analysis of the 313 respondents is presented in Appendix 1. In the previous chapter (see Table 4-1), these respondents also rated their parents and the environment in which they were raised with regard to twenty specific qualities.

Each of the 313 women was assigned a score and corresponding rank based on their evaluations of the parental environment in which they were raised, as detailed in chapter 4. For example, a score of 20 (the highest possible) for Mary Anne means that she rated her parents as providing a nurturing environment in regard to all twenty measures. In sharp contrast, Bonnie's score was 0 because she rated her parents as not providing even one of the nurturing components. The 313 women were ranked from 1 to 313 according to their respective scores. The respondent with the highest score was assigned the highest rank, and the lowest scorer was assigned the lowest rank.

TABLE 5-1

ATTRIBUTES DERIVED FROM A
CONTENT ANALYSIS OF "SUCCESS" ESSAYS:
WOMEN WITH ALPHA VS. BETA PARENTS

Alpha Women % Indicating (Rank)	Beta Women % Indicating (Rank)
Perseverance 48 (1)	Perseverance 76 (1)
Education and Training 38 (2)	Education and Training 30 (2)
Self-reliance 28 (3)	Self-reliance 26 (3)
Helping/Caring 26 (4)	Advisers 18 (4)
Saving/Investing 24 (5)	Ethics 16 (5)
Goals 22 (6)	Enjoyment 14 (6)
Responsibility 22 (6)	Goals 14 (6)
Advisers 18 (8)	Spiritual 14 (6)
Enjoyment 14 (9)	Responsibility 12 (9)
Integrity 8 (10)	Helping/Caring 12 (10)

For illustrative purposes, Alphas were designated arbitrarily as those respondents who ranked in the top 50 of the 313 according to their scores, and the Beta label was assigned to women who had scores that placed them in the bottom 50. For Alphas, the average score was 17. For Betas, it was just 4! How did the women in the Beta category ever overcome the odds? How did they become successful in spite of having "parents from hell"? In part, their essays about success answer these and many related questions.

As might be expected, a significantly higher portion of the Beta women emphasized perseverance as a success factor. This seems to reflect in their responses to discouragement, fewer opportunities, and a general lack of a nurturing parental environment. Webster's defines *persevere* as "to persist in a state, enterprise, or understanding in spite of counterinfluences, opposition, or discouragement." It is an important attribute for both Alphas and Betas, but especially for the Betas who had to learn to persevere in a nonnurturing home environment that was anything but conducive to their future success.

FAITH, THE TENACIOUS

Consider her profile, then ask yourself, "What are the odds that this woman would ever become a successful adult?" Faith's parents possessed just two of the twenty nurturing qualities studied. Yes, they did encourage Faith to earn her own spending money—she had little choice if she wanted to wear decent clothes. They also gave Faith "much responsibility"—along the lines of "we don't care what you do." And what could be worse for a girl than to be regularly beaten by her parents? Faith was beaten repeatedly by both her mother and her father. Faith made a decision during her sophomore year in high school. She believed that eventually she would be permanently injured or even killed by her abusive parents, so she chose early emancipation. She left home, quit school, and began working in the food industry. Faith discovered that the food, the employers, and the diners didn't care if their server had dropped out of high school. They would not hold it against her even if they knew that their server was the product of abusive parents. No matter your background, if you give people good service you will be rewarded.

There is more to Faith's profile than parental beatings. Her parents taught her nothing about saving and investing, and they spent every dollar they earned. Her home was filled with disharmony, shouting, and arguing. Her mother and father constantly battled each other over the slightest issues. They had no respect for themselves, each other, or their daughter. Both parents were also very pessimistic about their future. They were chronic complainers and seemed to hate just about every part of their married life. Neither had any compassion for Faith, and they paid little attention to her except when they thought she'd done something wrong.

Faith did not take to the strap very well. She was always strong and spirited. When she was being punished, she wrestled and screamed right back at her abuser. She was a tiger even in her youth. Faith never believed, not for a moment, that she deserved to be beaten.

The Beta women often overcame things that would destroy spirit, pride, and ambition in most people. Case studies such as Faith's are of particular value because people like her often make the greatest mentors and coaches. They are role models.

Faith never looks back at her past with regret. She never wastes time thinking about how her childhood home could have or should have been. She uses the memories of her family experiences only to tell her story of success and encourage other women to overcome the adversity of their pasts.

Faith shares many of the beliefs that other Beta women possess. All focus on the future, learn from the past, and don't dwell on it. They don't hate those who abused them. They use their time and emotional energy in more positive, productive ways. This is what Faith did early in her career. Instead of filling her mind with hatred for her parents and her horrible childhood, Faith redirected her enormous emotional energy, extraordinary courage, and strength of spirit to build a career as a business owner. She strongly believes that one's background should never define one's future.

> Do not accept your future as when you were young. Every statistic was against me! I should be on welfare. I should be part of the state correctional system!

Yes, given the large doses of abuse and humiliation Faith received as a girl, one might expect that today she would be on the dole, in jail, or walking the streets. But not Faith. Even in her darkest hours as a young girl, she kept telling herself:

> Somehow, someday . . . I don't know exactly. I will not settle for less than I'm worth. . . . [I must] believe.

Faith does not mince words. She does not coddle those who use the past to justify their current lack of success.

> Don't use [the past] as your excuse. It's so easy just to say, "I was born poor, . . . I had bad abusive parents, or I lack education. . . . I could not finish school."

Faith is living proof that if you lack a college or even a high school degree you can still succeed in America, but she is the first to point out that education does make things easier in terms of succeeding in the economy. However, one's lack of education should never be used as a self-defensive bullet point:

So you could not go to school. You say, . . . I'll never get ahead because I started out too low on the food chain. If you do, you will lose. . . . You are a quitter. . . . You don't even want to try.

Faith was never a quitter. She found a career that rewards performance, not one's upbringing or pedigree. Imagine right now that you are sitting in your car in line at the take-out window of a fast-food restaurant. Guess what? Faith owns this store and several others. She knows that as long as she provides great food and service, people will continue to patronize her many restaurants. They want service, not a background check on the owner.

According to Faith, too many people in this nation of opportunity allow other people's assessments to dictate the course of their lives. And many are skilled at inflating their shortcomings. Go ahead, constantly remind yourself of each and every conceivable flaw, all the possible impediments to your becoming successful. The outcome is predictable. Even when she was starting out on her own, Faith did just the opposite. She recognized that success is a function of controlling how one thinks, and she was determined to think success.

If you are determined that no one will stop you . . . if you fail, try again. . . . Never accept less of yourself. Never!

It is difficult to envision becoming an economic success when your childhood environment was strictly Humbleville. But Faith dismisses the common belief that only those already rich from inheritances succeed in life.

No one is better than you! They might have it easier than you because they had a better start.

In other words, do not degrade yourself. Do not lose confidence in your ability to succeed. Just because others may be better educated or have wealthy parents does not mean they are superior to you. You will succeed if you are determined.

If you are tough, if you believe in yourself, if you let no one tell you you can't.

Faith indicated that no matter how bad one's beginnings, no matter how many failures one encounters, success is still attainable.

Never accept what has happened in the past as your fate. Keep telling yourself . . . you will do something, and do it well.

There is hope for all, but you must understand that it is very difficult to succeed if you allow a wretched past to dictate your future. Bury the ugly ghosts of the past as Faith did. She trained and conditioned her mind to envision a successful future. If you do, she says:

Nothing is impossible if you believe in yourself. Use this value [of yourself] like an anchor. You will make mistakes . . . learn from them. Then move on with your quest. . . . Don't dwell on past mistakes. Otherwise you will waste time and energy.

Faith is a living testimony that success comes to those who have the iron will to make it happen, who really want to succeed. She is amazed at the large number of people who don't know what controls the door to success in this country.

You are the loom that weaves the tapestry.

It's your work and your thought processes that control the quality of what you are and what you will become. Your tapestry may not be what you would like when you are young, but according to Faith, you can always change what is being woven.

Last year, Faith achieved the one-in-one-thousand designation. Only one household in one thousand generates a net annual realized income of $1 million or more. Yet given her unfortunate upbringing, one might predict that Faith is a bitter, miserable human being. She is not. She loves her career, her family, her many friends, and her success in general, which is even more enjoyable since she moved from the back of the pack to take the lead. The pride, high self-esteem, and confidence she displays go to those who set high goals and achieve them, as Faith has done.

Faith is also a very generous person. Last year she donated more than 10 percent of her income to charity, more than twice the total percentage that her household allocated for motor vehicles, clothes, and vacations combined. She also gave considerable sums to her children, nieces, and nephews. She has funded their private school and college educations and has provided them with forgiveness loans to purchase homes.

Faith is a woman in control. She earns 80 percent of her household income; her husband earns the other 20 percent. She and her husband own a home valued near $300,000, and they have no outstanding debts—no mortgage, no auto loan, no boat loan, no home equity loan. She is a fastidious keeper of records and can tell you how much her household spends each year on food, clothing, transportation, utilities, and all other categories of expenses.

It may seem odd that Faith the multimillionaire would be so concerned with expenditures, but it's not peculiar at all. Control of one's mind and money is a key to becoming successful. Faith would have never been able to go from economic ground zero to her current status without being in control of her mind, her emotions, and her financial resources. She learned to live a spartan existence during her salad years while she was building a business.

Faith always looked toward the future. Her long-term goal of financial independence was always more important than owning expensive clothing, motor vehicles, or even a luxury home. You will feel deprived only if you convince yourself that you are deprived. For those who keep reminding themselves about that, Faith has these big words of advice:

Get over it!

Faith never wastes her precious time or emotional energy opening the old wounds inflicted by her contemptible parents. She has conditioned her mind and established a strong will so as not to be a perpetual victim of a past that no one can change. Instead, Faith does something much more positive. She takes time each day to count all her current and future blessings.

You can do what Faith did if you have perseverance, tenacity, and courage, but it also helps if you begin your work experience early in life. Be wise like Faith. You might select a successful restaurant owner to work for, one who is willing to be your mentor. Work hard, and be responsible. Start at the bottom, busing and cleaning. Work your way up to waiting tables. Learn from your mentor how to operate a business. Learn to prepare food if you are so inclined. Then consider, as did Faith, opting for self-employment.

MARIA McFRIENDLY OF THE 900 CLUB

An exclusive club . . . the 900 Club—only those millionaires who scored below 1000 on their SATs are admitted. Scores under 1000 define less than spectacular performance. A minority of millionaires fall into this category [yet] . . . it's possible to become an economic success with scores that are mediocre or worse.

What if we tell people with low SAT scores that they can succeed? Perhaps then more would become economically successful one day. (The Millionaire Mind, p. 120)

It was the third time that Maria McFriendly had opened an envelope that contained her SAT scores. In three attempts, she'd never reached four figures. She always scored "somewhere in the 900s." In middle school and high school, Maria was never a candidate for talented and gifted programs, nor was she encouraged to take any advanced-placement courses. However, she worked very hard and generated a B average in high school.

Maria's parents had an unusual attitude about their children. They believed that children are genetically programmed either to achieve or not to achieve, and according to them, Maria did not possess the qualities necessary to be a major success in life. In fact, they often communicated this belief to their daughter. They believed that she would never amount to much in life and that the results of the standardized tests supported their opinion.

In terms of income, it was possible for Maria's parents to pay at least a portion of their daughter's education, but they decided not to do so because they believed she was not the type to get much out of college. In spite of her B average in high school, Maria's SAT numbers were below the norm for the region where she attended school. High academic achievement was the soup of every day. What was a parent to do?

Several times during her high school years Maria's father suggested that she transfer out of the academically oriented high school and enroll in the local vocational high school. After all, he reasoned, what was the sense of Maria laboring along in an academically oriented high school of excellence? He often asked why she was attending a high school whose curriculum was designed for students who were college material.

Maria's father figured that Maria's only chance to earn a living would come through her learning a trade. He told her she should become a hair-dresser or a secretary, saying, "After all, it's still a living." Maria refused to budge. She graduated, although not at the top of her class, from a public high school of academic excellence. Later, her application to a local college was accepted, and she graduated with a 3.2 grade point average. But that is by no means the whole story. Maria worked the entire time she attended high school and college. Her parents never gave her as much as one dollar for her college expenses, providing her only with food and a place to live. To this day she has never accepted any form of economic assistance from them, not even a well-used chair or lamp. In her family, exemptions from household chores and tasks were allocated to the children based on academic performance, so Maria did a lot of chores and housework. According to her parents, she was a very long shot to succeed in life, so they acted accordingly. Why invest in a child who was positioned on the lowest rung of the academic caste system?

However, standardized tests don't measure some qualities that explain success in life, and even as a youngster, Maria had many of those assets. Can you imagine how difficult it is to succeed in life when even your parents bet against you? Both her parents were perfectionists when it came to academic achievement, and their Maria was not at all perfect in that regard. Maria did have heart, tenacity, drive, ambition, and discipline. She also had a lot of plain and simple common sense.

Just where do Maria's parents rank on the nurturing-to-nonnurturing parent scale? Of all the successful women interviewed, Maria's parents are among the bottom five. You could call them ultra-nonsupportive parents. To say that they provided Maria with a nonnurturing environment is a gross understatement. If I were writing a book on how to encourage daughters to fail in life, Maria's parents' actions could fill up several chapters.

Maria was wise enough to create her own support system. She had many wonderful friends, and she received a lot of encouragement from some of their parents. Maria reasoned that she was always going to be treated like a poor relation by her own family. In the eyes of her parents, she was inferior, and she knew there was nothing that could be done to change the way her parents evaluated her. But Maria disagreed with her parents' assessment of her. In her own mind, she was a much better person than her mother and father had ever imagined, and she proved her evaluation to be more accurate than her parents'.

Maria relied heavily on her friends for psychological support along the way. They were a critical part of her self-evaluation during her formative years. Maria honed her skills at making friends, having lots of friends, and keeping friends, and she was well liked. Her friends and most of their parents thought much more of Maria than her own parents did, and she worked very hard at galvanizing these relationships. Today, she credits these relationships with enhancing her self-esteem.

Maria was the ultimate "favor" person. She was always doing favors for her friends and actually sought out friends in need. If someone needed a date with a cute guy, Maria was motivated and bold enough to introduce herself to the targeted male. Later she would bend his ear about the great qualities of her girlfriend, and always the close of the sales pitch was "You two should really get together."

Yes, Maria excelled at matchmaking, but she also exuded confidence when she was making a pitch. She was absolutely at her best when pitching, selling, and networking on behalf of her friends.

As a side note, I have a theory about this. Successful women who were raised in a nonnurturing environment, the Beta women, often excel in businesses that involve some form of promoting, protecting, or supporting others, such as customers or clients. If your self-esteem is tainted by your parents, you may find it easier to sell on behalf of others. Perhaps deep down in your psyche you remember that once you were judged to be inferior, not as worthy as others. But if you have to raise money for disabled or abused children or some other noble cause, you might fight like a tiger for donations. Or if you are an employment agent, your task is to find jobs for others. You might not fight for your own employment, but you could be a successful advocate for others. It's not for you; it's for others. In your mind, those others are very, very worthy.

Even when she was in school, Maria was never out of work. Her motives for working were strong. She enhanced her self-esteem by earning her own money, and she disliked asking her parents for spending money. In her mind, it was degrading to take money from people who did not respect her. Of course, working also gave her an excuse to be out of the nonnurturing home environment that her parents provided. Later, when Maria realized that she would have to pay 100 percent of her college expenses, working became even more of a necessity. It was survival.

Who got Maria all those countless jobs she held during her years as a student? She did it all on her own. She could always find jobs—even summer jobs when the market was very tight for applicants. She was both resourceful and bold in securing employment. Maria did more than scan the newspaper's employment opportunities. She often found jobs by making intense cold calls to managers of successful businesses, whom she identified as leads from newspaper articles.

But Maria was never just all about Maria—she sought out friends in need of part-time jobs as well as full-time summer positions. Here again, Maria excelled in filling these types of needs. Every time she found a job for herself, she would "sniff around" for economic opportunities for others. In high school, many of Maria's friends considered her to be the placement office that the high school lacked. She was often on the move, upgrading from one job to a better opportunity, but she always tried to leave a job "in good standing" with the employer. What if her departure would leave Maria's employer shorthanded? Not to worry—she had a solution. Maria always had a stable of job-seeking friends to fill vacancies.

Maria was a whiz at finding a place for human resources. In fact, she always thought it ironic that she helped her friends find jobs because many of them were the daughters of successful business owners who had countless job opportunities within their companies. More often than not, "the girls didn't want to work for Dad and Mom." Not to worry; Maria solved their problems.

One of the more humorous episodes occurred when Maria was in high school. She landed a wonderful summer job at an exclusive country club, and she had to fib when asked if she had her own transportation to and from work, since the club was situated some distance from her home. There was no public transportation available, and Maria did not own a car or have access to her parents' cars. No problem. Maria found jobs at the club for two of her closest friends. Of course, it was no accident that both of these friends, daughters of wealthy business owners, had their very own motor vehicles.

Later, during her junior year in college, Maria found yet another part-time job for herself that had a major influence on her ultimate career choice. She was hired to bolster the clerical staff at an employment search firm, and she moved quickly from clerical work to matching the human resource needs of employers with those of the labor market.

She excelled at this job. Actually, she had been training for such a position by finding jobs for friends. That was a hobby—how nice it is to get paid to do what one once did for free. Today Maria still gets great satisfaction from her vocation of finding suitable talent for major corporations. After graduating from college, Maria began working full-time for a staffing firm. In less than two years, she was their top producer. Before she was thirty years old, she went out on her own.

Owning and managing her own staffing firm was an easy transition from being an employee. Once she had some on-the-job experience, Maria felt an urge to go it alone. She did not need or like the structure and narrow job parameters that were part of working for someone else. Maria recognized early that she was the industry, the product. She was the matchmaker. To her, expensive office settings and related overhead had little to do with being a productive matchmaker. Her clients did not care if she worked out of her kitchen or a luxury office downtown. They wanted results, and Maria always gave them what they needed.

Her business thrived from the start. She never had to borrow to start her own company because her most important asset was Maria, not expensive overhead. Today, Maria's household has a net worth of nearly $4 million. Last year her staffing company paid its forty-two-year-old owner a salary of just over $300,000. Maria's husband, an assistant manager of a discount department store, added another $75,000 to the household income.

The couple and their children live well below their means. The home they recently purchased went for $299,000, and the house matched the $199 watch she wears! Given the couple's low propensity to spend, Maria does not feel pressure to produce, produce, and produce higher and higher levels of revenue to keep up an opulent lifestyle. That would take away the great pleasure and satisfaction she gets from being a matchmaker on her own terms.

Part of her success can also be attributed to her choice of market niches. Maria realized that she could be most productive focusing her energy and that of her employees within a target market segment. She and her firm specialize in staffing the intellectually gifted, matching candidates with firms that are interested in hiring individuals with advanced degrees in physics, chemistry, engineering, science, mathematics, and other scientific disciplines.

So it is somewhat ironic that Maria, who was often told she was *not* intellectually gifted, *not* college material, has the key role in finding jobs for those who *are* considered intellectually gifted. It is Maria who finds economic opportunities for physicists, chemists, and engineers who have doctorates and even postdoctoral experience. Remember, no matter how smart or well educated the individual, even a genius can't make a living without a job!

One might expect that Maria would feel uncomfortable associating with all of these brilliant people, but she is not. Long ago she realized that desire, perseverance, hard work, empathy, and the ability to get along with people were key attributes for success. What continues to surprise Maria even today is that some of the most intellectually gifted people in this world lack many of those qualities. So what if someone has impeccable credentials, with a dozen advanced degrees? If that someone has a history of being an unproductive worker, his/her credentials mean very little.

That insight is one reason that Maria has succeeded in the staffing business. She never endorses a candidate who has a history of being subpar on a job, no matter how many degrees the candidate has earned. Her clients appreciate this, and Maria's company has many outstanding corporate clients. What Maria learned early in her life is a crucial factor in explaining her success. Making friends and attracting and retaining clients is all about having perseverance and empathy for others' needs and knowing how to satisfy them.

Today Maria is a successful business owner even though she was never considered intellectually gifted by her parents. She acts as a matchmaker for those who are supposedly gifted, but gifted or not, one cannot provide food, clothing, and shelter for a family without a job. So who is the more important element in this equation? Is it the out-of-work genius or Maria, the advocate?

CINDY CINDERELLA

You are at a graduation ceremony. It's standing room only here at this large public high school of excellence. The top ten graduating seniors are seated up front on the stage. The principal introduces all ten and details the many accomplishments of each young scholar. Six are women; four are men. They are all smiling. It's a happy time. It seems to take forever just for the principal to list the many awards and scholarships that these youngsters have won.

At least one of the young women is more deserving of recognition than any of the others onstage, but today there are no awards given for courage, tenacity, valor, integrity, or beating the odds. Cindy has all of those qualities and more; hers is a Cinderella story. She achieved and excelled. She came out on top in spite of being raised in a home environment that was anything but conducive to success. Perhaps the other students onstage that day were raised in a nurturing home environment, but not Cindy Cinderella. She had to beat the odds to earn her place. Cindy made the high school honor roll every single time, was an active student leader, and participated in extracurricular activities—all this while working part-time jobs. She always had a summer job, including waiting tables at exclusive resorts far from home. She liked the pride and confidence associated with earning straight A's, and she enhanced her self-confidence by leading others. Also, she enjoyed working with others and playing sports. Her jobs even contributed to Cindy's self-esteem and the pride that goes with being self-reliant. But there may be another reason for her proclivity to work. During her school days, Cindy's friends often used the same expression to describe her lifestyle:

When I call, she is never at home.

How right they were. But "never at home" was not an accident—Cindy planned it that way. It was all part of a stealth strategy for dealing with her unfortunate home environment. Cindy's father could objectively be classified as Ogre One. Ogre One frequently verbalized his beliefs that he was overqualified for his job, his wife, his sons, and his daughters. But in reality, he suffered from an acute case of low self-esteem. If you just happened to look at him the wrong way, Ogre One would interpret it as a serious insult, a threat to his self-image, and the lightning bolts would start. Of course, there were different forms of his emotional lightning. Shouting and throwing objects were two of his favorites, and he was very democratic; he distributed his curses and his hurled objects equally among all of his family members. At other times, Cindy's father was cold and withdrawn. He never had much to say unless he was provoked.

Cindy figured out a way to reduce the probability that she would be the recipient of Ogre One's lightning bolts. She always had a high mathematical aptitude, and while still in middle school she developed "Cindy's lightning-bolt share model." Stated simply, the probability of receiving a lightning bolt of abuse from Ogre One was inversely corre-lated with the distance between him and the competing recipients. In other words, the relative share of Ogre One's attentions that Cindy, her brothers, her sisters, and her mom received were predictable. Who got the lion's share of the lightning bolts? The person who was closest in physical distance to Ogre One.

Thus, Cindy figured that if she was out of the house each morning before Ogre One got out of bed, the probability of receiving a lightning bolt was zero. So Cindy joined study groups and clubs that met early, well before school started. Part of Cindy's motivation came from the results generated by her lightning-bolt share model. The same answer also applies to Cindy's activities after school—participating in sports and working at night and on the weekends. She was an outstanding babysitter and pet minder, and her clients often took her along on sum-mer vacations to watch their kids. Later, Cindy worked summers far from Ogre One, waiting tables at luxury resorts in the Rocky Moun-tains. She was well recompensed for such services, and that's how she paid for all her college tuition, board, clothing, and other expenses.

What is ironic about Cindy's stealth strategy for dealing with Ogre One is that he never got it. He never figured out what Cindy was doing. Ogre One thought that Cindy was just an overly ambitious girl, and he never suspected that his daughter deeply resented the way he treated his family.

Ogre One often bragged to friends and neighbors about his Cindy's academic achievements. Sometimes he actually tried to take credit, as a father and mentor, for her success in school. Yes, he did influence Cindy's performance in the classroom, but it was not the product of his coaching and mentoring. She excelled because she wanted to do more in life than survive. She'd witnessed what the lack of a good educational background had done to her mother, who was completely financially dependent on Ogre One. He alone doled money out to her, often begrudgingly.

So Cindy said, "Not me." She reasoned that she would have to earn a scholarship if she wanted to have any hope of going to college. Oth-erwise, she might end up like her mother—dependent and "always-in-denial Dotty."

Cindy recognized that her family had problems when she was quite young, and that was the rationale behind her stealth approach. When she was in seventh grade, she wanted to enter her school's science fair.

After school one afternoon, she was assembling the posters for her project on the kitchen table when Ogre One came in. He inquired about why Cindy had not set the table for dinner, and she responded, perhaps flippantly, that first she needed to put the final touches on her project. Hearing that excuse, Ogre One flew into a rage. He ripped apart the posters and hurled a series of lightning bolts at his frightened daughter. This episode made a lasting impression on Cindy. She recognized the benefits of keeping a good distance between herself and Ogre One, and that was the beginning of her stealth approach. She was too young to leave home, and she lacked the educational background that could enable her to earn a decent living on her own. So Cindy decided she would bide her time and learn to live in the home of Ogre One.

Where was Cindy's mother when Ogre One was shredding Cindy's science project, and why didn't she shield Cindy from the verbal assault? Cindy's mother was a weak woman. She "never wanted to interfere when Father was disciplining the children," and she always tried to smooth it over with rhetoric:

All families have their little disputes once in a while.

Cindy soon learned to discount her mother's words. She babysat for many families and spent time with the families of friends. There were no Ogre Ones in any of their households. Cindy realized that she could not count on her mother for protection or as a role model for a strong woman, but she was too proud to tell anyone about the problem. She dealt with it. She overcame it.

Men like Ogre One are a clever bunch. They are marginally abusive—brutal up to or near the threshold, but just under the legal definition of child abuse. Unlike physical abuse, verbal punishment does not involve blackened eyes, bruises, or physical trace evidence. Ogre One seemed to know just where the lines of demarcation were. And there are no laws against Ogre One refusing to pay for his children's college education, let alone sports uniforms, fees, and hairstyles. Yet his refusal was not for lack of earning a decent living—he earned above the average. However, Ogre One was a dysfunctional loser when it came to saving and investing. What he made, he spent. How could he fund a college education? He was a self-described "working man of modest means" who could afford to have cases of beer delivered to his door every Saturday afternoon. Then add the cost of purchasing, financing, and operating his bass boat. And, of course, Ogre One and his wife were not only drinkers but also heavy smokers. No, there was not much left for college funding. It's all about priorities.

Fortunately, Cindy was exposed to several role models who were strong women, including several of her teachers and professors. One woman in particular, whom Cindy worked for in her teens, was a woman "in charge" of both her household and her business, which made a strong impression on Cindy.

Cindy did more than endure the years of living in a nonnurturing environment. She turned a bad situation to her advantage. Cindy had a roof over her head, and she had a plan to "stay out of harm's way and study like the dickens." Her plan worked, and Cindy completed college with honors. The discipline and strong work ethic she developed contributed to her success as a self-employed business owner. She operates her own money-management and financial consulting company and has great passion for her business. It contributes much to her high self-esteem and pride, and it also represents freedom. It's a protective barrier against all the Ogres out there feasting on women who lack the education and tenacity to go it alone.

What Does It Mean to Be a Beta Parent?

The Alpha and Beta women were asked about their respective parents' financial practices. Their responses are telling.

> Beta women are nearly two and a half times more likely (61 percent versus 26 percent) than Alpha women to say, "My parents lived above their means."

They were not income poor, but they claimed to have precious little or no money for their daughters' college expenses. Most were not lying when they made such statements. The parents of Beta women were dysfunctional in many respects. They often ran households that were grossly inefficient. There was little planning, poor organization, constant friction, little savings, and no investment strategy. Beta parents were so busy dealing with their own discontent that they devoted little time or effort to providing their children with a nurturing environment. Putting money away for the future, even the near future, was rare. They were distracted, always engaged in recurring economic fire drills.

The parents of Beta women tended to be hyperconsumers. Their budgeting system was simple enough—they spent until their income was depleted. They were also heavy users of consumer credit. Is it any wonder there was no money for tuition? Surprisingly, Beta women report that most of their parents, in spite of their hyperconsumption habits, had very little, if anything, of lasting value.

If they did "own" a home, it was heavily mortgaged. Beta parents tended to be big spenders on consumables such as clothing, snack foods, alcoholic beverages, eating out, vacations, boats, motor vehicles, and consumption-related interest charges on loans. They were surrounded by the chaos associated with recreational shopping and impulse buying.

I recall interviewing millionaire Teddy Friend for *The Millionaire Next Door*. Teddy's parents were ultra Beta types. After the couple had worked for more than fifty years, they had near zero net worth, and they'd smoked three packs of cigarettes each day for forty-six years. If they had invested this cigarette money and then reinvested the dividends in Philip Morris [now Altria] stock during the same period, the $33,190 they'd spent on cigarettes would have been worth over $2 million in Philip Morris stock. Instead, both developed emphysema.

It is no wonder that only one in four of the Beta women ever received as much as one dollar for college expenses from her parents, although the majority were clearly college material. Beta women scored about 30 points higher on their SATs than did the Alpha women (1,194 versus 1,165). Most nonsupportive parents who were heavy smokers, drinkers, eaters, gamblers, or compulsive shoppers considered these activities more important uses for their income than educating their own children. Some of these parents had an uncontrollable compulsion to fund their favorite hobbies, and they used these activities as an excuse for not having much contact time with their spouses and children. Perhaps these parents did not realize it, but their hyperconsumption habits acted as a substitute for educating their daughters. In sharp contrast, many Alpha women reported that their parents, and in many cases grandparents, began funding their college accounts before they were born. The ignorance of the Beta women's parents is no excuse.

They were very self-absorbed, focusing on their own problems, their misery. Often they used hyperconsumption as medicine for that misery. Yet overconsuming, overeating, smoking, and drinking were never permanent remedies.

While Mother shopped for clothes hour after hour, Dad was always hunting, fishing, boating, playing cards, and always drinking, but not necessarily in that order!

There is nothing wrong with these activities until they become compulsions, substitutes for a happy home life and the love and respect of one's spouse and one's children. Then the parents are guilty of not providing a nurturing family environment. Most parents of Beta women did not abuse their children in the legal sense of the word, but these women had parents in name only who had little interest in them, showed them little respect, and gave them little encouragement.

Unfortunately, a child in such a home can't call 911 and report the behavior of her parents. Unfortunately, it's not a crime for parents to refuse to provide tuition and encouragement to their children. The Beta women began to realize their parents were dysfunctional even before entering high school, and they were determined that their own lives as adults would be very different. So in a way, these highly nonsupportive parents were role models for how not to behave. Their daughters saw firsthand that their mothers had little choice. They had to stay married because of the fear they could not "go it alone," since most of these moms did not have the education or job training to land a well-paying job. They were trapped. Beta women in these situations promised themselves that they would not follow in their mothers' footsteps. They were determined to become self-sufficient adults.

CHAPTER 6

Alpha Women vs. Beta Women

*I*n terms of economic productivity, Beta women are just about as successful as Alpha women. Given their respective average ages (fifty-one years for Alphas versus fifty-two years for Betas) and their total annual realized income ($410,793 for Alphas versus $417,707 for Betas), the expected net worth of the Alpha women was $2,095,044, versus $2,172,076 for the Beta women.[1] Contrast these figures with their actual levels of net worth. For Alpha women it was $4,771,864, versus $4,720,125 for the Beta women. Alpha women have a net worth that exceeds the predicted number by a multiple of 2.28, versus 2.17 for Beta women. This difference between Alpha women and Beta women is not statistically significant.

You will recall the definition of the term *Balance Sheet Affluent:* people in this category have a net worth that is at least two times their expected level given their age and income. Fully 62 percent of the Alpha women—versus 54 percent of the Beta women—are in the Balance Sheet Affluent category, but the accomplishments of Beta women deserve special attention because most Beta women succeeded without the benefit of a college education. Only 40 percent graduated from college, versus 72 percent for the Alpha women.

Are they happy? One would expect that Beta women would not be as satisfied as Alpha women. They were the products of parents from hell, and 64 percent reported having had to remove themselves from at

---

[1] Expected net worth = 1/10 (age) x annual realized income

least one bad marriage. Both Alpha and Beta women report that they did in fact encounter many obstacles along their journey to Successville. Ask these women a simple question:

How much time do you spend in a typical month thinking about "how things could or should have been?"

For the large majority of both types of women (82 percent for Beta, 85 percent for Alpha), the answer is zero; they never look back. This is one of the key reasons why they are both satisfied and successful. Given the negative experiences encountered by Beta women, one might expect that they spend much more time than Alpha women wallowing in the past with a thousand regrets—"If only this, if only that." That simply isn't the case for most Alpha and Beta women. They do not conjure up past moments of pain and suffering. They may have learned from the past, but they know that it is history, and history cannot be changed.

What do Beta and Alpha women suggest to those who aspire to succeed?

You can spend time planning for and thus guaranteeing your next reversal, your next failure, by constantly thinking about past failures and reversals. Or you can train yourself to always focus on your dreams.

CONSUMPTION HABITS

Most Beta women had parents who did not teach them how to save and invest money properly. In fact, their parents were "flakes" when it came to financial planning and budgeting. Beta women reported that their parents tended to live beyond their means by a ratio of nearly two and a half to one. Also, most Beta women (two of three) had parents with little or no empathy for the needs of others (especially those economically less fortunate). In nine of ten cases, Alpha women had parents who were just the opposite with respect to empathy. Probably as a result of these factors, Beta women spend more money on consumer goods than do Alpha women. Conversely, Alpha women donate more money to noble causes. However, both Alpha and Beta women are in fact quite frugal when compared to the high-income population in general, and both are above the norm regarding their eleemosynary behavior.

In terms of their consumption habits, Alpha women spend at a level in line with an American family that earns just over $100,000 annually. Beta women have spending habits more in line with a household that has an income of about $135,000. But again, both Alpha and Beta women have, on average, annual incomes in excess of $400,000.

Consider for a moment the annual realized income of the top quintile producers in this nation. The average income of this top 20 percent of our population is just over $100,000. This same group has an outstanding mortgage balance on their homes of just under $140,000. Only about one in four are millionaires. How do Alpha women and Beta women fit into this picture? First, consider the fact that half of the Alpha women have a net worth in excess of $3.3 million, versus $2.9 million for Beta women. Also, both Alpha women and Beta women have average incomes that are four times higher than the average for the income producers in the top quintile for all households in America. When it comes to outstanding mortgage balances, Beta women are more frugal ($135,348) than those in the top income quintile ($138,000), and Alpha women are even more frugal ($90,778). But what types of homes would one expect these women to own?

What is the most these women have ever spent for a home? The typical Alpha never spent more than $271,100 (median, defined as fiftieth percentile); the typical Beta, $349,995. The median home price in various geographic areas of America in 2002 was approximately $151,000. The people who spent that amount have a net worth that is less than 10 percent of the net worth of these millionaire women. If these women followed the lead of the typical home buyer in America, they might be expected to live in homes that are priced at least ten times higher than the median purchase price, or $1,510,000. Yet in reality, these wealthy women paid only a fraction of this amount: 18 percent for Alpha women, 23 percent for Beta women.

Actually, the median figure for the most spent for a home by these women is fairly typical of the median prices paid for a home in several areas of the country (see Chris Horymski, "Home Economics: The Smart Money Real Estate Index," *Smart Money*, February 2002, pp. 70–74):

Minneapolis/St. Paul: $292,100
Sacramento: $292,300
Denver: $297,500
Chicago: $315,500
Seattle: $330,800
Washington, D.C.: $352,500
Nassau and Suffolk Counties, N.Y.: $371,300
Orange County, Calif.: $386,800
Boston: $397,200
San Diego: $399,600
Los Angeles and Long Beach: $478,800
Oakland, Calif.: $675,800

Both Alpha and Beta women are rather frugal in terms of their consumption habits, but they are extraordinary in regard to the wealth they have accumulated. Their average levels of net worth place them in a fraction of the top 1 percent of wealth holders in America. Yet most live in a nondescript home in a middle-class neighborhood. They follow a very low profile lifestyle. Their neighbors have never earned more than $100,000 a year and have a median net worth that is about one-fifth of theirs.

What is the most that these women ever spent, for themselves or anyone else, for a suit of clothing? The median value for Alpha women is $384, versus $550 for Beta women. What about for a pair of shoes? Again, Alpha women report paying less, $146 versus $174 for Beta women. What about the most they ever paid for a wristwatch?[2] For Alpha women the answer is $341. The Beta women paid much more: $1,185.

If you earned more than $400,000 a year and had a net worth of several million dollars, how much would you allocate for an automobile? Why not buy a Porsche 911 Carrera? This car ranges in price, depending on the options included, from $67,900 to $83,630. Certainly the price of this high-grade sports car is within your economic range. After all, you are a millionaire. You have an income that exceeds the purchase price many times over. But a Porsche might not fit the pattern of your other consumption habits. Would it be appropriate for

---

[2] Several respondents who reported paying in excess of $1,000 for a wristwatch added a handwritten comment on the questionnaire,—e.g., "purchased as a gift for my husband's birthday" or "for an anniversary gift to my former husband."

someone who lives in a rather modest home to own an expensive car? For most Alpha and Beta women, the answer is no. It's not what these people are about.

Or look at it another way. The average income of a Porsche 911 Carrera owner is $113,000 (see Lorraine Farquharson, "Me and My Car: Porsche 911 Carrera," *Wall Street Journal*, June 5, 2002, p. 3). That is approximately one-fourth the income of the women profiled. Given this ratio, perhaps these women should have automobiles that cost four times the average selling price of a 911. One might thus expect both Alpha and Beta women to report that the most they ever paid for a motor vehicle was in the neighborhood of $300,000! In fact, the opposite is true. The most the Alpha women paid for a motor vehicle was $38,588, versus $42,375 for the Beta women. Sorry Alphas and Betas: this is just not enough for you to qualify for membership in the 911 Club. What sales pitch is supposedly effective in attracting prospective buyers of 911s? According to Farquharson's article, the answer is this:

Sales pitch . . . turn heads. Stop traffic. Inspire deep feelings of lust and envy in those around you. After all, it's a Porsche. (p. 3)

Well, neither Alpha nor Beta women are interested in spending big bucks just to turn heads or conjure up lust among friends. To most of these women, showing off and displaying their economic success is a good case of "poor taste." They have little need to demonstrate that they are at the top of the economic food chain. Their pride and high self-esteem comes from being successful business owners, having the resources to be financially independent, and helping family, friends, and employees. In general, these women don't associate with people who need to display success through the flashy consumer goods.

No, these women prefer to drive motor vehicles that range in price from the high thirty thousands to the low forties. Now, the average price of a new car today is about $23,000, so these women do spend more than the average. But they have incomes that exceed the norm for the population of new car buyers by more than ten times.

If not a Porsche, if not a Range Rover HSE, if not an S-Class Mercedes-Benz, what do these women drive? They can usually be found behind the wheel of an Acura sedan, Buick LeSabre or Park Avenue, Chevy Tahoe, Dodge Durango, Ford Explorer or Expedition, Infiniti

I35, Lexus ES 300, Lincoln LS, Mercedes-Benz C-Class sedan, or Toyota Avalon. These are fine automobiles, and they are above average in terms of quality and price. With respect to overall value, they fit nicely into the consumption patterns of Alphas and Betas.

On average, Alpha women donate $41,778 to noble causes each year, versus $25,814 for Beta women. This translates into 10.2 percent and 6.2 percent of their respective incomes. Where do these women rank along the "giving scale"? The top 20 percent (top quintile) of the income-producing households in America have an average income of $101,602. On average, they annually donate only 2.4 percent of their incomes to noble causes. Alpha women also give 6.2 percent of their income to their adult children, grandchildren, brothers, sisters, and parents; Beta women give 5.6 percent.

ABOUT THE DIFFERENCES

Why is it that Alpha women tend to spend less money than Beta women? Consistently, Beta women report spending more on motor vehicles, clothing and accessories, and homes. Beta women described their parents as "living above their means." Alpha women did not. Beta women had parents high on the "flake scale" when it came to running a household. Most gave little priority to saving and investing, and it's no wonder they never taught those skills to their children. How could they? They had little knowledge of the processes. Beta women were raised in a dysfunctional environment, with one chaotic event after another, crisis followed by crisis. Often their parents would punish them one day and give them a dollhouse the next. It was all part of the unstable nature of these parents, going from hot to cold, up and down.

According to Beta women, their parents never wanted to spend a lot of time with them. At best, they were cold and indifferent in relating to "their girls." If these parents felt any guilt about ignoring or mistreating their children, they did the substitute act. They bought them gifts in place of allocating precious time and affection to their Beta daughters.

Some Beta women undoubtedly still carry the emotional scars from the substitution acts perpetuated by their parents. Is that the reason they have a stronger need to spend more on their automobiles, watches, suits, and such than their Alpha counterparts? Could it be that their purchasing habits and consumption behavior are in fact substitutes, second-generation forms of substitutes for the parental love they did not receive?

HUSBANDS OF THE FORMER VARIETY

Alpha and Beta women share something else in common: nearly all (95 percent) have been married at least once. However, divorce is much more frequent among the ranks of the Beta women. Of those who have been married, 64 percent have been divorced at least once, as opposed to 50 percent of the Alphas. Of those divorced once, three in five of the Betas remarried and remain so, versus three out of four Alphas. There are a lot of reasons for these divorces, but one issue is more compelling than all of the others. It appears that both Alpha and Beta women tend to attract a certain type of suitor, who shall be referred to as "Marginal Bob."

SPEAKING OF MARGINAL BOB, HOW DID YOU KNOW?

A telephone conversation with a Beta woman:

> DR. STANLEY: Mrs. Tone, I would like you to review the manuscript for my latest book. It profiles many successful women like yourself, and it contrasts two types of self-employed businesswomen who have achieved financial success—Alpha women, who come from loving and nurturing homes, and Beta women, who are the products of parents who were anything but nurturing.
>
> MRS. TONE: Tell me more about the Beta women.
>
> DR. STANLEY: They became successful, in large part, by sheer will and determination. They are tenacious. Most had to pay for their own college expenses. They were economically productive early in life—they had to be. Typically, their fathers had little use or respect for them. Often their mothers were "weak sister" types.
>
> MRS. TONE: What about their married life?
>
> DR. STANLEY: Many married Marginal Bob.
>
> MRS. TONE: Who is Marginal Bob?
>
> DR. STANLEY: He is actually a prototype, a man who typically exploited his wife, especially economically. He tried to dominate

her, but he also disrespected her. That's why most Beta women divorced their Marginal Bobs. Many of these Beta women are outstanding marriage partners. They have strong character and pull more than their own weight, and they are also forgiving and unselfish. They were not very good judges of the character of the guys they first married, though. Often these Beta women were not socialized in the ways of judging the quality of potential spouses. Their fathers made horrible role models. Also, Beta women did not date a whole lot in high school and college. They were studying and working too hard.

MRS. TONE: But why call him Marginal Bob?

DR. STANLEY: Because he is marginal—a marginal husband. He's not the type who physically abuses his wife, but he is a very marginal partner. Some other women might stay married to Marginal Bob, but not the Beta women. They can be pushed. They can and do forgive. They do want to make their marriages work, and they can be exploited economically. They often blame themselves for their Marginal Bob's faults. However, they have a certain threshold. Marginal Bobs often underestimate the strength and resolve of their Beta wives. The Bobs think they can train them to accept increasing degrees of exploitation. They go from marginally acceptable to unacceptable as husbands.

MRS. TONE: I would be delighted to review your manuscript. But let me interview you for a moment. How do you know so much about my first husband, and how did you know that his name was Bob? *(Laughter and more laughter.)* Let me tell you about my own Marginal Bob. All the time we were married, his salary was used exclusively for purchasing his boats, his accessories, his trucks, his mountain cabin, his outdoor equipment, and his supplies. My salary paid for all other purchases for our family—my money was for all. His income was for his pleasure.

DR. STANLEY: Did you at least enjoy boating?

MRS. TONE: I hate boats. I dislike water. I can't swim, and I'm not interested in the least. He bought three rather expensive boats while we were married. I never set foot on one of them. I never laid eyes on his cabin. Bob spent most weekends without us— out on the boat and at the cabin. He would order a boat in the fall, then be gone for a week or two the following spring, taking delivery out of state. He spent a lot of time playing with his toys. He was the king, and we were his servants. He bought toys with his money and lived on mine. He had little respect for me and was ambivalent about our children.

DR. STANLEY: Could you tell me something about the home environment that your parents provided for you?

MRS. TONE: You have that one down as well. My father never respected me or my mother. He was really, really marginal, cold and aloof on his very best days.

MARGINAL BOB AND BETA WOMEN

Many Beta women made a mistake about their choice of spouse early in their lives and married Marginal Bob. By definition, he was a marginal husband at best.

Marginal Bobs are exploitative, and they are attracted to Beta women. They see many wonderful features associated with being married to Beta women, who are hardworking and unselfish. As young women, Betas worked and studied. They did not date a lot of fellows, so they were not experienced in determining if a suitor was a prince or a frog, aka Marginal Bob. Marginal Bob is just the opposite of the Beta woman.

He is often the product of an overindulgent mother who spoiled him. She spent a lot of money (more than she had) on her Bob, and he could do no wrong. She also convinced him that he was far superior to others. He was raised to be an expert in charming a woman and begging for her forgiveness. And Beta women will testify that no one was more adept at asking and gaining their forgiveness than their very own Marginal Bobs.

Marginal Bobs tend to be economic underachievers who relish the idea that their wives provide the lion's share of the housework, the child rearing, and the household's income. As a rule, this is more income than the Marginal Bobs could ever earn on their own, since they have little interest in working hard. They do enjoy spending money, especially to fulfill their consumption needs and enhance their overinflated egos. Bobs are charter members of the "Persuasion" Club. They often designate their occupation as sales professional, sales consultant, or marketing professional. They often change jobs, and they enjoy the freedom that certain commission sales jobs offer, including flexible working hours. There is no doubt that many Marginal Bobs are charming, with the high potential to be productive as sales professionals, but rarely does their actual performance approach their potential. Nevertheless, they did a great job prospecting and closing the marriage proposal they made to one or more Beta women.

Yes, Marginal Bob could sell anything if he had the discipline, but he never made it for very long selling time-shares, condos, automobiles, insurance, health club memberships, or vacation packages. Other Bobs believe that they possess creative genius, but they rarely succeed as artists, musicians, actors, or writers. There is nothing marginal about their egos, though, and many are at least marginally narcissistic. They believe that others are obligated to indulge them, and they do not have the work ethic, integrity, or tenacity to succeed.

Marginal Bob never felt the real need to succeed; he does not have to. He knew his wife, the Beta woman, would always heavily subsidize his lifestyle needs and forgive his transgressions. Always.

Why do so many Beta women end up married to Marginal Bobs, ignoring the signs that he is marginal at best? Even a Phi Beta Kappa graduate from a competitive college can make mistakes selecting a husband. The theory is that Beta women tend not to be well socialized in the art of judging the character of men. Remember that all during their teens, in high school, and maybe in college, they studied hard and worked hard, earning their way. While other young women were learning about men by dating frequently, Beta women were not. Instead they were fully implementing their strategy of learning and earning to become independent someday. The terrible irony is that this strategy left them vulnerable to the solicitations of the Marginal Bobs.

There is another explanation of why Beta women often marry Marginal Bobs. Remember Cindy Cinderella and her father, Ogre One, profiled in the last chapter? Unfortunately, Ogre One is often the adult male whom the Cindys of America use as a reference point. Yes, even Marginal Bob might be better than Ogre One. Why do Beta women strive so hard to become successful business owners? In part, it is their need to excel and maintain their pride and high self-esteem. It's also in order to maintain freedom from Ogre One and Marginal Bob.

TWO DECADES WITH MARGINAL BOB:
REFLECTIONS OF AN ALPHA WOMAN

Beta women are more likely to marry a Marginal Bob than are Alpha women, but the experiences of some Alpha women are nonetheless compelling. Consider the case of Ms. Foote, an Alpha woman. She is a highly successful businesswoman who was married to a Marginal Bob for twenty years. Like many leaders who marry Marginal Bobs, she had a high degree of tolerance, thinking she could somehow bring out the best qualities of her Bob. Yet like most of her cohorts, Ms. Foote finally reached her own high threshold of tolerance regarding her husband's transgressions.

Ms. Foote was kind enough to share her many candid insights about dealing with Marginal Bob. She did so in hopes that other women will learn from her mistakes.

RECOGNITION . . . IS HE A MARGINAL BOB?

DR. STANLEY: Do you think it's possible for a woman to recognize that her suitor might be a Marginal Bob?

MS. FOOTE: That is my incentive . . . to help other women of the next generation . . . [to suggest] what signs they may be able to identify. . . . If I knew back then . . . [I] wouldn't have married my husband. . . . [I] must protect my daughter from making the same mistakes. When I met my husband . . . I was blind in love . . . [I] cannot for the life of me think of all the warning signs. . . . Even now in hindsight [I] could not have recognized [his faults] because I wasn't looking for those things. Had I been able to know what was really going on with his parents, I could have seen it. . . . Yes, you can see a lot from the parents. Make sure your daughters look at the parents [of their suitors] before they make a decision [about marriage].

DR. STANLEY: How did your relationship evolve?

MS. FOOTE: You have a strong woman who becomes a high-wage earner . . . you have a man who is predisposed . . . has the characteristics [of a Marginal Bob]. . . . Then the woman becomes the enabler and allows the man to take the path of least resistance. . . . I think that as the relationship develops . . . as things happen . . . as life impacts you, that is how you . . . get into those roles.

DR. STANLEY: Could you tell me something about your husband's parents? How was he raised?

MS. FOOTE: [He was] raised to think of himself as superior . . . ultimately, he saw himself as superior.

DR. STANLEY: Was he in fact superior to you?

MS. FOOTE: No . . . no, he wasn't! . . . [I] did not see it at twenty-one. . . . [That] might have been naive on my part. . . . [We] attended college together . . . graduated at the same time. . . . We were both twenty-one at the time.

DR. STANLEY: Let's return to our discussion of his parents. How did your husband interface with his mother and father when he was growing up?

MS. FOOTE: He was his mother's pet . . . his mother's favorite child. . . . She doted on him. . . . I think she probably, not unlike the Democratic Party, . . . paid to capture voters. . . . She enabled him and she doted on him . . . took care of him financially . . . still did until recently. . . . [She] really enabled him. . . . She fed him the thinking that he was superior . . . also that he could never do anything wrong . . . absolutely . . . even though they saw a lot of the things he was doing wrong.

DR. STANLEY: Could you give me an example of some of the things he did wrong?

MS. FOOTE: The first time there was adultery . . . infidelity . . . I asked him to leave our home. I said, "You go home [to his parents' home] right now." . . . So his mother knew immediately about [her son's] . . . adulterous behavior. . . . His mother knew what had happened but failed to take a tough stance. . . . She was her son's good friend, not a disciplinarian. . . . [She] always believed that there were extenuating circumstances [concerning her son's transgressions].

BOBS WERE RAISED TO BECOME BOBS

More often than not, Marginal Bob's parents lived well above their means. There was often discomfort and disharmony over money issues. His parents had a great need to display a lifestyle that was incongruent with their true economic means, and they were highly leveraged in terms of their outstanding debt balances. They had difficulty making ends meet. This should not be interpreted as meaning that all Bobs come from humble economic backgrounds. Actually, just the opposite is true—most of their parents just outspent their incomes. Ms. Foote's Bob is quite typical, but she was raised by parents who had a very different orientation toward spending and saving.

> MS. FOOTE: [My father] didn't have a car unless he could pay for one hundred percent of it in cash at the dealership. . . . The same with [my parents'] home . . . no debt. . . . [This was] totally different from the economic environment my husband had grown up in. . . . They borrowed and leveraged everything and that was how we got in trouble financially . . . the leverage he exhibited during our own marriage.

Typically, Marginal Bobs are trained by their parents to become high-grade Income Statement Affluent hyperconsumers.

What happened when Ms. Foote, a woman of Alpha parents, married Marginal Bob? Her folks were savers and investors. Her dad was a very successful, high-income-producing professional. Her mom was a strong woman who was an active fund-raiser for a variety of noble causes. Both parents were frugal; they were high-grade Balance Sheet Affluent types. They lived well below their means, and few would expect from their outward appearance that they were quite wealthy. They were also people of integrity. They trusted people and saw the best in others.

This couple instilled in their children the golden rule: have integrity and empathy for others. During this time, however, Marginal Bob was taught how to manipulate and use people to his advantage. He looked at people the way a wolf looks at meat, and those who had a lot of meat made the best targets. The ones who were the most naive were especially attractive to predators like Bob. Of course, he felt that he was superior to his spouse and that she would be willing to accept his predatory behavior. Her function was to indulge him. He expected it to be this way, given his self-image as a prince.

When Ms. Foote and Bob married, he became the major financial decision maker. She did not object, in spite of the fact that her income was as high as and eventually higher than his. She assumed that Bob was just as enlightened about saving and investing as her father, but Bob was very different. He spent all the couple's income and more. In short order, he even depleted his wife's savings. At one time, the couple nearly had to declare bankruptcy; that is when Ms. Foote took control of her own finances. But then Marginal Bob began stealing from his wife, forging her name to financial documents, and deceiving her in many other ways.

Why did she ever marry Marginal Bob? Of course, love was a big part of it, but she'd been raised in a family where love and trust were part of her everyday surroundings. She'd assumed that her relationship with her husband would be similar to the environment in which she'd been raised. She was very, very wrong.

BOBS ARE MASTERS AT BEGGING FOR FORGIVENESS

It is one of the major characteristics of the Marginal Bobs—they are highly proficient at asking forgiveness for their many transgressions. They are very cunning at hiding their activities, but what happens when they are caught red-handed? Bobs are confidence men, sociopaths. They can anticipate the need for forgiveness, and they know what buttons to push.

Some of the women profiled herein reported being married to a Marginal Bob for twenty years or more, and they forgave their husbands countless numbers of times. Then some transgression pushed these women beyond the threshold of their tolerance. Up to that time, however, they were subjected to some of the most effective apology themes imaginable.

> Ms. FOOTE: Just when I was ready to say, "That's it," there was that beautiful letter, the trip to Europe, the confessions of total love and "how you saved my life." . . . Very sentimental . . . with the cards and the flowers.
>
> DR. STANLEY: Could you reflect upon an instance that was particularly memorable?
>
> Ms. FOOTE: One time . . . he came by to pick up my car to have it washed. I handed him my keys. He came back, dropped off the keys, and then left. . . . At the time, I did not think anything about it. But later when I picked up the keys, I noticed that these were not my keys. . . . Keys on a new key chain. . . . I went out to the driveway. . . . He had bought a new car for me . . . what a way to ask for forgiveness. Bought me a new car. . . .

But later . . . I found out that he paid for it with my money out of my personal checking account. . . . He was always doing things like that.

BOBS SEEK OUT WOMEN WHO HAVE LEADERSHIP QUALITIES

Leaders tend to see the best qualities in people, thinking they can mold people, train them to become better and more proficient at their tasks.

> MS. FOOTE: [I] always think I can bring out the best in people . . . it's what I do. . . . I'm such an optimist that I always failed to look . . . I don't ever look for the bad in people. I always look for the good in people . . . I would always fall into the trusting category because [my parents] told me to [trust people]. . . . [I] went to Sunday school . . . [and they] taught to follow down a straight and narrow, moral road. . . . I thought everybody that I would love and be associated with could be trusted to have the same moral fiber. . . . I didn't think to raise the hood of the car, examine his family's history, and look down into the wiring and say: "Where is this going to go wrong?"

Having trust, confidence, and belief in the good of people is all part of being an effective leader, but Marginal Bobs are trained to disguise themselves. Their inherent lack of integrity is not always easy to detect, especially in the early stages of a relationship. And, of course, strong leaders have strong egos. They have great confidence in their ability to judge the character of other people, and if there is even a hint that their assessment is wrong, these women always feel that they can change each and every Marginal Bob.

Having leadership ability is, in fact, a two-edged sword. A leader who does not trust people will not have a long tenure, but too often female leaders put too much blind trust in a suitor like Marginal Bob. This is, of course, exactly the type of woman that Marginal Bob seeks to capture.

> MS. FOOTE: Oh yeah . . . trust in my personal relationships and with my business. Plus, I always think I can make everything better. . . . Today it still dogs me . . . what did I miss? What could I

have seen before our marriage that I didn't see? I need to know.
. . . Part of the reason for this conversation [is that] . . . I need
to know . . . what kind of predatory characteristics to look out
for so that this doesn't happen again. . . . If we'd had all the
money in the world, there probably still would have been the
adultery . . . but perhaps not the stealing and forging of signa-
tures. . . . But maybe all the money in the world wouldn't have
been enough, and he would have gone through all of that.

MARGINAL BOBS UNDERESTIMATE THE STRENGTH
AND RESOLVE OF SUCCESSFUL BUSINESSWOMEN

How did Ms. Foote find the strength and determination to go beyond
being married to Marginal Bob? First she gives much credit to her
mother.

> MS. FOOTE: My mother told me to buck up. . . . There was never any
> whining, no complaining in our house. . . . [If you] stubbed your
> toe? She'd say, "It's three feet from your heart . . . buck up . . ."
> Yet up until my marriage nothing really bad had ever happened
> to me. When my husband had his first affair, she said, "This is
> going to be a stiff pill for you to swallow . . . buck up and get
> on with it!" . . . I'd tell my mother, "You know, I'm going
> through a hard time. . . . We almost had to file bankruptcy."
> . . . My mother [told me to] buck it up. . . . There was no sym-
> pathy . . . there was no "My poor, poor daughter." When the
> divorce went through, I made some mulling comments about
> "poor me." She said, "Well, would you rather have cancer . . .
> have your breast removed?"

Ms. Foote's mother preached strength, never weakness. She always
reminded her children that no matter how bad things seem to be, someone else has it much worse. She reminded her daughter of all the
women who had similar Marginal Bob stories but who did not have the
high-income-producing ability that she did. Ms. Foote also had great
support from her children, a very successful career, and many accomplishments in taking leadership roles for several noble causes.

DR. STANLEY: What were some of the other factors that helped you during this transition?

MS. FOOTE: Absolutely . . . doing so well in business [and] overcoming discrimination against women . . . gave me strength to deal with this. . . . My job, it gave me a harbor, a distraction . . . something I could totally lose myself in while the wounds healed . . . so I didn't have time to think about it. The self-esteem did help me heal well. . . . [It] came first from my parents [and was] instilled in me very early. . . . I wasn't going to let him destroy that. Plus my job also . . . gave me strength . . . training me to lead.

Ms. Foote also used her leadership skills to help those in need. It was her sensitivity to the needs of others that helped her handle the pains generated by dealing with Marginal Bob.

MS. FOOTE: [There is one] accomplishment of which I am most proud . . . something that I am so passionate about. . . . Child care is one of the most important things . . . women [need] . . . to be able to work and build self-esteem. Quality child care for women from housing projects. . . . Our program started with fifty thousand dollars . . . two years later, we crossed the one-million-dollar mark.

Today, Ms. Foote often reflects on her mother's sage advice about dealing with reversals in life. What does Ms. Foote know full well? That even during her most painful experiences, she was still much better off than those women she is helping today.

III.

About Their
Benevolent Nature

CHAPTER 7

Generous *and* Wealthy?

PRIORITIES ACCORDING TO MRS. E.

*L*ike most of the other women profiled herein, Mrs. E. is a successful, self-employed business owner. In her mind, success is more than being financially independent, more than earning a sizable income, and more than the pride, ego enhancement, and high self-esteem she experiences as the owner of a very productive management consulting firm that counsels senior officers of prestigious firms. It's even more important than the respect and accolades she often receives from various trade and professional associations. According to Mrs. E., success also means having the ability to share the wealth and support noble causes. How can one become financially secure and still donate considerable amounts of one's income, time, and energy? Allow Mrs. E. to answer this question.

It's possible to do well financially and to do good things for others; these are not mutually exclusive goals.

Mrs. E. was raised by parents who taught her to be charitable and include charitable giving in her household budget and financial plan. They were frugal, and they imparted that virtue to Mrs. E., who can afford to purchase just about anything offered in the consumer market because of her extraordinarily high level of income and wealth.

Her parents also trained her to deal with success. Both her mom and her dad were religious and very generous, and they told their children countless times, "Always celebrate your success first by helping those less fortunate." It is for this reason especially that Mrs. E. has been able to achieve financial security and, at the same time, give generously.

Yes, Mrs. E. was raised to be different from most people in our hyperconsuming society. They look at an upswing in their cash flow as an economic opportunity to acquire more and more consumer artifacts. What's the first thing that pops into your mind when your boss gives you the great news? Maybe he says, "Johnson, you will be receiving a $10,000 end-of-year bonus." Or: "Calhoun, you just made partner. Gone are your days of earning $50,000 a year. As partner, you will receive at least $250,000 annually." Most likely, the first thing that Johnson and Calhoun think about is buying a home or a new car, or going on vacation.

It's very predictable. An increase in cash flow generally translates into significant increases in consumption. Is it any wonder that only a small portion of Americans are financially independent? We have been well trained in how to dispose of cash. Yet some people, like Mrs. E., were trained to respond in a different manner. She invests more and gives more at peak economic periods of her career. Mrs. E. was well trained by her parents to always be very humble. Mrs. E. is, in fact, very successful in business, but she receives no satisfaction from purchasing so-called luxury goods. Mrs. E. does not need to brag. She feels no compulsion to conspicuously display the trophies and related status artifacts that supposedly denote success in this country. Mrs. E. allocates her hard-earned dollars in another way: she gets a great deal of satisfaction from donating a substantial portion of her income.

Mrs. E. believes that a significant component of success is one's ability to give more, to increase the percentage of one's income that is donated to noble causes as one's income rises. Do you want to be successful? Then follow Mrs. E.'s suggestion:

Be generous and gracious with what God gives you.

Mrs. E.'s interesting philosophy about wealth says that much of it is on loan from God, and clearly it is not accumulated in a vacuum. Success comes from standing on the shoulders of others, including parents, professors, and employees. So Mrs. E. believes that wealth should be shared if only for the simple reason that many shoulders, in addition to the millionaire's, created his or her wealth.

Perhaps you are thinking that Mrs. E.'s "others," specifically her parents, were wealthy and that she inherited more than a strong eleemosynary orientation. Perhaps Mrs. E. is one of high society's contributors. Sorry; Mrs. E. does not fit this profile. She inherited very little in terms of wealth, but she received many other more important things. Her parents molded their daughter into a leader and placed great value on her becoming an independent person. They taught her to be a caring and forgiving person and to have strong religious faith.

Mrs. E. tells of the values her parents instilled in her:

> To establish and maintain a lifelong commitment to core principles . . . honesty, integrity, respect for others. . . . Keep your priorities in order with family and faith at the top of the list. . . . Know the difference between justice and righteousness and understand the role that each should play in your life and the lives of others.

By now you may have a good grasp on understanding the character of Mrs. E., but a bit more information will likely be valuable. Our society has not always been kind, economically, to women or to people of color. Only about one in ten of the million-dollar businesses (judged by gross annual revenue) operating in America are owned and managed by women, and blacks and Native Americans overall account for a disproportionately small percentage of millionaires in this country. As a forty-eight-year-old woman of color, Mrs. E. has defied many probabilities to become a millionaire business owner. She does fit one piece of the statistical profile, however. Like others in her cohort, she is part of one of the most generous groups in American society:

Out of twenty-six ancestry groups studied, African-American women gave a significantly higher proportion of their annual income (10.1 percent) to noble causes. The average overall for successful women business owners in general is just under 7.0 percent.

You can imagine that it was not always easy for Mrs. E. to achieve. Even today, there are far too many negative stereotypes about the abilities of women, Native Americans, African-Americans, and others. While Mrs. E. was growing up, people were not always kind to her. Far from it. But her parents instilled in their daughter the strength and resolve to overcome the biting comments and hurtful exclusions. Mrs. E. suggests to those who want to succeed:

Do not make popularity a goal . . . but always be confident in who you are, what you stand for, and in what you believe.

In many ways, Mrs. E.'s success in life is the product of her positive view about life, her happiness, and her enormous ability to forgive. Mrs. E. never expressed one word that even hinted at hating or getting even with those who tried to degrade her, and she is anything but a cold and callous person. Mrs. E. is a woman of great compassion, integrity, courage, and character.

Why did Mrs. E. take so much time to complete a lengthy essay on how young people can become successful adults? Note that she works sixty to seventy hours per week and is an active fund-raiser. She's a single mom with all the related responsibilities, and she spends about five hours each week planning and managing her investments. She also has many other responsibilities and activities, including helping her older children start their own businesses.

All this and she took time out to tell her story. It's not about boasting, and it's not to enhance her own reputation. Mrs. E. is passionate about helping others achieve. It is one of her most important goals. She has helped mentor many ambitious young people. It's all part of her philosophy of giving to others. She hopes that her profile and suggestions will inspire those who feel that the odds, the mathematical probabilities, are against them.

Always strive to do your best, and when your best isn't good enough, find peace in knowing that you did all that you could.

It is amazing that women like Mrs. E. are often overlooked by noble causes. Imagine if fund-raisers asked her and others like her to use their skills to help write grant proposals. Yes, ask them to use their extraordinary writing and speaking skills for the cause. They could be formidable assets, but their potential is largely ignored by most charities.

YES! IT'S GENEROUS *AND* WEALTHY

Mrs. E. is not alone in her beliefs about giving and accumulating wealth. Cliff C. Jones wrote a book in which he discusses the multiple benefits that donors receive from being generous (*Winning Through Integrity* [Nashville: Abingdon Press, 1985]). He concludes that people who annually give at least 10 percent of their income to a noble cause are likely to: 1) gain much respect; 2) have more joy and happiness in their lives; and 3) encounter increases in their wealth and net worth. He contends that as part of the process of giving, generous people discipline themselves in terms of becoming astute managers of their income as well as their wealth.

Just what does the empirical data tell us about the relationship between giving and accumulating wealth?

Is contributing to charitable or noble causes a complement or a substitute in regard to accumulating wealth?

The answer seems logical enough. Consider these case examples: Tina Patron (TP) is a generous person, and she donates at least 10 percent of her income each year. Olga Price (OP) donates far less, at most 1 percent. All else—income, age, and several other wealth correlates— being equal, Olga should have a higher level of net worth, so logic suggests that giving to noble causes is a substitute, not a complement, to accumulating wealth.

Well, so much for college-classroom and economic-textbook logic. All things are not equal in such situations. My data from two groups of high-income-producing women suggest that giving and wealth are indeed complements, not substitutes. All those surveyed had annual realized earned incomes of $100,000 or more, and all were owners and managers of their own businesses. Each respondent was randomly selected from my national-survey database, and two groups, each containing survey data from 100 women, provided the empirical base for this analysis. As detailed later, on the average both groups were similar in terms of age and income.

The first group of 100 women was labeled "ten percenters" (TPs, Tina Patron types). They gave at least 10 percent of their annual realized income to charitable and noble causes each year. The second group of 100 women was labeled "one percenters" (OPs, or Olga Price types); they gave 1 percent or less. Thus, on average, TPs contributed $41,543, while their counterpart OPs contributed just $2,355.

You may logically conclude the OPs would have considerably more wealth accumulated. They are not "burdened" with doling out $41,543 annually. Again, so much for logic. In spite of contributing 10 percent or more of their annual realized income each year, the TPs have a higher level of net worth than do the OPs: $2.03 million versus $1.96 million (see Table 7-1).

TABLE 7-1

NET WORTH AND INCOME CONTRASTS:
TEN PERCENTERS VS. ONE PERCENTERS

DEMOGRAPHIC CHARACTERISTICS	TINA TYPES Ten Percenters (TPs)	OLGA TYPES One Percenters (OPs)
Net Worth (Average/$000's)	$2,031.9	$1,954.9
Annual Realized Household Income (Average/$000's)	$254.9	$270.4
Net Worth per Dollar of Income	$7.97	$7.23
Age (Average)	51.9	49.2
Income as a Percent of Net Worth	12.5	13.8
Expected Net Worth[1] (Average/$000's)	$1,322.9	$1,330.4
Ratio: Actual/Expected Net Worth	1.54	1.47

[1] Expected net worth was computed via the wealth equation: Expected net worth = 1/10 (age) x annual realized income.

This variation might be explained if TPs had higher annual incomes than the OPs, to offset the large amount they contributed; but that is not the case. Actually, the OPs have a higher total annual realized household income than do TPs ($270,400 versus $254,900). How can it be possible? The Tina Patron types, those who give 10 percent or more of their income annually, earn less yet have a higher level of net worth than the Olga types, the one percenters. TPs are different from OPs. An examination of the financial lifestyles of these two groups answers this question:

Why do TPs have more wealth than OPs?

The data indicates that TPs are able to produce more wealth per dollar of income than the OPs are ($7.97 versus $7.23), but it's not just one form of financial behavior that explains these differences. TPs and OPs are different in their respective orientations toward spending in general. It is more than just variations in giving that separates these two groups.

Consider again the actors in this study of contrasts. Olga Price, the charter member of the one percenter group, pays higher prices for a variety of consumer products than does Tina Patron. These types of products depreciate in value rapidly. Tina Patron has a different income-allocation orientation, spending more money in categories that tend to enhance her wealth. Olga Price spends more money on consumer items like wristwatches, suits, and shoes, while Tina Patron allocates more for investment advice, asset-management services, investments, and pension funding.

Remember, while you examine this data, a simple rule:

People allocate their dollars in ways they feel will give them the greatest satisfaction.

Those who receive enormous satisfaction from giving to noble causes can be expected to give generously, and vice versa. Those who believe they will receive much satisfaction from buying products will likely allocate their dollars in an attempt to enhance their happiness via consumption.

If you spend big on products, you have fewer dollars remaining with which to save, invest, or even donate.

Who is more frugal when it comes to allocating income dollars to purchases of clothing, accessories, and motor vehicles (see Table 7-2)?

TABLE 7-2

THE MOST EVER SPENT FOR CLOTHING AND ACCESSORIES:
TEN PERCENTERS VS. ONE PERCENTERS

ITEM	TINA TYPES Ten Percenters (TPs)	OLGA TYPES One Percenters (OPs)
SUIT OF CLOTHING		
Median Price:	$294	$338
Average Price:	$479	$680
PAIR OF SHOES		
Median Price:	$114	$131
Average Price:	$137	$146
WRISTWATCH		
Median Price:	$276	$345
Average Price:	$1,220	$1,748
MOTOR VEHICLE[1]		
Median Price:	$34,700	$35,108
Average Price:	$38,685	$37,458

[1] One percenters are more than twice as likely as ten percenters to lease their motor vehicles.

Respondents were asked about the most they ever spent (the actual median sale price) for a suit of clothing ($294 versus $338), a pair of shoes ($114 versus $131), a wristwatch ($276 versus $345), and a motor vehicle ($34,700 versus $35,108). In all four situations, the Olga Price types, the one percenters, paid more. Since they donated considerably less money than the Tina Patrons, the ten percenters ($2,355 versus $41,543), it appears that spending and giving are not complements but substitutes.

There are other measures of frugality regarding consumer expenditures. Who lives in the most expensive home? Once again, it's the Olgas (see Table 7-3). They live in a home that has a median current market value of $321,900, while their counterparts, the Tinas, own homes that have a median current market value of $298,900. What is the most they have ever spent on a home? Again the Olga types are the "high price"

TABLE 7-3

CONTRASTS IN HOME VALUES, PRICES PAID, AND MORTGAGES: TEN PERCENTERS VS. ONE PERCENTERS

ITEM	TINA TYPES Ten Percenters (TPs)	OLGA TYPES One Percenters (OPs)
CURRENT MEDIAN MARKET VALUE OF HOME OR PRIMARY RESIDENCE:		
Median Price:	$298,900	$321,900
Average Price:	$321,429	$346,104
MOST EVER SPENT ON A HOME (ACTUAL SALES PRICE):		
Median Price:	$201,500	$253,900
Average Price:	$288,700	$315,300
Percent with an Outstanding Mortgage Balance on Primary Residence:	69%	79%
Median Mortgage Balance for Those with Mortgage on Primary Residence:	$60,714	$126,200

leaders. The typical one percenter (50th percentile) paid $253,900 for her most expensive home, while the ten percenters paid much less: $201,500.

Credit use is another measure of frugality. Which group is more likely to have a mortgage on their primary residence? Who has a larger mortgage balance outstanding? The answer to both questions is the Olga types, the one percenters (see Table 7-3). Nearly eight in ten (79 percent) of the one percenters have an outstanding mortgage on their homes. A somewhat smaller percentage (69 percent) of ten percenters do also. However, the typical ten percenter with a mortgage has a much lower balance than the typical one percenter (median balance of $60,714 versus $126,200).

As noted in Table 7-4, the Tinas contribute seventeen times more money annually than do the Olgas. The Tinas also gave $15,200 to their adult children, grandchildren, parents, nieces, and nephews. The Tinas gave a combined total of $56,700 to noble causes and to relatives, while the Olgas gave only $10,200. Again, the Tinas have on average less annual realized income than the Olgas ($254,900 versus

TABLE 7-4

INCOME ALLOCATIONS:
TEN PERCENTERS VS. ONE PERCENTERS

Annual Amounts Allocated
(Average/$000's)

Income-Allocation Category	TPs	OPs	Who Allocates More?	Ratio: More Allocated/Less Allocated (%)
Contributions to charities or other noble causes	$41.5	$2.4	TPs	1729.2%
Gifts of cash or equivalents to relatives	$15.2	$7.8	TPs	194.9%
Income taxes[1]	$73.5	$88.2	OPs	120.0%
Interest paid on loans[2]	$4.6	$5.0	OPs	108.7%
Mortgage payments[3]	$14.7	$19.1	OPs	129.9%
Club dues	$1.7	$2.3	OPs	135.3%
Fees for financial advice or asset management	$7.8	$3.8	TPs	205.3%
Pension or annuity contributions	$21.6	$16.2	TPs	133.3%
Investments[4]	$35.1	$28.3	TPs	124.0%

[1] Includes federal, state, and local income taxes.
[2] Includes annual interest paid on all personal loans, including home equity loans but excluding mortgage loans.
[3] Includes mortgage payment on all noncommercial residential properties owned.
[4] Excludes pension or annuity contributions.

$270,400). Isn't it ironic that the Tina Patrons have a higher level of net worth ($2,031,900 versus $1,954,900)? How is this possible?

Look at it another way. Reduce the average income of both groups by the amount of their respective contributions to noble causes alone. The average "real" income for TPs then is transformed ($254,900 less $41,500 for contributions) to $213,400, while the income for OPs becomes $268,000 ($270,400 less $2,400). Using these "real" income figures, take a measure of each group's economic productivity. Divide the "real" income figures for each group into the respective net worth. The results indicate that the Tina Patrons generate on average $9.52 of net worth for every dollar of their income. But the Olgas are not nearly as productive. They have accumulated, on average, only $7.29 for every dollar of their income.

Some portion of this difference can be explained by the previously described variations in consumption patterns. Taken separately, on a one-time purchase basis, these differences may not appear to be substantial. Yet over time, the composite of a few extra dollars spent here and there can and do add up to considerable amounts of money. In reality, neither group has what could be considered an extravagant lifestyle. Both groups are rather frugal, especially given the fact that their respective average income characteristics place both in the top 98.5 percentile for all American income producers. Nonetheless, TPs are decidedly more frugal than OPs.

The Olga Price types also paid 26 percent more for their most expensive home than did the Tina Patron types (a median of $253,900 versus $201,500), and a more expensive home is associated with a large number of "more expensives," including taxes, maintenance costs, and the size of the mortgage balance ($126,200 for OPs versus $60,714 for TPs). More expensive homes are typically situated in more expensive, higher-status neighborhoods, and home owners are often expected to have more costly furniture and accessories.

Differences in the cost of a home are significant, but this variation is not enough to account fully for the reason that TPs are more economically productive than OPs. Perhaps their respective allocation of income dollars accounts for the difference. According to Table 7-4 the Olgas allocate more money for categories that are substitutes to accumulating wealth. In contrast to the Tinas, they spend more of their annual realized income on things that are impediments to building wealth: income taxes ($88,200 versus $73,500); interest paid on loans ($5,000 versus $4,600); mortgage payments ($19,100 versus $14,700); and club dues ($2,300 versus $1,700).

Yes, OPs spend more for taxes, products, pleasure-related services, and interest on loans, which are all negative correlates of building wealth. What about those income-allocation categories that are positive correlates of wealth building? As you suspected, it's the ten percenters who allocated more dollars than the one percenters to: fees for financial advice and/or asset management ($7,800 versus $3,800); pension or annuity contributions ($21,600 versus $16,200); and investments ($35,100 versus $28,300).

The patterns are predictable. Very often, those with high incomes who spend more also invest less and accumulate less. Conversely, those who spend considerably less can and do invest more and accumulate more. As a result, they are able to give more. But there is something even more basic than spending and investing. The Tinas are different types of people from the Olgas. More than two-thirds of the Tinas—68 percent—versus only 46 percent of the Olgas indicated that they were raised by parents who taught their daughters how to be frugal, to save, and to invest. These parents also taught them about their obligation to share and the resulting joy derived from such behavior. TPs spend more money than OPs for financial advice or asset-management services because their parents taught them that when it comes to investment expertise, one must pay for high-grade advice and management.

Don't think that TPs blindly turn over control of their portfolios to investment managers. They are very deliberate when selecting investment advisers, and they usually deal with several. TPs spend money on investment-related periodicals and reports that are produced by objective third parties, so they have several checks and balances with which to evaluate the success and relative performance of their advisers.

TPs, on average, spend about 25 percent more time per week than OPs managing and planning their investments. This translates into just over one hour more per week. But OPs, in general, have less experience with investing, and they do not have the same informative periodicals that TPs purchase. Plus, OPs are much more passive. Their philosophy about becoming financially independent is less complex. In contrast to TPs, OPs are more prone to believing that being frugal, earning a good income, and saving and investing alone will translate into becoming wealthy. Certainly their system worked, because they are wealthy in terms of net worth. But TPs are even wealthier, although they give substantially more money to noble causes. More than eight in ten (82 percent) TPs have an estate plan that specifies "significant donation be given to charitable causes," while only 47 percent of the OPs have made such provisions. In fairness, it is important to note that the intentions and goals of the OPs regarding wealth are not nearly as well formulated as those of the TPs.

Both TPs and OPs have had and continue to have a very strong long-term goal of becoming financially and psychologically independent through owning and managing their own businesses. Both planned for this to happen. Members of both groups wanted to enhance their self-images, their self-esteem, and their pride and dignity, and they did so in large part through success in business. However, OPs are much more one-dimensional in regard to goals and intentions. Beyond maintaining their independence, what do they plan to do with their wealth? Most "have not given it much thought" in spite of the fact that "you can't take it with you." They have yet to formulate a firm set of goals and intentions concerning the disposition of their wealth. Few in either group intend to spend, spend, spend on themselves.

Conversely, TPs have given considerable thought to "What now, since I am already rich?" Most have advisers who have helped them formulate questions. Their families and eleemosynary causes are typically part of their distribution plans.

The Tina types donate on average $17.29 for every $1.00 given by the Olgas. Could it be that the TPs' giving is a substitute for spending more on products and so-called pleasure-related services? They seem to get great satisfaction from giving rather than consuming more and more. The Tinas know better how to leverage their income into wealth for themselves and others in need than do the Olgas.

In summary, what can be said of the TPs, the more generous, and the OPs, the less generous? Within each age and income cohort:

- TPs tend to spend fewer dollars on the impediments to building wealth: income taxes, homes, clothing and accessories, motor vehicles, mortgages, interest on personal loans, club dues, and vacations.
- TPs allocate more money to the foundation stones of accumulating wealth, including investments, pension or annuity contributions, and fees for professional financial advice and asset-management services.
- TPs spend less on themselves while giving more to needy causes. Yet they tend to have higher levels of wealth.
- Most TPs can identify the origin of their acumen concerning finances and their proclivity to give to charitable causes. They were raised by parents who taught them how to accumulate as well as share wealth.

CHAPTER 8

Learning to Give

hy is it that some people give substantial amounts to noble causes while others do not? Most of those who give at least 10 percent of their income (TPs) were raised by parents who had a strong eleemosynary orientation. Yes, their parents were givers. Plus, they taught their children to do likewise. Also, nearly two-thirds (66 percent) of the TPs, versus only 52 percent of the OPs (those that give 1 percent or less), indicated that their parents had a close affinity for at least one religious organization. Their parents taught them to appreciate the importance of financially supporting these types of organizations, as demonstrated in the case studies profiled in this and other chapters.

The parents of TPs also taught their children how to plan, budget, and allocate their financial resources. Actually, charitable giving and financial planning are part of the same process for most TP households—one cannot give if one spends all her income. Conversely, those who have the strongest orientation toward giving also tend to be savers and investors. Their domestic income allocation, including charitable giving, saving, and investing, is all part of the same financial plan.

CHRISTY

Christy has always been a very charitable person. No matter what the condition of her family business might have been, she was always in the

TP category because she was trained by her parents not only to save and invest but also to give. In fact, saving and giving were both part of the integrated financial education she received from her parents, a socialization process that was an important part of her upbringing. Her earliest recollections of this process, as a young girl, still bring a smile to her face, and even recalling those days generated tears of joy.

> *We [the entire family—Mom and Dad, sisters and brothers] would sit down the first Sunday afternoon of each month . . . we'd all sit at the table after church and Sunday dinner. We didn't have much money. . . . We would always take a look at Daddy's [monthly] paycheck and then start doing our homework [financial planning and income allocation].*

Her mom and dad taught Christy to place high priority on empathy for the needs of those less fortunate.

> *I had two strong, fabulous parents. . . . The first things funded were their pledges. Regardless of anything else, Mom and Dad would always pay their pledges . . . always donated 10 percent of their incomes.*

Then her dad's paycheck would be earmarked for all the current bills that were outstanding.

> *We would then work our way down through all the bills.*

After all the bills were taken care of, upcoming expenses for the month were estimated. Dad's income dollars were allocated to key categories.

> *I remember one time my mother said . . . [we] need this amount for groceries. . . . [I] can make it with less, but I hope you like beans. And we ate a lot of beans that month.*

Yes, the family members ate a lot of beans, but they never failed to give generously to noble causes. Living the "a lot of beans" lifestyle also enabled Christy's mom and dad to fund much of the expenses of sending their children to college.

Sitting at the kitchen table . . . I knew how hard it was for them to save for us to go to college. We would sit down on Sunday, and we would all look at these staggering amounts [estimated dollars for college fees and tuition] . . . a whole lot of digits.

How did Christy's mom and dad typically respond when they considered these numbers? They smiled while earmarking a good portion of their household's income to the "children's college fund." If her parents had not allocated that money, it might have been impossible for their children to attend college. At the same time, the children were socialized about the importance of sharing and being generous to others who were less fortunate.

Dad, he would look up and smile . . . and mother too . . . while the checks were being written [for the college funds]. I had tears in my eyes. . . . It made my heart break with joy. . . . It was not easy for them. But each time Dad would write a check [for the college fund], he would smile and say . . . I love writing checks that will pay these bills for tuition . . . you can do this for your kids someday.

Christy did follow her dad's advice, and her own children are being exposed to the same "kitchen table" planning process. Christy is also very generous in supporting noble causes, and it's very likely that her children will follow her lead.

One of the reasons for Christy's success today is the nurturing environment that was provided by her parents. They demonstrated respect for each other and for their children. Christy's folks were frugal, and they planned and accounted for every dollar of their income. Their children were treated more like adults than infants and were always included at the Sunday planning meetings.

Each child would make his or her proposal to the other members of the family planning board. If Christy needed a new notebook or shoes, she would have to explain the rationale behind her request. Each child had to plan for the meeting and conceptualize a logical theme for funding. If they could not, then no money would be earmarked for the item.

Imagine if all children grew up in an environment like Christy's. They would have begun learning how to run a business meeting before they were ten years old! But they would also have learned about how to plan disbursements, how to budget, and how to have considerable empathy for the needs of others. They would become especially sensitive to the key qualities of leadership. Christy's parents were fine role models in this context.

The monthly meetings were not just about budgets and financial details. There were discussions about household tasks, and Christy's parents made doing chores fun. For example, her dad would often ask with a smile:

"Who will help me clean up the yard?" He really made it fun to work . . . yard work or household tasks. He was the first one out the door to start raking leaves.

Her parents would also inquire about the goals their children had set for themselves concerning courses in school.

[I] had to look them [Mom and Dad] in the eye and tell them how I was doing in school . . . if I was trying my best.

Christy is raising her children, who are financially much better off than Christy's mom and dad, in the same manner. Nevertheless, they are being trained to appreciate the values taught to Christy.

There are certain advantages to being raised by parents of modest means. It forces caring parents like Christy's to budget and plan and invest for the future of their children. They began college funding for each child before he or she was born. Without such forethought, her parents would have never been able to fund all those college educations. This is especially significant given the fact that the family always donated at least 10 percent of its income each and every month of their adult lives. Knowing that they had an obligation, a strong need to make donations, made them all the better planners and investors. They became experts in getting the most out of each dollar of income. Is it any wonder that Christy has so much respect and appreciation and admiration for her parents?

What if Christy's parents had had very different standards? What if they'd had a substantially higher income, perhaps in the low- to mid-six-figure range, and were Income Statement Affluent? Income Statement Affluent parents do little or no budgeting or planning. They spend a lot and save little, if at all. Mom and Dad are hyperconsumers, and through their consumption habits, they communicate to the children that they evidently have a great deal of income. Why else would they spend so much?

When Income Statement Affluent parents contact me, they want to know why it is that their kids don't seem to appreciate them. Should these kids have great appreciation for all the expensive products and services they have received from Mom and Dad? No! Not if the children have been given the impression that their parents have more income than they know what to do with.

Income Statement Affluent parents who never teach their children the value of money produce Income Statement Affluent children. So what if your mom and dad bought you a new car? You say, "It's no big deal, no economic pain, they can afford it. Just look at the way they spend. They don't have to plan or deliberate." If the household spends a lot on consumer goods, it will have little or nothing to give to eleemosynary causes. Again, selfish parents produce children who lack empathy for the less fortunate.

Does this mean that all parents who have high incomes are destined to produce spoiled, selfish, and unappreciative children? No, it's not the size of the income or the magnitude of wealth that is so crucial in such situations. The important factor is how well Mom and Dad train their children to adopt the important values about charity, thrift, saving, and investing. Mom and Dad can certainly be well off financially and still teach these lessons.

But as in Christy's case, parents must take the time to share these values. It's not difficult—parents can be creative in explaining the value of money and its alternative uses. After all, there is "magic" in the compounding of interest and dividends over the lifetime of an investment! There's also magic in the way that one dollar added to educational funding can eventually generate fifty or even one hundred dollars or more of added income for the recipients over a lifetime.

The parents who never take the time to teach their children about the value of money usually don't understand or practice money discipline, thrift, or generosity themselves. So how could they be expected to raise their children with these values? Christy's parents spent just an hour or two per month formally teaching their children about money-related values, but each day their children also observed their parents actually practicing what they preached.

HELEN OF ORANGE

The following anecdote was supplied by one of my successful self-employed businesswomen, Helen of Orange. Her family donates at least 10 percent of its income to charity each year, and it also gives much time and human effort to helping causes that assist the poor. Helen, her husband, and their children are active volunteers for such activities.

Helen indicated that her "giving nature" was something she acquired from her kind, charitable mother. When Helen was young, her parents would give her four gifts for her birthday, but one of them Helen was to give away to a child in less fortunate circumstances. Once Helen asked her mother why she could keep only three of the gifts. Her mother informed her, "The baby Jesus received only three gifts on his birthday." Helen never asked that question again.

THE GENEROUS BEVERLY BISHOP

Beverly is so generous because she was raised that way, and one particular event had a major influence on her. When she was ten years old, Beverly was playing in the front yard of her parents' home. She looked down the street and noticed something strange. A family—mother, father, and children—was milling around in front of their home among piles of cardboard boxes, furniture, lamps, and clothing. Beverly did not understand what was happening, so she went inside and asked her mother about it.

Her mother knew immediately what it meant. She'd known that the family was having a difficult time making ends meet, but she was surprised that they were being evicted from their house. Beverly was shocked when her mother told her the neighbors had lost their home.

Without hesitation, her mother went to the family and insisted that they change addresses. She then helped the entire family of four move into Beverly's home.

I acquired my need to help others from my parents, especially my mother. We were always cash poor, never wealthy, but my mother was a very giving person. Once a neighbor family was really down financially. They were thrown out of their home. Evicted . . . with no place to go. My mother made wooden pallets for them to sleep on . . . [and we] kept the family at our house. Fed them, took care of them until they got on their feet financially. Even though we had a small house . . . three rooms . . . my mother made room for them. It was how she was raised.

Beverly also mentioned another interesting incident. Once again her mom demonstrated great empathy for those less fortunate.

My Cuban boyfriend was talking to my mother . . . about all the Cuban exiles living in basements, halls . . . [including] children. . . . Mother invited them over for Sunday dinners. Sunday after Sunday my mother's dining table was full. . . . The house was full of Cuban exiles.

Beverly's mother instilled in her children this strong need to help others, but it was more than a proclivity to give to those less fortunate. Beverly also learned how to be a leader and how to take the initiative in helping others, as did most of the wealthy women who have a charitable orientation. They take the lead role in initiating and organizing the giving process because that's the way they were raised. Most often, their mothers were of strong character and were role models of leadership.

Beverly's mother took the evicted family into her own home, and she fed people who had lost everything. She never once complained about having so many mouths to feed in so few square feet, and she never worried about getting a tax write-off for being kind. Nor did she even yearn to have her story and her picture in the local newspaper. She helped her neighbors because she felt it was the proper thing to do for families in dire straits. She shared her home and food because it gave her satisfaction and pride, but in the process, she also accomplished something else: she did a masterful job of teaching her daughter Beverly how to be a very strong and generous woman.

Just how charitable is Beverly? On an annual basis, she donates about 30 percent of her income to noble causes. That 30 percent exceeds the total she allocates annually to mortgage payments, interest payments on other loans, motor vehicle purchases, insurance, clothing, vacations, and utility costs combined. In terms of percent of her income devoted to noble causes, she allocated more than eight times what the typical highly compensated professional does.

Beverly has never owned a vehicle whose cost exceeded $22,000; she drives a pickup truck. She can carry a lot of toys for hospitalized children in the back of a truck, and that's one of her favorite pastimes. That is why Beverly's good friends often joke about the worst place a toy shopper could be during the holiday season:

> *You never want to be standing in line behind Beverly when she's on a mission, checking out of the toy store with multiple shopping carts fully loaded.*

Giving is a personal thing to Beverly—it enhances her self-esteem. It is one of the rewards that she receives from being a top producer of income. Her high income and frugal lifestyle enable her to be so very generous. Unfortunately, not all high-income producers have Beverly's extraordinary interest in supporting noble causes.

CHAPTER 9

Intrafamily Gifts of Kindness

J often use the term *nurture* to describe the behavior of parents in supporting, encouraging, and otherwise developing their offspring. Most millionaire women and men take nurturing beyond this standard definition by providing their children with a variety of "economic acts of kindness" long after they have reached adulthood. Millionaires often also provide substantial economic subsidies to other family members, including grandchildren, nieces and nephews, and less fortunate brothers and sisters.

Women and men differ in the degree to which they provide family members with economic gifts, as presented in Table 9-1. As might be expected, women are significantly more nurturing than men, allocating nearly 5.0 percent (median) of their annual realized income to their adult children, grandchildren, nieces and nephews, brothers and sisters, and other relatives. Men who are millionaires allocate a smaller portion, less than 2.0 percent, of their annual income.

Nearly nine in ten (89 percent) of millionaire women have provided their adult children with interest-free loans. Only 60 percent of millionaire men have done the same. Over time, most interest-free loans usually become forgiveness loans, which do not require repayment. About two-thirds (65 percent) of millionaire women have provided their adult children with financial assistance in purchasing a home, but only about half (51 percent) of the millionaire men did the same.

There is usually a progression in "lending" money to one's adult children. Typically money is provided in the form of a low-interest loan;

TABLE 9-1

MILLIONAIRE WOMEN VS. MEN:
ECONOMIC OUTPATIENT CARE GIVEN BY PARENTS TO
THEIR ADULT CHILDREN OR GRANDCHILDREN

	Percent of Millionaires:	
	Women	Men
1. INTERGENERATIONAL TRANSFER OF CASH OR SUPPLEMENTAL INCOME BENEFITS		
Periodic gifts of cash in the amount of $20,000 or more	43%	27%
Interest-free loans	89%	60%
Cash or forgiveness loans to start or enhance a business	44%	26%
2. INTERGENERATIONAL HOME OWNER'S SUPPLEMENTS		
Financial assistance in purchasing a home	65%	51%
3. SECOND-GENERATION EDUCATIONAL ENHANCEMENT		
Funding of tuition for children's undergraduate college education	78%	80%
Funding of tuition for children's graduate college education	31%	29%
4. THIRD-GENERATION EDUCATIONAL ENHANCEMENT		
Funding of tuition for grandchildren's private grade school and/or high school	54%	44%
5. TRANSFERS OF PRIVATE ASSETS		
Gifts of farm or timber land to adult children or grandchildren	9%	5%
Gifts of shares of family or private business to adult children	30%	16%
6. INTERGENERATIONAL TRANSFERS OF VALUABLES OR COLLECTIBLES		
Gifts of gems, precious metals, or coin or stamp collections	56%	25%
Gifts of family engagement or wedding ring or diamond	41%	NA
7. TRANSFERS OF SECURITIES		
Gifts of publicly traded securities to adult children	63%	37%
8. PLANNED INTERGENERATIONAL TRANSFER OF WEALTH		
Establishment of trust accounts for children or grandchildren	59%	35%

then the low-interest loan becomes a no-interest loan; next, the no-interest loan is often converted into a forgiveness loan. Forgiveness loans in turn often precipitate financial assistance in purchasing a home, which translates into making mortgage payments for one's adult son or daughter. Finally, it is often the outright gift of a home that results in an increase in the variety and size of economic outpatient care (EOC) given by parents to their adult children and grandchildren. It's unfortunate, but parents who attempt to prop up the social and economic status of their adult children or subsidize their lifestyles find that they must continue to do so for a lifetime and beyond.

Often, at least one of the adult children of millionaires never becomes as economically successful as his or her parents, and the parents respond by taking aggressive domestic action, giving these children economic outpatient care. They heavily subsidize their adult children and allow them to live well above their economic means. Subsidizing the consumption lifestyles of adult children weakens their ambition and motivation to achieve. In turn, they become more and more reliant upon the dollars doled out by their wealthy and well-intentioned parents.

In some extreme cases, these highly subsidized economically under-achieving adult children find themselves facing a dilemma. They become the guardians for elderly parents who are incapacitated, and they live in fear of having to lower their own high-consumption lifestyles. What if the money that their parents put away for high-quality assisted living begins to reduce the number of dollars earmarked for the children's economic outpatient care? What if Mother requires years and years of intensive assisted care? What if the size of Mother's estate is being eroded by medical and related health-care bills as well as poorly performing investments? These issues may well be perceived by the heavily subsidized daughter or son as a major threat to their lifestyle.

THE DILEMMA

Such cases are not unusual today in America, and people contact me about these and related issues. They reveal their own, often bitter experiences. They also tell of family conflicts that are caused by the particular manner in which wealth within families is distributed.

Millionaire women are very generous in providing economic acts of kindness to their adult children, but frequently they are too kind. The typical millionaire produces three children. In terms of achievements, they are not all likely to be equally productive. What is a mother to do when one of her three adult children is unable to maintain even a modest form of middle-class lifestyle, yet the other two children had no problem achieving on their own? More often than not, it is Mom who will take the blame. She reasons that it was her fault that her "Beth" or "Bob" never finished college, never had much ambition, was never wise in selecting a spouse, was never lucky at finding a suitable job, never succeeded in operating the antiques business that Mother bankrolled, never seemed to be able to purchase a home without being heavily subsidized, never succeeded as a day trader, and so on.

Their mothers often refer to these sorts of children as "poor Beth" or "poor Bob": "Poor Beth and her husband can't afford to purchase a home. They need some financial help." Or "Poor Bob and his wife, they need a new roof but don't have the money. I'm going to pick up the tab." The "poor" preface denotes pity, but what about the sisters and brothers of Beth and Bob? They are the productive ones, and they, too, blame Mother for spoiling Beth and indulging Bob. When they speak to me about "poor Beth" or "poor Bob," it is not in ways that connote pity. The preface "poor" rings with sarcasm and contempt for the giver and taker of economic subsidies. Yes, they see things differently from Mother, who, in their minds, is the root cause of Beth's and Bob's dependency and unproductive lifestyle. They reason that Mother gave Beth and Bob too many fish and never taught them how to fish on their own. Beth's and Bob's productive siblings will tell you that they are self-sufficient because they were not indulged, not overprotected, never spoiled.

Why is it that a disproportionately large percentage of the oldest children are the most productive? Is it because they received more attention from their parents? Or is it that they had to learn to do things for themselves while their parents were devoting much—often too much—time, energy, and money to doting on Beth and indulging Bob?

Usually the Beth and Bob types receive economic subsidies from Mother throughout their lifetimes and even beyond. They, the weak of character, are further weakened. They are likely to receive the lion's share of Mother's economic handouts during her lifetime, as well as a disproportionately large share or, in some cases, all of their mother's estate. Thus, even after they pass away, these mothers continue to weaken their weakest children. The strong get little or nothing, and they expect that. Receiving little or no economic outpatient care from an estate tends to strengthen the strong.

There is a difference between being kind and being overindulgent, which can create much friction within a family. It is the weak versus the strong, with Mother, the self-made millionaire, in the middle. Mother is well intentioned. She thinks that her Beth should have the same socioeconomic lifestyle as her more productive children. She believes that her money can accomplish that and that her productive children will understand, even encourage, the subsidies that she gives to her Beth and her Bob.

Money handouts will not make an unproductive child productive. And no matter how many times she refers to "poor Beth" this and "poor Bob" that, her productive children will not change their views. In fact, the more she tries to persuade them to change their definition of "poor," the more friction is created.

There is another problem that many of these mothers never anticipate. Over the years, they will have doled out much of their economic resources to the weak Beth and the dependent Bob. When it comes to the late stages of their lives, do they really think that Beth and Bob will provide for them? Will they be willing to provide first-class assisted living for Mother that might require them to reduce their high-consumption standard of living? Remember that Mother trained them to appreciate a lifestyle that was far above their own self-generated resources. What will it be, Beth and Bob—your lifestyle or your mother's health care? The answers to these and related questions point in one direction. Everyone who can afford it should use the services of a top trust company and estate attorney. These professionals should be employed to make certain that even if one is incapacitated, one's golden years are at the gold level indeed.

Why do people need to tell me about their own experiences, revealing that family conflicts are caused by certain forms of economic outpatient care? They hope that by reporting the evils of overindulgence they can help others not to make their mistakes. Typically it is the strong, productive daughters and sons who reveal certain family secrets. Their mothers, the self-made economically successful women, also share their concerns and opinions. They all have a strong need to tell their stories about the unproductive sister or brother who exploits the wealth and good nature of their mother. The sad tale that follows is a consolidation of many such revelations.

RESTITUTION AND EXTORTION FAMILY STYLE: BETH AND BOB, THE PRO FORMA EXPLOITATIVE COUPLE

Mother, aka Mrs. M., gave her daughter Beth and her son-in-law Bob cash for the down payment on the purchase of a home. The couple received more than $150,000 or about one-half the purchase price of the home. At that time, Mrs. M. reasoned that the couple's earnings would enable them to pay the balance of the purchase price in monthly mortgage payments.

Within two years of buying the home, Beth gave birth to the couple's second child, and then decided not to return to work for a year . . . or two or three. Beth explained to her mother that the couple would not be able to pay the mortgage on their home. What were they to do? Mrs. M. suggested that she would make the mortgage payments until Beth was working again. Eventually Beth returned to work part-time. She gave birth to a third child and then another. How was the couple to make ends meet now that there were four children to support?

Mrs. M. thought she had a solution to the couple's dilemma. What if she could enhance her daughter's self-esteem and make things a bit easier for Beth and her family? Mrs. M. thought both of these things could be accomplished just by writing a check, so she paid off the entire balance on Beth and Bob's home. In an instant, Beth and Bob owned outright a lovely home in a nice middle- to upper-class neighborhood. After paying off the mortgage, Mrs. M. made it clear that there would be no more housing subsidies, no more economic outpatient care— unless, of course, they had a dire economic emergency.

For nearly two years after paying off the mortgage, Mrs. M. gave Beth and Bob little in the way of direct economic outpatient care. She did, however, transfer some of her wealth indirectly, in another form. These transfers were precipitated by what might be called a series of economic emergencies.

Beth and Bob often complained to Beth's mother about the poor quality of the public schools in their district. They explained that the lack of a good education at the elementary and high school levels would reduce the probability that their children would gain admission to a quality college or university. Bob also sent certain news clippings to Mrs. M., and the theme was always the same: "Drugs Present at Local Public High Schools," "Problems at Local Public School," and "Assaults at High School." Mrs. M. responded to these revelations by agreeing to pay for all of her grandchildren's private school tuition.

Other than this, Mrs. M. deflected Beth's requests for more direct forms of economic outpatient care. She did "help out" when the couple purchased a new SUV, but for several years Mrs. M. was otherwise insensitive to the couple's requests for cash subsidies.

Mrs. M. began to believe that Beth and Bob were finally making it on their own. However, they were a conniving pair. Using his short-lived job experience in the insurance and financial-training area, Bob devised a plan to loosen his mother-in-law's purse strings. Bob and Beth took out a series of equity loans on the home that Mrs. M. had bought for them—after all, they owned the home outright with no mortgage clouding the title.

Equity loans! Equity loans! What a wonderful idea. How else could they pay for their new camper and vacations to Mexico and the Bahamas? How else were they supposed to pay for his-and-her water-craft and their storage? How else could Bob even think of upgrading to a top-of-the-line all-terrain vehicle? Don't forget the cost of operating and maintaining two cars and one SUV. And, of course, it's rather expensive to clothe four kids who attend upscale private schools.

After more than two years of outlandish consumption financed by home equity loans, the couple could not pay off the loans on their own and were faced with the loss of their home. Without additional support for their hyperspending and their outstanding debt, Beth and Bob would likely have to sell the house. But Bob had anticipated that Mrs. M. would have no alternative but to pay off the equity loans for them. Otherwise, she risked having her daughter and four grandchildren living on the street.

What happened when they dropped this bombshell on Mrs. M.? She was angry and emotionally distraught, but as Bob had predicted, she eventually capitulated and began paying off the equity loans. In her mind, she had no choice. Call it what you like, but in essence it was economic outpatient care via extortion.

In regard to Beth's problems in life, Mrs. M. always felt that she was at fault. How else could it be that her son and older daughter were so productive, while Beth accumulated little and had a marginal husband, major debts, and very low self-esteem? Mrs. M. reasoned that she had devoted too little time to raising this daughter. During Beth's formative years, her mother had been involved in running her business; she had also spent a lot of time caring for her own mother during a long, painful terminal illness.

Mrs. M. still feels that some children need more nurturing in order to succeed in life and that some children are programmed at birth to succeed. So it was with her two other children. It seemed that they were always well behaved. They were straight-A students from day one. Given these experiences, Mrs. M. expected that Beth would develop into a successful adult just like her brother and sister. When Beth first ran into problems in elementary school, Mrs. M. thought this was just a short phase. She soon realized that Beth's personality traits and needs were very different from those of her other children. Accordingly, Mrs. M. pampered Beth. She forgave her and indulged her, unwittingly exacerbating Beth's problematic tendencies. Mrs. M. realizes this today, but what is a mother to do? Beth cannot maintain a middle-class lifestyle without major doses of Mother's economic outpatient care. In every case where Mrs. M. attempted to remove Beth from her dependency on economic outpatient care, Beth and her creative husband took countermeasures that proved successful. Whenever there was even a hint that the economic-outpatient-care valve would be shut off, Beth and Bob figured out a way to open it even wider.

Over the years, Beth developed a great deal of resentment toward her brother and sister. Both were economically productive, had strong marriages, and were well educated. She was terribly jealous of them and their successes. Beth's brother had graduated with honors from a prestigious college and then attended law school. Beth's sister had also been a scholar in her undergraduate and graduate studies. Mrs. M. had paid for much of these educational costs, although some were covered by scholarships.

Beth blames her mother's lack of encouragement for all her problems. What other reason could there be for Beth's not attending college? In her mind, she'd been shortchanged by her own mother. She and Bob strongly believe that she is owed a great deal of economic restitution.

Obviously, Beth's logic is faulty. Mrs. M. wanted all her children to attend college. She started college funds for each of them prior to their births. So what happened to all those accumulated dollars in Beth's college fund? Mrs. M. maintained this fund even when Beth was no longer a minor; but even when Beth reached her twenty-first birthday, she never inquired about it. Then she married Bob, and months before the couple married, he got wind of the existence of Beth's college fund. He told Beth that all the money in the fund, well over $100,000, was hers and pointed out that Mrs. M. could not stop Beth from accessing it.

When Beth and Bob confronted Mrs. M. about disposition of the college fund, she had no choice but to relinquish control of the money. Predictably, the couple ran through it in short order.

The lump sum of restitution was not enough for Beth and Bob. After all, think of the lifetime differences. What would a person like high school graduate Beth be expected to earn as opposed to her brother or sister with advanced college degrees? Beth and Bob felt that Mrs. M. should make up the difference. Call this life-cycle restitution. How else could the couple maintain the same standard of living Beth's brother and sister enjoyed?

Mrs. M. never agreed to provide the couple with a monthly fixed-dollar dose. She doled out money to the couple when they convinced her that they had a serious need. If Mrs. M. balked, she was treated to a variety of distasteful, psychologically painful actions that she found particularly distressing after her husband passed away. Both her son and other daughter and their families lived far away in other parts of the country, but Beth and her family lived near Mrs. M. She had frequent contact with Beth and her grandchildren, which was very comforting to Mrs. M. This fact made some of the actions taken by Beth and Bob to precipitate more and more economic outpatient care all the more potent.

A RUNAWAY BEST-SELLER

What if Beth and her husband, Bob, wrote a book on how to extort economic outpatient care successfully? Imagine that Beth and Bob are so proud of their book they agree to be interviewed on the nationally televised *Barry Prince* talk show.

> BARRY: Good evening. Tonight we have a very special couple as guests for our entire program. They are the authors of the runaway best-

selling book *Getting Your Fair Share and More*. They, like all of the guests on our show, have been injected with our own special formula of "one-hundred-proof truth serum." Beth, how did you convince your mother to pay for so many expenses?

BETH: I look at it this way: What can I conclude if Mother thinks so little of her grandkids that she won't help with their school expenses and transportation? To her, these kids are Cinderellas, inferior to my brother's kids—my kids are not worthy. Yet Mother is always coming over to visit her Cinderellas. She always wants to be here for their birthdays, on holidays, weekday evenings, weekends—you name it. The soft sell did not work, so we decided to place Mother on the cold turkey program. That's what we call chapter 6 in our book: "The Cold Turkey Program."

BOB: Beth's mother is addicted to our kids, but in a lot of ways she treats them like Cinderellas. She'd probably prefer to be with her son's children, but they live on the other side of the country.

BARRY: Okay, but explain what you mean by "cold turkey."

BETH: Like it says in our book, the "Cold Turkey Program" is an extreme method. It may have to be deployed when one or both grandparents are stonewalling. If Mother has an addiction, one must capitalize upon it. So we decided to cut her off from contact with us and the children. Mother was always invited to the birthday parties for our kids. Too often she took over the event. She planned things without asking what our kids wanted to do in terms of activities, prizes, and games. So when the next birthday was coming up, we did not invite her.

BARRY: Did she inquire about why she was not being invited?

BETH: Oh sure, but I never told her that it was because she refused to help us with the new car and private school expenses. I just said we were having our parties at places like McDonald's and such, and there was limited seating. I also told her that she should call before she, as she calls it, stops by for a few minutes.

BARRY: What did you do when she called and asked if she could stop by?

BOB: Oh, let me do this one. It's all in the book. You have to ask yourself about your immediate objective. You want to get her off the phone in a heartbeat before she asks to stop by. One of the best ways of doing this is what we call the "Embarrassment Method." Say she calls one Saturday; right after she says hello you might say, "Oh, I have a room full of neighbors here right now." She feels embarrassed that she has interrupted something. It works every time. Or "I'm waiting for an important phone call from our son John's teacher." Again, she's off the phone in a second. Or "I'm just walking out the door to pick up the kids from karate lessons. I have been late picking them up the last two times." Again, she's off the phone. Or "Something is burning on the stove." This is a really effective method during dinnertime.

BARRY: Don't you think these tactics are a bit cruel?

BETH: We talk about this in the first chapter. Cruel, maybe, but always remember that you're fighting for your pride and what is rightfully yours. You deserve it; you must demand restitution. You're fighting for your kids, and as my psychologist says, you're fighting for your self-esteem. The ends justify the means—he has often said that.

BARRY: How long have you been counseled by a psychologist?

BETH: For ten years. Mother pays for it all, and she should. He often tells me that it's Mother's fault that I did not go to college. He said I was an extremely bright person with great potential.

BARRY: Interesting. But let me return to our discussion of cold turkey methods.

BETH: Barry, we have gotten hundreds of letters and e-mails from other Cinderellas. They shared some of their own cold turkey methods. Let me just read a few from the book. It's under the heading "Cold Turkey: Excluding the Grandparents." That is, excluding them from: vacations with children and grandchildren, Little League baseball games, church events, school plays, and holiday celebrations. I could go on and on with these cases from Cinderellas.

BARRY: But, Beth, don't you worry that your mother will get angry and completely cut you off from more restitution?

BOB: It can happen. It happened with my first wife, but we didn't have any kids. It's the kids, the grandchildren, who are the real lever in getting restitution.

BARRY: Well, Beth and Bob, this has been really illuminating. That's all for tonight, folks, and thank you, Bob and Beth.

A Letter from a Cinderella

Re: My mother, my sister, and your words, ringing in my ear

Dear Dr. Stanley:

*You mentioned that those parents who provide certain forms of economic outpatient care have significantly less wealth than those whose adult children are economically independent. Also, that the more dollars adult children receive, the fewer they accumulate, while those who are given fewer dollars accumulate more (*The Millionaire Next Door, *pp. 142–143).*

My parents, especially my mother, did precisely what you predicted:

> Distributors of EOC often conclude that their adult children [mainly my sister] could not maintain a . . . high-consumption lifestyle without being subsidized. [My sister and her husband] are playing the role of successful members of the high-income-producing upper middle class, yet their lifestyle is a facade. . . . [They] are high-volume consumers of status products and services, from their . . . home in upscale suburbia to their imported luxury motor vehicles . . . from their country club affiliations to the private school they select[ed] for their children. [My sister and her husband] are living proof of one simple rule regarding EOC: It is much easier to spend other people's money [my parents' wealth] than dollars that are self-generated. (*The Millionaire Next Door, *p. 143)

My sister and her family have been indulged by my parents for all her married life, for more than thirty years. She and her husband are the case of your Mary and Lamar revisited. My sister and her husband, in their mid-fifties, still want more EOC. Without it they will be unable to continue with their charade.

As you stated:

> The real problem [for my mother] . . . is that her daughter's family is in a situation of economic dependency. Mother has difficulty with the fact that her daughter married someone who is unable to earn a high income. . . . Daughter and grandchil-

dren may not be able to live in an environment congruent with mother's upper-middle-class background. So Mother is determined to enhance the environment of her daughter's family. (*The Millionaire Next Door*, pp. 145–46)

My sister and her family, like Mary and Lamar, are living in an upper-middle-class fantasyland (The Millionaire Next Door, p. 148). I'm four years older than my sister. I'm the Cinderella Sarah you wrote about; my sister is the sister you contrasted.

People often ask . . . how offspring of the same parents can differ so much when it comes to accumulating wealth. How could Sarah and her sister be so different? . . . Much of the difference . . . can be explained by variations in how parents relate to each of their children. [Sarah's father] encouraged Sarah to become . . . [an] accumulator while fostering the opposite trait in her sister. . . . He strengthened the strong daughter while weakening the weaker one. When Sarah left home, she burned her bridges. She received no outpatient subsidies. She had no choice but to learn how to "fish" for herself. And she taught herself very well. At the same time, her sister became progressively more dependent on Papa for . . . money. . . . The real tragedy is the helplessness of those who come to depend on outpatient care. (*The Millionaire Next Door*, pp. 189–90)

My husband and I, along with our three children, are self-made decamillionaires. We opened a business soon after we were wed, and all three of our children started working in it when they were in their early teens. They have worked ever since, and are millionaire shareholders. We went public in 1996. Our children always worked for what they have accumulated. My sister's children, like their mother, never worked for a living. She was given every luxury by my parents. She "married poor," so my parents made up for it year after year.

As in your discussions of economic outpatient care, my parents first made a large down payment for my sister's home, but the "poor family" could not make ends meet. So my parents eventually paid off the entire mortgage.

Over the years, my parents have paid for almost every conceivable expense that my sister and brother-in-law have incurred: mortgage payments, private school tuition, expensive dental work, braces for their children, music lessons, cars, and cosmetic surgery.

The economic outpatient care never stopped. On and on it went. Now for more than three years my widowed mother has been in and out of hospitals and nursing homes. Twice they thought that she would never recover, but somehow she held on to life. She is currently residing in a third-class nursing home. She has had a series of strokes and suffers from Alzheimer's.

I know that my mother always worried about being disabled, so she did put a good amount of money aside for her own health care. I understand that the money was enough to provide her with quality care for years. My sister, who was given every form of EOC, now feels threatened about the prospects that the well is drying up. She is in complete control as my mother's guardian . . . and has power of attorney.

My mother, at one time, did have enough wealth remaining to enjoy a decent life and quality care during her last remaining years, but that care is being repeatedly compromised by my sister. She is worried that her inheritance is being eroded; she wants to make certain that there is money remaining for her. She continues to reduce the quality of care my mother is entitled to receive.

Sincerely,
Cinderella

A REPLY FOR CINDERELLA

Dear Cinderella:

Note that much of what Sarah did for her parents was not included in the text of The Millionaire Next Door. *The interview I conducted with Sarah ran nearly three hours, so I could only print a bit of what she said. Sarah did more than "turn the other cheek," and I suggest you do the same. She too was cast out, essentially disinherited, and her sister and her sister's children were given major doses of EOC. Yet when Sarah's mother and father were terminally ill, she oversaw and made certain that they both received high-grade health care. Later she did the same for her sister, the sister who received all the EOC from their parents. Sarah's sister squandered all of the EOC and inheritance she* received, but Sarah paid for much of her parents' high-grade care. Sarah also paid for her sister's children's education and weddings.

Why did Sarah do so much for her parents, the people who'd disinherited her? In part, it's because Sarah is a woman of great character and integrity, but there is more to it than that. Sarah never resented her parents for giving all the EOC to her sister, nor did she resent her sister for being on the dole for all those many years. No, Sarah felt that indeed she was the fortunate daughter, and you should feel the same way.

Like you did early in your life, Sarah opted for early emancipation from the confining pressures of her mother and father. She disobeyed her parents and she worked. You did also. You went the entrepreneurial route when your parents wanted the "lady of leisure" act for you. They blamed your spouse for influencing your disobedience. So what if they objected to your choice of mate? It's time to forgive. It's time for you to step in and make amends. Restore your mother's dignity by placing her back in the first-class nursing facility where she began her terminal health-care experience. Take control of your mother's future. You have the strength and financial means to more than counter your sister's unconscionable behavior. Unconscionable behavior is perhaps a better term to use at this juncture than embezzlement.

Regardless of what you call her actions, forgive your sister. Again, you are the lucky one, the more fortunate sister. You did what you really wanted to do. You set your own goals for being independent and achieved them. This partly explains your high levels of pride and self-esteem, but your sister's goals were shoved down her throat. Is it any wonder that she has low self-esteem? Your focus is on achieving; hers is on consuming. She is consumed by consumption.

You were indeed lucky. Your parents' efforts to mold you into a lady, a nonworking suburban country clubber, were futile, but that made it more difficult for your sister to follow your path. Because of your early emancipation and related acts of domestic treason, your parents became all the more resolute. They were determined that your sister would toe the line, and they had more time and energy to devote to molding her, since you left home early.

As a leader, you should take the initiative. Help your mother. Yes, help the woman who repeatedly turned her back on you and your children.

Forgive and take pity on your sister. Today she is in a constant state of fear and panic related to her own possible economic disaster, and that's *what compelled her to cut back on the quality of your mother's care. Your sister is like most women who are dominated and taken care of by their parents. Most constantly "whistle past the graveyard" and never envision that the EOC will someday dry up, as it did in your family.*

The choice is yours. You will not get another chance to save your mother from spending her last few days in squalor. In the future, you can think of your sister's behavior and lifestyle in Shakespeare's terms:

How sharper than a serpent's tooth it is to have a thankless child.

But it was also Shakespeare who wrote:

The quality of mercy is not strain'd.

Many people in your situation selected the "mercy" route, but they reconciled with their parents and siblings at an earlier stage in life.

Today you have a great opportunity. You alone can prevent yet another generation, your children and your sister's children, from having animosity and resentment toward each other. Tell your children not to resent their aunt—your sister—and their first cousins. So what if their cousins received cars, private school tuition, musical instruments, braces for their teeth, cosmetic surgery, and, of course, lots of cash from their grandmother? So what if your children did not? Explain to them that these items of EOC were pushed upon their cousins, and that they had to trade their independence and pride to continue receiving them. The EOC their cousins received should not perpetuate the family estrangement.

Finally, remind your children often about the dangers of too much EOC. It can destroy ambition, drive, and pride, and those who live in fear of having their EOC cut off often panic. Their very way of life is being threatened, so their fear is unrelenting. It's almost like the fear of losing one's life. It should not be surprising that for those who have long depended on EOC, the choice is not all that difficult.

What to do when it becomes a matter of choice—should Mother's standard of living be lowered or one's own? Too often, Mother's is the answer. Becoming economically successful and financially independent is a much better route than accepting dependence on EOC, but being successful financially is not satisfying if one is filled with hate and resentment toward one's siblings. Shakespeare also said,

Nothing emboldens sin so much as mercy.

It's a matter of time and allocation of mental energy. Your sister spent much of her time planning for shopping. You spent yours planning to achieve and succeed. She spent her time trying to predict the amount and category of EOC her family could receive next time. You spent your time and emotional energy balancing a business and raising your kids to be independent. That is why you are a satisfied and economically successful woman.

Thank you for sharing your case history. I wish you and your family much love and harmony.

Regards,

T.J.S.

CHAPTER 10

The High Price of Being Controlled

JOHN AND MR. MEAT REVISITED

*J*ohn was profiled in *The Millionaire Mind* (pp. 271–76). His case study precipitated many letters from interested readers. John is a self-made multimillionaire and a senior officer of a Fortune 100 corporation, but his financial success was not the impetus for the letters I received about his case. Instead, they concern a decision John made years ago when he was a senior in college.

THE MEAT OF THE PROPOSAL

John waited patiently for his turn. I had just completed a two-hour seminar, and many members of the seminar class approached me as I prepared to leave the podium. I noticed that John kept allowing people who were behind him in line to move ahead. Finally he was the only person left. It was obvious that he wanted a private audience.

. . . Even before his career started, John was confronted with a tempting proposal, one that he turned down. He never regretted his decision. . . .

When John started his senior year at a state university, he had a steady girlfriend, Becky, also a senior. . . . John and Becky developed a great affection for each other. So the couple decided the Christmas holidays would be a good time for John to meet Becky's parents.

Becky's father was the founder, owner, and manager of a highly successful meat-processing and -packing company. . . .

After a long Christmas day, Becky and her mom retired for the evening. Becky's two sisters and their husbands had already left for their nearby homes. That left John and Becky's father sitting and talking in the den. . . . Becky's dad thought he was the luckiest man in the world—he was "Mr. Meat" in that part of America.

. . . For nearly two hours, Mr. Meat spoke nonstop. John sat and listened politely to what seemed to be a well-rehearsed sales presentation, apparently the same one that Mr. Meat had made to the two young men who were now married to his other daughters.

Mr. Meat's deal was more involved than just an employment opportunity. It was a proposal for a programmed lifestyle. John paraphrased in detail what Mr. Meat had proposed, playing the part of Mr. Meat for me. It reads like a classified advertisement in the *Wall Street Journal*, but that's the way John described it. . . .

Employment and Lifestyle Opportunity:
Son-in-law and Senior Executive Wanted

"Mr. Meat," the owner of a highly successful, privately held meat-processing company, seeks qualified man to marry his daughter Becky. . . . He must be:

1. *Willing to work for his father-in-law, Mr. Meat. . . .*
2. *Agreeable to living near Mr. Meat and his family and adjacent to Mr. Meat's other married daughters and their husbands. Applicant and his wife, Becky, will be given a home of their choosing.*
3. *Excited about the prospects of vacationing each summer with Mr. Meat and his entire family. . . .*
4. *Willing to work closely with Mr. Meat and his two other sons-in-law. The applicant may be given some equity in the business, with the prospect of taking over when Mr. Meat retires.*

This is a once-in-a-lifetime opportunity as well as a lifestyle and lifetime obligation. Becky's hand will be given only to the applicant who accepts employment from Mr. Meat. Those unwilling need not apply.

John listened to all of it. Then Mr. Meat made the "assumptive close," as it is called in Salesmanship 101: "I know exactly what you are thinking. You are saying to yourself, 'John, you are the luckiest guy in the world.'" Why would he think otherwise? After all, Mr. Meat was two for two.

John was never actually given a real opportunity to respond that night—Mr. Meat thought he had signed up another son-in-law. So John . . . left for his parents' home the next day. . . .

John waited until he and Becky were back at the university to break the news. There would be no engagement and ultimately no marriage with the family plan. Becky was true to Mr. Meat more than to her beau's wishes. . . . She was not interested in marrying someone who would take her outside the lifestyle designed and programmed by her parents.

Why did John turn down what some might call an opportunity of a lifetime? . . . He has a strong need to be independent. He found it insulting that anyone would propose to dictate his lifestyle. Mr. Meat was in love with the meat business, but John had no affection for it, nor was he marginally impressed with any part of Mr. Meat's operating style. . . .

John . . . wondered about the productivity of hiring executives based on who they married. If Mr. Meat's two other sons-in-law were losers, who would pick up the slack? Common sense told John that nepotism was not the best way to select and promote executives. He was particularly incensed by the potential domestic problems that were likely to occur. John and Becky would be given a home by Mr. Meat, but whose name would be on the deed? How would domestic disputes be handled? . . .

. . . Disputes would probably be handled outside the home, inside the court of Mr. Meat. . . . Given John's ambition and need to be independent, he clearly made the proper decision. Today he is a successful corporate executive and has reached millionaire status on his own. John realizes that it's the struggle, the self-made journey to success, that makes us strong. Subsidies from the Mr. Meats can make one dependent. What if Mr. Meat dies suddenly?

Having reviewed John's case, you may now be able to predict the themes of the letters I received in response to it. One paragraph inspired most of the letters that were written.

> *What if it turns out that [Mr. Meat] has no intention of giving his businesses to his sons-in-law? Worse, what if he is merely looking for dependent stooges to dominate? How many Mr. Meats have dangled the prospect of business ownership in front of the noses of unsuspecting candidates? How many of these candidates were looking for love and marriage but not emasculation?*

Even when promises are meant to be kept, there are no guarantees in life. There is no absolute certainty that twenty years from now you will end up with a windfall from your father, mother, grandfather, wealthy aunt Anne, or father-in-law, aka Mr. Meat. Wealth in any form can and often does disappear—businesses fail, key business leaders die or become incapacitated. But what if you sit back, relax, and anticipate that a sure windfall will come your way in just twenty years? You may not strive and make your own way in the economic arena. Very often, young women give up careers on the advice of their husbands, who designate themselves as the career and financial leader of the family.

As a woman and recent college graduate, what would you do if Mr. Meat's one and only son proposed marriage? Of course, the deal would be promoted with an attractive theme. "You will never have to worry about money or financial issues; one day, you and I will own the business outright. Mr. Meat will make certain that this becomes a reality. Someday we will be Mr. and Mrs. Meat.

> *Survey data are very clear that many people who select a spouse because of the wealth factor are eventually disappointed. Sometimes the parents of the spouse leave little or no wealth. Other times, the parents only act rich but in reality they are "big hat,*

no cattle" types. It's better to marry for love, respect, and ambition than for a spouse's ancestors and their financial artifacts. (The Millionaire Mind, p. 276)

THE CASE OF FAY J. NAIVETE

Fay did marry for love, but shortly after she married Rodney, he made another proposal. He convinced Fay to become part of his father's business plan. Fay accepted the proposal. At the time, she had great faith in her husband's judgment about career and money issues.

Dear Dr. Stanley:
    . . . My father-in-law, a millionaire, owned restaurant franchises, commercial properties, distributorships. . . .
    . . . He promised my husband and his all too easily persuaded wife to work for him. Eventually we were supposed to take outright ownership of the businesses.

Fay and her husband worked for Rodney's father for nearly twenty years, and they helped him build these businesses. All the while, Fay and Rodney were assured that these operations would be theirs once Rodney's father retired, but there was never a written contract concerning these issues.

Over the years Fay occasionally asked Rodney why there was nothing in writing, and his reply was always the same. Rodney and his father believed that contracts were for strangers and not for doing business with family members. Whenever the subject was broached, Rodney's father would always say, "Trust me . . . not to worry . . . trust me." It was indeed unfortunate for both Fay and Rodney that no written contract was ever cast.

Can you believe it? [My father-in-law] just retired and sold it all! Am I the only person in this world . . . so stupid . . . such an idiot?

According to Fay, her father-in-law controlled her family's life for almost twenty years, and she strongly maintains that the couple helped make her father-in-law a wealthy man. Even after selling the businesses, he still maintains the "Don't worry" philosophy, promising that his son Rodney, will eventually, absolutely, positively receive an inheritance from dear old Dad. But what will Fay and Rodney do for a living in the meanwhile? Perhaps they will be able to manage one or more of the restaurants that were sold to the new owners. Why not? They have been doing so for nearly twenty years.

Fay's situation is not as unusual as one might imagine, although most business owners who promise to pass their companies on to their offspring actually do so. The timing of such transfers, however, is not always congruent with the promises made to the offspring.

It doesn't matter if your father-in-law is the reincarnation of Honest Abe Lincoln—get the promise in writing. Otherwise there is always some probability, no matter how small, that you will end up like Fay and her husband. Fay thought that she could rely on her husband's judgment. He promised that if she followed his lead, working long hours, often on holidays and weekends, she would be transformed, just like Cinderella. Instead Fay's dream of becoming a financially secure business owner turned into a pumpkin.

THE BUSINESS OF GREAT EXPECTATIONS

Dear Dr. Stanley:

My husband and I just finished reading The Millionaire Mind, *and I noticed that he, his parents' only son, has all of the character qualities of these successful people, except that he has yet to risk everything financially. The problem is that he has followed his father in his business, always with the promise that he could earn the right to purchase it from his dad.*

At this point, although my husband has put money toward the company and been wholly faithful and regularly cutting-edge in his work, making the company the success that it is today, his father is now refusing to sell out to him. He has even turned to accusing him falsely of wrongdoing within the business to keep him in his place, as it were. It is clear that my in-laws have no intention of ever "retiring," or giving up what they now clearly consider to be "theirs," although they seem to want my husband to remain with them to help maintain the financial success. My husband pointed out the story of "Mr. Meat" in your book, finding many similarities in that scenario. At this point, my husband is forty-one, and the first of our four kids is in college. So we have some serious decisions to make.

Anyway, thanks so much for your fascinating research! Your book is on our gift-giving list for this year, for many different people.

A.W.

WHAT TO THINK ABOUT BEFORE JOINING YOUR FAMILY'S BUSINESS
by Dr. Craig E. Aronoff
Founder and Head of the Cox Family Enterprise Center

Joining the family's business is never a decision that should be made lightly. The rewards can be great—a clear shot at the top spot, financial security, a chance to work with people you love while building your family's legacy, and more. But the risks are great too—if things don't work out, both the economic and emotional costs can be huge. Blurred lines between family and business roles and goals create complexities that can result in family-rending conflicts and business disasters.

Before joining the family business, members of the younger generation should ask themselves a series of questions. Remember, you are taking a job and just because it's in your family's business doesn't ensure that you are making a good career move. Here are some questions to think through:

- Why am I doing this? Your answer should focus primarily on business-related reasons. If you are thinking "My family needs me" or "Working in the family business will be easier than working elsewhere," we recommend thinking again. You may be walking into an unintentional but painful trap.
- Does it offer the career I want? Does it fulfill my personal goals? Do I like what the business does? Will I find the work meaningful and challenging? Before you join the family business, you need to think clearly about yourself, your goals, and what you find fulfilling. If your family business offers a way to apply your passions to your career, go for it. If not, consider another calling.

- Can I make a real contribution? Can I bring meaningful skills, talent, knowledge, and experience to the business? Businesses thrive because of value added by each employee and the company as a whole. If you bring real value to the table and the capability to build more, bring it on. Other rationales—blood, family expectations, ease of getting the job, a sense of entitlement—are not sustainable and lead to trouble.

- Can I work with my family? Do we communicate openly, honestly, and effectively? Can we resolve conflicts that inevitably will arise? Do I understand that being "a good son or daughter" is different from being an effective manager? Some believe that strained family relationships can be improved by family members working together. More often, the opposite results. If you lack good relations and solid communication, your joining the family business can put you in real jeopardy.

- If things don't work out, am I confident that I have other opportunities and the freedom to seek my fortune elsewhere? Dependency is a horrible trap and an invitation for abuse. You should be of independent mind—psychologically and economically prepared to leave if frustrations become too great.

- Do you understand what you are getting into? A potential successor should enter the family business in response to a specific, formal offer to fill a job that exists. If responsibilities are cloudy or a position is being created for you, steer clear. Conditions and criteria for advancement should be explained, as should the methods for determining compensation and the opportunity to become an owner.

Don't join the family business because of promises or expectations. Plans go awry under the best of circumstances. Even if you inherit a business, in reality you must earn it through work, commitment, and contribution. Following in the footsteps of a parent is a tricky and difficult challenge. Know what you are getting into and be thoughtful about the seriousness of the commitment you are making. If you are satisfied you've done your homework and you still want to proceed, you have a shot at a career that combines the best—or the worst—of all worlds.

GREETINGS FROM TEXAS: FOCUSING ON THE MEANING OF SELF-RELIANCE

You must develop self-reliance now. Otherwise, sometime in the future you will have to deal with the inevitable consequences of this lack. In the long run, there are few, if any, benefits to being dependent on others, but there are a multitude of reasons why you should strive to become self-reliant.

Attention, women! This is a wake-up call. You can love a man with all your heart and admire his sincere intentions when he tells you, "I will always be here for you," but never, ever believe him or anyone else who tells you:

You never have to worry about money. Let me take care of all the economic issues for you.

or

You do not need to concern yourself with ever being on your own or paying your own way. That's why I'm here.

Attention, married women, in particular. The odds are about four to one that your husband will die before you do, yet too many women believe what their husbands have told them about their future. Far too often men condition their mates into becoming progressively more and more economically and emotionally dependent upon them. These economic and emotional issues are in fact close cousins.

Women, whether you work outside the home or not, you must develop budgeting, saving, and investing skills. You must not accept the "there is no reason for you to concern yourself about issues of money" answer from your significant other. You must insist on sharing the responsibility for investing your way to financial independence.

If you don't know how to deal with money, it will not matter if your husband leaves you well off financially. You may not even be certain how to judge those professional money managers who want you as a prime client. If you do not have investing skills, you, the millionaire widow, will likely be uncomfortable, even frightened, about the prospect of having to deal with money issues for the first time in your life.

During nearly thirty years of interviewing millionaires, I have found that, in some cases, little has changed regarding men's attitudes. More than 80 percent of the economically successful men are married, and most see their role as being the economic leader, investment manager, and provider for their families. So it is not often easy for the wives in these situations to assume some of the control of the household financial decisions.

It is in the best interests of you and your family to develop and constantly hone your fiscal skills. That takes more than writing checks, paying bills, and balancing your household's checkbook. Even budgeting and budget-planning skills are just good economic defenses, not wealth builders. To accumulate wealth and hold on to it, one needs to know how to select the right investments and reject the losers; how to research and evaluate various investment opportunities; and how to judge the skills and integrity of those who position themselves as professional investment experts.

These skills can be acquired only with experience. Nearly all the self-made millionaires I have interviewed have told me much the same thing. All made mistakes early. They made errors when selecting investments and investment experts. In fact, I have never interviewed a millionaire who had a perfect lifetime batting average regarding the selection of the ideal investment advisers.

Yes, you will make mistakes. You will be lied to. You will deal with some financial advisers who talk only about integrity. Over the years, however, you will become progressively better at judging the wide variations in veracity that exist among professionals in the investment industry. Investing skills come to those who practice, but women often feel otherwise. Too many believe that a good academic background is all they need to make them instant investment experts. Too many women today think that if they are college graduates they will never become economically or psychologically dependent on a mate.

Over the years, I have interviewed many wealthy widows. Mrs. Kelly Lyn M. was one of ten millionaire widows who recently participated in a three-hour focus-group interview I conducted. Her husband, a senior officer of a Fortune 500 corporation, had died suddenly of a heart attack about eighteen months prior to the interview. He and Kelly Lyn were both in their early sixties at the time of his death.

The couple met while they were in college. Kelly Lyn graduated with honors from a private college of high academic excellence, and shortly afterward, she got married. Kelly Lyn taught school for two years prior to giving birth to the first of three children, and she has not worked outside the home since then. The only money-related tasks that she was involved in during her married life were paying household bills, balancing the household checking account, and purchasing certificates of deposit whenever her husband told her to do so.

Today Kelly Lyn is a wealthy woman with a current net worth that places her in the decamillionaire category. It's safe to assume that Kelly Lyn is financially independent; however, in spite of her wealth, she is not emotionally independent. Of course, she is still distraught about the loss of her husband, and this is understandable, but her emotional discomfort stems from more than the loss of the love of her life. Kelly Lyn's discomfort comes from the harsh realization that she has very little knowledge of money and investment concepts.

So there sat Kelly Lyn in the focus-group session, among a group of her peers. She was an attractive, well-spoken, and intelligent woman, but she could not hide her fear. A large trust department was now making most of the investment decisions for her. Yet all during the interview, she put on a brave face.

DR. STANLEY: Let's change gears for a moment. Perhaps someone would like to discuss the sources of their investment ideas.

MRS. KELLY LYN M.: Oh, my husband taught me about investing.

DR. STANLEY: Mrs. M., would you like to expand on that for a few moments?

MRS. KELLY LYN M.: Certainly. When my husband died, we had about $1.5 million in cash, plus a lot in stocks. Fred always said . . . we needed to have a backstop . . . [and] foundation stones . . . [and take] little risk. . . . [I] adhered to his ideas.

DR. STANLEY: How did you eventually invest that $1.5 million?

MRS. KELLY LYN M.: All $1.5 million in CDs . . . in $100,000 CDs . . . but . . . never in the same place. Fifteen [$100,000 CDs] at fifteen different banks. I understand that the FDIC upper limit is $100,000. Plus it's spread out . . . [in] fifteen banks.

It is not unusual for people, especially people in their golden years of life, to want to protect the value of their financial assets. It is a bit extreme for Kelly Lyn to take the time to patronize fifteen different financial institutions in the acquisition of her many $100,000 CDs, but she was so fearful of losing any of her money, she overdid it. However, even the FDIC insurance and the use of fifteen different banks could not completely reduce her fear about losing money.

> MRS. KELLY LYN M.: Dr. Stanley, can I ask you something about my CDs . . . the FDIC insurance . . . ?
> DR. STANLEY: Certainly.
> MRS. KELLY LYN M.: Beyond the FDIC [insurance on deposits] should I buy additional insurance [on the fifteen $100,000 CDs]? . . . I count on those CDs. . . . Would I be really justified in that? Should I insure my deposits with additional insurance?

Her husband is no longer there to make all the decisions for her, and Kelly Lyn was almost in a state of panic about the money. She felt that her husband would never forgive her if she was "underinsured." With regard to stocks and bonds, however, Mr. M. had made some arrangements for the future. On the advice of his estate attorney, he'd contracted with a large trust department to oversee his widow's investments in stocks and bonds.

> DR. STANLEY: Mrs. M., let me ask about your investment decisions concerning stocks, for instance.
> MRS. KELLY LYN M.: Oh, here once again, my husband taught me.
> DR. STANLEY: Specifically what did he teach you about investing in stocks?
> MRS. KELLY LYN M.: To have a trust department [an asset-management company within a commercial bank's trust department] take care of that.

After the formal interview, Kelly Lyn told me that her husband had a bookcase in his office filled with books about investing and related financial planning. Yet all during their marriage, he never encouraged his wife to read any of this material. Kelly Lyn trusted his decision to be the sole investment manager for the family. Today, she knows full well that her husband's judgment is her source of fear.

It is unclear why Mr. M. left his wife of forty years in the dark about investing. Some men do this so as "not to trouble" their wives with the stresses that are often associated with investing money. They see themselves as being much stronger psychologically than their wives and firmly believe that men are generally superior to women in matters of money. These well-intentioned husbands do a disservice to their wives. Perhaps unknowingly, they seek to prove their tenuous hypothesis about the inferiority of women. Often this is a matter of their need to control their wives long after they become widows. Some call it dominance from the grave. Such men leave behind a will and corresponding estate plan that is in reality a futile attempt to become immortal.

There is yet another type of husband, the nurturing type. Mrs. Maddi S. was also present in the focus-group session that Kelly Lyn attended. Her late husband, Mr. S., was nearly twenty years older than Maddi when they married. At that time, Maddi was successful in her profession of selling residential real estate and Mr. S. was a wealthy business owner. It was he who encouraged Maddi to start her own business and master key financial concepts. He taught her well, fully realizing that his young wife would likely outlive him by many years.

He told her that inheriting an estate was not as satisfying or comforting psychologically to a widow as generating wealth from her own business, so he persuaded Maddi to progress from selling real estate to owning and managing a real estate management company. Maddi states:

> *[Inheritance is] not sufficient . . . not enough. [A husband must] . . . keep a wife informed. My husband encouraged me to be my own person. . . . [I] did that, . . . thank God. . . . Dear God . . . other women, I feel so bad for them. . . . It's pitiful . . . someone else doing their thinking.*
>
> *I was lucky. . . . My husband encouraged me to learn. . . . [I] had a career of my own [in real estate sales] . . . [and] now manage real estate.*

Maddi's enlightened, nurturing husband saw that selling real estate was a hunting-gathering occupation. Unless she made sale after sale, she would not receive any additional income. Thus, she had to hunt and gather income every day. Sales can't be inventoried, and there are no guarantees in commission sales. But if Maddi owned her own real estate management company, she would have a steady stream of income from contracted fees. Maddi's husband helped transform his wife from a hunter and gatherer of sales commissions to a cultivator of future revenues. Mr. S. was never a controlling husband. He recognized that Maddi's pride, self-esteem, courage, and confidence would be greatly heightened if she owned and managed her own business.

Maddi mentioned that it was very difficult emotionally to lose a husband, but over time this wound is healing. Other widows, however, confront constant fear and discomfort each and every day, in spite of their financial independence. Their fear stems from having little control and possessing no real ability to earn their own way. Even the best-laid plans of husbands, outstanding estate attorneys, and trust departments are not substitutes for being self-reliant. Eventually even the strongest of the strong, like Maddi, will likely become disabled and unable to care for themselves. Often these strongest of the strong outlive most, if not all, of their relatives and friends. So who is to care for them? The most enlightened women I've interviewed have a detailed plan; they did their homework. They sought out those attorneys, accountants, and trust departments that had the highest levels of integrity and the very best track records for taking care of the needs of the disabled and terminally ill. It's much more than a legal and financial service. The best people in this business make certain that their clients are very well treated, or as another respondent recently stated:

> *Mrs. Lulu S. saw firsthand the care . . . the unselfish kindness. These trust people did much more . . . than they are ever paid to do. . . . You will never find one of their clients complaining about lack of concern. . . . [I] wouldn't want to be a health-care provider that did not deliver outstanding service to even one of their clients. . . . [Trust] personnel are constantly visiting clients in hospitals . . . [and] special-care facilities. [Sadly,] often they are the only visitors.*

In this context, the use of a high-quality estate attorney, trust company, and accountant cannot be overstated. Even if you have a loving family whose members are all committed to caring for you if you are incapacitated, you will still need professionals to take some of the burden off their shoulders. And you will need seasoned professionals to ensure that your wishes are carried out when you are deceased.

CHAPTER 11

The Gift of Gifts: Demonstrating Empathy for the Real Needs of People

I can usually predict the gender of the letter writer. If the letter states, "My case is must-reading," and declares it should be published in one of my forthcoming books or asks how the writer can become an economic success, it was written by a man. Women usually don't write on behalf of themselves but instead suggest that someone else's case study be profiled. Only a minority of the women who contact me ever ask how they can enhance their own wealth and success in business.

Most of the successful businesswomen profiled in this book have a habit of helping others. They do more than give to noble causes and provide financial assistance to relatives. They give real thought to the gifts and favors they bestow on others.

If you owned a business, what gifts would you like to receive from a friend, relative, or spouse? What if you were having some difficulty getting the business off the ground or getting it back on track? Wouldn't it be wonderful if your friend wrote a letter profiling your many accomplishments and it was published in a best-selling book? Thus, your reputation and the sales volume of your business would both be enhanced. Letters of this type are the gift of gifts. Such letters cost only a few cents, but they do take time and effort to compose. They require real empathy, and they are priceless.

The examples included in this chapter illustrate the true meaning of empathy and giving to others. It is understanding exactly what is troubling a friend or relative and taking action to answer the need.

THE MOTHER'S DAY GIFT: A LETTER FROM DEBORAH

Suppose you are a mom and a successful self-employed business owner. What will your children likely give you this Mother's Day? They know you like flowers and chocolate; but what will they come up with this year for their mom?

Ms. Driskill, you never imagined what a great gift your daughter, Deborah, would select. It was not at all expensive, but it took a bit of time and a great deal of empathy and appreciation. Deborah wrote the letter of letters about her mom, and she also promoted her mother's achievements.

> *Dear Dr. Stanley,*
>
> *I believe that Ms. Cynthia Driskill would be an excellent subject for you to interview for your forthcoming book about women who are self-made millionaires. Ms. Driskill founded her company, CDG & Associates, Inc., . . . in 1981. . . . [The company] currently has almost one hundred employees.*
>
> *Ms. Driskill has a wonderful story to tell, and it is truly a "pulled herself up by her own bootstraps" tale, which I, her daughter, . . . personally attest. She is also currently a contender for the . . . Entrepreneur of the Year Award.*
>
> *Thank you for considering using Ms. Driskill as material for your new book, and I look forward to conversing with you.*
>
> *Sincerely,*
> *Deborah Driskill*

A GEM OF A SISTER-IN-LAW

Recently you decided to bite the bullet—you quit your job and joined the ranks of the self-employed. No more monthly paychecks from your employer; you are all alone. You just "bet the farm" that your business will succeed. And it better succeed, because in order to fund your company initially, you doubled up on your mortgage and dipped into your family's savings and pension plans. You also wrote IOUs for the money you borrowed from your children's college funds.

Family and friends alike complimented you on your decision to open your own business. They care about the prospects for your future and that of your family. Some even have a strong urge to send you some type of "best of luck with your new enterprise" greeting. Others want to send you a small gift, a symbol that they wish you well. What type of gift would you like to receive in honor of opening your very own business? Any and all greetings, "best of luck" cards, and gifts will surely be welcomed. All of these items are symbolic of the love, admiration, and support your family and close friends have for you.

You take inventory of the many gifts you have already received. There are a great many self-help books and tapes, including:

- *Business Management for the Beginner*
- *10,000 Ways to Succeed in Business*
- *Motivating the Business Commando Inside You*
- *Business Strategy 101*
- *Opting for Self-Employment*
- *Overcoming the Fear of Self-Employment*

It is nice to have so many caring relatives and friends, but you feel guilty because they went out and spent their hard-earned dollars for these gifts. Although you were delighted to receive three coffee mugs that said "Boss," just a card or telephone call would have been sufficient. You could read the message in a card in a few seconds, but all those books! You do not have the time to do much reading.

The books, tapes, cards, and coffee mugs are all arranged neatly in your office, but the most valuable, important gift you received cannot be displayed. It is an intangible gift that came from someone who has a deep understanding of the needs of people in your situation who have recently opted for self-employment.

What is your number one need as a new self-employed business owner, and how might someone help fill that need? You need to generate income. What a great gift idea—something to enhance the revenue of your new business. Call this gift "revenue enhancement," and the giver a "revenue enhancer."

> REVENUE ENHANCER: I would like to increase your revenue by distributing these materials to people whom I believe need what you are selling. I hope you don't find this presumptuous. I'm sure that all your current suppliers, your CPA, attorney, and others whom you patronize have already begun distributing your promotional materials to their clients, customers, and friends. Am I right in my assumption?
>
> NEW BUSINESS OWNER: You are the only person who has offered to enhance my revenue.
>
> REVENUE ENHANCER: Perhaps you should think about changing your long list of suppliers.

THE GIFT OF GIFTS

Dear Dr. Stanley,

My story is about my brother-in-law Ed. When Ed was fired by the BMW dealership for being "too slow" [in repairing automobiles] he and his wife, Kay, started their own BMW repair business. . . . I happened to be visiting with my family when they opened the business. . . . [I] knocked on doors. . . . I canvassed the suburbs [high-income residential neighborhoods] and talked to everyone with a BMW in their driveway. . . . They were all thrilled to give an honest, thorough repairman their business.

Ed was slightly oxygen-deprived at birth. His parents were told he would not be able to participate normally in life. He also had what is now known as dyslexia. Back then it got him in the "slow" class in grade school and shop class in high school. Before he was ten years old, his parents would always come out of stores to find him under the hood of a stranger's car, inspecting their engine. By the time he graduated from high school, he was employed as a car mechanic and began specializing in BMW repair. He then purchased a two-story house to live in. . . . [He] paid the mortgage by renting out the second floor to college students. Ed also began investing his wages in the stock market and bought a horse. . . . Later he sold the house at three times what he had paid for it, the race horse at double what he had paid for it.

His bride, also labeled "slow" in our educational system, owned a lovely home in the Chicago suburbs, had a new car, no debt, and a job as a med tech she had held since college graduation. She had financed her entire college bill herself. You might guess what these two have done as a married couple. They bought a prime lot here long before it was developed and now have built a gorgeous home with their own hands. Because they enjoy working together, they sometimes buy run-down property, remodel it, and sell it for a large profit. [Shop class came in handy!]

They have three daughters who have no idea how wealthy their parents are. Ed and Kay give all the credit to God and are staunch churchgoers. No one in their community has any idea of their wealth. From time to time, Ed will purchase a BMW from a customer, and repair and restore it to sell cheaply to a nephew or niece.

Do we, his family, care that he was in the "slow" class in high school? Do the BMW owners who entrust their cars [to him] care that he isn't articulate? They are very glad to find an honest *repairman.*

Sincerely,
Ruby

What type of gift would you like to receive—yet another set of motivational tapes? Or would you prefer the gift of gifts, revenue enhancement? It is all about taking time, as Ruby did, to understand people's real needs. She wrote a letter about Ed's capabilities that brought in new clients and attention for his business—the gift of gifts.

THE CALL OF CALLS

You are worried. It is the first time you ever flew solo, but you just had to start your very own real estate brokerage firm. You started your career selling residential real estate twenty years ago. Initially, you envisioned just making a few extra dollars on a part-time basis. Before long, however, you were selling full-time. Within three years, you were the top producer among all those seasoned veterans who worked for your broker. Often you annually outperformed all the other agents in your office combined.

Yet you never felt totally fulfilled, even after winning many awards for your efforts. You made an outstanding living, but selling was just not enough. You wanted to do something that would allow you to fully use all of your skills, abilities, and leadership qualities. You needed to be challenged, and in spite of your success, merely selling no longer satisfied your desire to excel.

You have spent a lot of time over the past few years thinking about making a change—opting for self-employment was not a knee-jerk decision. But you are worried, even though you studied, analyzed, and planned. Often, it is not easy making the transition from employee to employer. It takes courage, resolve, and resources. You also need to have a support system in place. Your real friends wished you well when you shared your thoughts about starting your own business, and what about your husband? He is a senior executive. Sure, he was supportive when you were selling real estate; would he feel differently if you became a major success among the ranks of self-employed business owners? Would he feel that his status was threatened if there were two senior executives in his household? Perhaps, as a subterfuge, he will patronize you and do the circumlocution dance around his true feelings. It is easy to tell your wife that you support her decision to become a business owner; it is quite another thing to demonstrate it. Supportive actions are priceless, especially when you are a newly minted entrepreneur.

One Tuesday afternoon when you are working, your husband is on the telephone. He is not making a call on behalf of his company; he is calling to support you and your business.

> DR. STANLEY: Hello, this is Tom Stanley's telephone answering machine. I'm sorry, Dr. Stanley is not here. . . . Please . . .
>
> MR. BOB Y.: Dr. Stanley, I read about your latest project . . . a book about women in business. . . . You might consider including my wife, Gwen. Her profile would make very interesting reading. Please call me at . . .

I did return his call, and in a few days I received a note from Gwen's very supportive husband. Once again, he highlighted the reasons why his wife should be profiled, and he enclosed several published articles and testimonials about Gwen's numerous achievements. She had clearly distinguished herself, but this is not the main reason why Gwen is profiled herein. My data bank is rich and contains information on over a thousand successful women. Gwen was profiled because her husband acted as her supporter, her unselfish advocate, and her apostle. He demonstrated his empathy for his wife's real need.

What would your preference be, if you could choose? Would you like to receive another box of chocolates or a dozen more roses for your next anniversary or birthday? Or would you prefer that your husband act as Gwen's did, as your greatest advocate?

FROM A THOUGHTFUL GRANDMOTHER

Dear Dr. Thomas:

I'm not sure that you are the Dr. Thomas I am looking for. . . . I own two books . . . about millionaires. . . .

. . . My grandson . . . has a high scholastic ability and a high IQ. . . . [He is] age sixteen and a junior in high school. . . . But [he has] never read a book about millionaires. . . . I want him to write a book review on The Millionaire Next Door. *I will grade it . . . [and] give him a cash gift according to the letter grade he receives.*

I'm sixty-nine. . . . [It] took me many years to save $500,000. . . . But his mom lives from paycheck to paycheck. . . . [I] want my grandson to focus upon the key point . . . [that] most millionaires live well below their means.

Sincerely,

Mrs. B.D.

Dear Mrs. B.D.:

Thank you for your interest in my work. Enclosed is an autographed first edition of The Millionaire Next Door *for your grandson. Please accept it as a gift for your interest in making our next generation of adults economically responsible.*

Regards,

Dr. Thomas J. Stanley

The inscription in the book said:

To the fine grandson of Mrs. B.D.,
Millions of Best Wishes!
Regards,
Tom Stanley

Dear Dr. Stanley:
*   The gift from you to my grandson of* The Millionaire Next
Door *arrived yesterday. I hope he keeps the book to refer back
to as a reference through life. . . . I am presently doing the same
regarding purchasing a home . . . a step up from my "starter
home"!*
*   Best wishes,*
*   Mrs. B.D.*

THE AUTHOR'S ADVOCATE: KAREN ANGELES

I was feeling pretty confident about myself. I was beginning to believe that I might even possess some talent as a writer. Why not? My book had been on the best-seller list for twenty-eight straight weeks. Then something happened that brought me back down to earth.

A review of my work appeared in a nationally distributed periodical, and the reviewer was not thrilled with the book. In fact, he went out of his way to emphasize his dislike for most of the frugal millionaires profiled in *The Millionaire Next Door*. He condemned them in part because they rejected the so-called high-consumption lifestyle. He felt that if one is rich, one should indulge oneself by purchasing high-status products and services. Of course, others, especially those who were not financially independent, felt the same way.

Fortunately, there are many others who enjoy their low-consumption, low-profile lifestyles. Mrs. Karen Angeles is one of those financially independent, strong-willed people. She takes great pride in her ability to think and behave in ways that suit only herself. She does not follow the crowd and has never been a slave to fashion.

After reading the above-mentioned review of *The Millionaire Next Door*, Mrs. Angeles wrote a rejoinder to it. She defended her lifestyle as a member of the Millionaire Next Door Club. Of course, in so doing, she acted as an advocate of the book. She also sent me a copy of her letter. This was my first contact with her, but if one day she showed up at my doorstep with a daughter who was selling Girl Scout cookies, I would order hundreds of boxes!

A LETTER FROM AN ADVOCATE
Letter to the Editor

Dear Sir:

Calling The Millionaire Next Door *a how-to book . . . completely misses the point. The book does not tell you how to get rich, it simply profiles some of the surprising habits of people who have accumulated substantial wealth. Financial success often combines shrewdness and hard work with the chance elements of luck, timing, and opportunity, which no book can help you assemble.*

When I read the book, I felt like someone had held up a mirror to my lifestyle, which is far from self-denial. . . . Rather, like the people described in the book, I find little value in the more expensive cars and the finer jewelry. The ability to afford more luxury items does not necessarily create the desire for them, even though advertising makes it appear that they immeasurably enhance one's life. Being able to afford whatever you want does not buy real satisfaction. People who have accumulated wealth through hard work and a thrifty lifestyle don't change their habits as their asset base grows.

The real contribution of the book, in my opinion, is for those of us who are fairly isolated running our small businesses and accumulating wealth to see that we are not alone in our spending habits. I have always thought it odd that my tastes have not kept pace with my bank account. The book shows that this is a common trait among a certain type of millionaire. The point is that not everyone finds enjoyment in self-indulgence, and when the choice is available, a group of people choose another path. I prefer rafting down the Grand Canyon and sleeping on its beaches to taking a luxury cruise, and I would rather buy real estate and stocks than designer clothes. This book shows that I am not as odd as I always thought in not following the paths of popular consumption.

Sincerely,
Karen Angeles

MR. EMPATHY

One of the greatest salesmen I've ever met is Peter Shorter. What was the source of Peter's empathy for the needs of people? His mother always had great empathy for others, and she was his role model.

Given the fact that Peter Shorter has great empathy, I was glad to respond to this request from his wife, Myra.

A Day to Celebrate His Birthday
Peter is 50 this year!!!!

You are invited to join in his fiftieth birthday celebration by sending cards, letters, notes, postcards, photos, or sharing details of a memorable or humorous event. (There are so many of these to recall!!) All correspondence/memorabilia will be compiled into a memory album and given to Peter on his birthday as a special remembrance of your being a part of his life during these past fifty years. Your personal expressions of congratulations, best wishes, and blessings will be a very meaningful gift to him on this special day in his life. (No gifts please!)

THIS IS A BIRTHDAY SURPRISE!!!

Please send your birthday greetings prior to June 3, using the temporary mailing address below. Please do not send birthday greetings to Peter's home address. You may also send an e-mail to the following address; it will be forwarded to Peter.

REMEMBER . . . KEEP THIS AS A BIRTHDAY SURPRISE!
(Please pass this letter to anyone who may be interested.)

Hello, Myra
Re: Peter Shorter

A MAN OF HUMOR, GREAT EMPATHY, AND COURAGE
I could focus on Peter's extraordinary ability to get people excited. Once he started a near riot during a talk he gave to one of my classes at the

university. That day he carried in two large duffel bags of his samples—ladies' fashion blue jeans. He had just gotten off a plane after visiting one of his top clients, J. C. Penney. Halfway through the talk, he began to throw "free blue jeans" to those coeds who asked him "good questions." Of course, I will never forget Peter's first call to yours truly . . . after he received an F to the third power on a midterm, which is an exponentially horrible F. Out of 10,000 students, only Peter had the guts to cold-call me (show up in person) at my home. . . . How did he ever get a B in the class when he received an F on his first exam? He persuaded me to drop one of the three exam grades given for the course.

But Peter Shorter is much more than me, me, me. He is really outstanding when it comes to helping and protecting the weak, the poor, the aged, the impaired. One notable case took place on an outbound fishing trip to Saranac, New York. We were on a forty-seat commuter plane out of La Guardia Airport. The plane was only about half occupied, so Peter, his brother Harry, and I spread out.

On board was the "poster child of ill-mannered flight attendants," Joyce the Barbarian. She asked Peter, "What are ya gonna drink?" Since it was still morning, Peter said, "I'll have a Beck's beer . . . it's the only beer I drink before lunch." She replied, "Well, it looks like you will get no beer, since we don't have Beck's." After she mentioned Beck's, Mr. Jim, two seats in front of Peter, piped up, "I'll also have a Beck's." As we determined sometime later, this fellow was eighty years old. He and his Seeing Eye dog were on their way to a class reunion at Union College. He was not only visually impaired, but he also did not hear very well. However, he did pick up the words "Beck's beer." The flight attendant then jumped down this elderly man's throat with a high-volume rant: "Can't you hear? We don't have Beck's beer!" That outburst was Peter's cue. He said to me that the flight attendant would not get away with punishing a defenseless senior citizen. Then he ran off the plane! Note that the propellers were already moving! I watched in amazement as he dashed inside the terminal. I felt certain that the plane would take off without Peter on board. I was about to give up on Peter flying with us. But then I saw him running in full stride out of the terminal. And Peter was not alone: he was carrying two twelve-packs of—you guessed it—Beck's beer, which he had "commandeered out of an unattended frequent-flier elite travelers' lounge"!

Upon entering the cabin, Peter first addressed the stated needs of

Mr. Jim. "Sir," Peter said, "I have that Beck's beer you requested." Mr. Jim replied, "Well, thanks, young fellow . . . your other flight attendant said that you did not have any Beck's." Peter responded, "I'm the senior flight attendant," and stated that "Joyce was new" and that "she would learn." Then while Barbarian Joyce was up front in the cockpit, talking to the pilots, Peter worked his magic. "Who wants a Beck's? Who wants a Beck's? We now have Beck's . . . lots and lots of Beck's." He passed out Beck's beer to nearly all the other passengers.

Shortly thereafter, Joyce entered and saw Mr. Jim downing a Beck's and immediately asked him where he had gotten the beer. Mr. Jim said, "Your colleague the senior attendant, the nice fellow served me a Beck's. I'll be ready for another one in a minute." After hearing those comments, I thought that she would "go postal." And she got real close to losing the little composure she had remaining.

"There is no other flight attendant on this plane," she screamed, "and we don't have any Beck's" With that Mr. Jim said, "Honey, you need to get more training and perhaps an eye examination." All during the flight Joyce interrogated the passengers: "Where did you get the Beck's?" Each time she got the same answer: "The other flight attendant, the senior attendant, the nice fellow served it to me." All during the flight, we were filled with laughter. Peter had done it again; he had made people, especially Mr. Jim, happy. Peter understood what Jim wanted and took action to fulfill Jim's need. Peter stood strong, protecting the weak, the elderly, the impaired, and most of all, the other passengers on the flight that day.

I hope the second half of his life has more good times, wonderful friends, and great laughs.

Tommy Stanley

IV.

The Choice of Choices

CHAPTER 12

Choosing a Business: Opting for Self-Employment

CHOOSING THE RIGHT TYPE OF BUSINESS

*W*hy do some small businesses generate large profits while others are marginal at best? There are many reasons, but one of the most significant relates to a very basic decision that is overlooked by those who operate unproductive enterprises. Many self-employed business owners simply choose the wrong type of business, one they are not suited to own and manage or one that by definition will not produce substantial profits.

Some business categories—entire industry sectors, in fact—are inherently more profitable than others. Even business owners with much affection for their offerings, great energy, and very high intellect can and do fail to generate profits because they made a very bad decision before they even opened their enterprises. They never studied the variations in profits generated by various types of businesses. So it might not matter that one has the desire and the ability. When the tide is going against you, it is much more difficult to reach your destination. On the other hand, those with less drive and fewer skills often succeed big-time because they are not sailing against the tide.

Building a business is like building a home. If the foundation rests on an unstable setting or is constructed with subpar materials, it doesn't matter if the rest of the home is perfect. It will never be a joy to its owner. Too often inexperienced future business owners are very narrow-minded about selecting a profitable industry. In particular, women are more likely than men to be attracted to the business of retailing products. They think to themselves, "Oh, how nice it would be to own my own store, to be loved by my customers, sell products that I am just crazy about and consumers will also love to purchase."

Why is it that so many marginally profitable or unprofitable businesses are owned by women? In part, it is because women business owners are significantly more likely to be in the retail trade than are men. Of the more than 2.3 million small business retailers in America, about seven in ten are owned by women.

The small business retail trade generates $185.2 billion in sales annually and accounts for nearly one in five dollars (19.1 percent) of all sales generated by small businesses[1] in America (see Table 12-1). "Wow!" you say. You might be impressed with this figure if you are contemplating owning your own retail store; unfortunately, all those dollars rung up on a cash register are not profit. Overall, the retail trade accounts for only 5.5 percent of all profits (net income) generated by all small business establishments in America. Look at another measure of profitability: on average, for every dollar in sales generated in the retail trade, only about 6.2 cents translates into net income.

In order for the typical retailer to earn just one dollar of net income, he or she must generate, on average, $16.25 in sales. That is $16.25 in sales, typically of products manufactured by others, for every dollar of profit to you, the retailer. Among the population of all small businesses, the retail trade has the lowest ratio in terms of percent of profits versus percent of total receipts: 0.29 (see Table 12-1).

For women to increase their chances of making a significant profit via business ownership, they must consider the most basic axiom in business:

There is a substantial correlation between the profitability of a small business enterprise and the overall profitability of the industry or sector in which the business operates.

To understand this point, consider the variation in profit margins between the retail versus wholesale trade as shown in Table 12-1. If a

---

[1] For the purposes of discussion in this section, small businesses refer to the 17,408,809 sole proprietorships operating in America.

TABLE 12-1

SMALL BUSINESS INDUSTRIES: RECEIPTS VS. PROFITS

Industry Sector	Percent of Total Business Receipts	Percent of Total Business Profits	Ratio: Percent Profits/Percent Receipts	Profit Margin: Profit/Receipts	$ of Sales per $ of Profit
Construction	15.9	13.6	0.86	18.4	5.45
Wholesale Trade	4.4	2.5	0.57	12.1	8.26
Retail Trade	19.1	5.5	0.29	6.2	16.25
Transportation and Warehousing	4.7	3.5	0.74	15.7	6.39
Finance and Insurance	8.9	6.9	0.78	16.7	6.00
Real Estate Rental and Leasing	4.4	8.8	2.00	42.7	2.34
Professional, Scientific, and Technical Services	11.0	21.7	1.97	42.3	2.37
Administrative and Support and Waste-Management Services	3.8	5.1	1.34	28.4	3.52
Health-Care and Social-Assistance and Child Day-Care Services	8.5	17.1	2.01	43.0	2.33
Arts, Entertainment, and Recreation	2.0	2.6	1.30	27.7	3.61
Other Services, Including Personal and Laundry Services	6.8	7.1	1.04	22.5	4.41
All Other Industries	10.2	5.5	0.54	11.5	8.70
All Industry Sectors	—	—	—	21.5	4.67

Source: MRI Database 2002 and Brian Balkovic and Michael Parisi, "Sole Proprietorship Returns 1999," *Statistics of Income Bulletin* (Internal Revenue Service), Summer 2001, pp. 12–13.
Note: Detail may not add to totals because of rounding.

woman contemplating owning a retail business wanted to double her expected margin of profit, she might decide not to go into retailing, with its 6.2 percent profit margin, and choose instead a wholesale business, with its typical profit margin of 12.1 percent. That is nearly twice the profit margin of the retail sector. Although about 70 percent of all small business retailers are owned by women, they own only about three in ten of the businesses in the wholesale sector.

How do these statistics relate to my studies of women who are millionaire business owners? The results are highly congruent, most notably the fact that a disproportionately small number of the millionaire women are part of the retail trade sector. Those who are millionaires, often multimillionaires, are much more likely to be involved in industries other than retailing. Table 12-2 illustrates a sampling of the types of businesses in which women millionaires are found in higher proportions, all of which have profit margins that are many times higher than the retail trade. Millionaire women are significantly more likely to be part of these industries that are, on average, much more profitable than retailing.

In Table 12-2 the professions are not included, because my national surveys of women business owners exclude those in the so-called status professions. Yet those engaged in these professions often generate substantial profit as measured in a variety of ways. (See for example, the various rankings of the profitability of 153 categories of small businesses given in Appendixes 2, 3, 4, 5, and 6.)

In terms of profit margin compared to average return on receipts, what is the most profitable small business category in America? Of the 153 industries studied, representing more than 17 million small businesses, it is the category entitled "physician's offices." The average profit margin for this industry is 55.5 percent (see Appendix 3). Keep something in mind when you examine these numbers. The profitability of industries and firms within those industries can and often do change, even within a few short years. Thus, it is advisable for those with an interest in this topic and those who might be contemplating starting their own company to review the latest profitability data published in the *Statistics of Income Bulletin*. An industry with high numbers of profitable firms often attracts more and more people, which can have a dampening effect on profits. For example, the number of men's and boys' clothing and furnishings stores more than doubled from 1984 to

TABLE 12-2

SELECTED CATEGORIES OF BUSINESSES OWNED
AND MANAGED BY WOMEN MILLIONAIRES

	Average Profit Margin (%)	Proportion of Profitable Businesses
Management Services	54.7	87.8
Consulting Services	54.7	76.0
Nursing Services	51.6	90.4
Counseling Services, except Health Practitioners	51.0	83.2
Real Estate Brokering/Agency Services	46.1	75.8
Real Estate Property Managers	39.8	86.1
Medical and Dental Laboratories	39.5	82.9
Child Daycare	39.1	86.5
Janitorial/Dust Control Services	32.8	88.9

1992. In 1984, all of the sole proprietorships in that industry made a profit. In 1992, however, only 82.7 percent were profitable. Its rank dropped from first to fifty-seventh among all the sole proprietorships studied. By 1998, just six years later, there were 29 percent fewer stores of this type still in business, and as expected, nearly all (96 percent) had a profit. (Also see *The Millionaire Next Door*, pp. 229–32).

With that in mind, why were self-employed physicians excluded from my surveys of business owners? For most people who are seeking to start a business, the "entrance requirements" for becoming a physician are too costly in time, education, and money.

The "legal services" profession, which ranks eighth in terms of profit margin, at 46.8 percent, was also excluded, along with these professions (listed here with their profitability rank and profit margin, respectively): 20th: dentists (37.5%); 22nd: podiatrists (36.0%); 24th: chiropractors (35.7%); 36th: architects (27.1%); 42nd: optometrists (25.6%); and 44th: veterinarians (24.4%). But keep in mind that those involved in these profitable professions are selling their intellect, their own information and advice, not other peoples' products.

If you have the desire, intellect, money, and time to complete medical school or law school, good for you. The American economy rewards the large majority of those employed in these professions, and for most of them, a pro forma business plan and profit estimates already exist. Many take their first jobs as associates or apprentices in professional organizations that are up and running. In that event, novices learn how to operate a professional service firm, and then they take those skills and go out on their own.

For most others seeking self-employment, it is not so straightforward. They have to select a business sector in which to operate, and all too often they become part of an unproductive industry. Too many industries provide only a slim chance for their members to earn significant profits; if one cannot earn, one cannot become financially independent. Just ask an associate of mine who could not wait to open his very own yogurt stores several years ago. Recently, he told me that these stores made little profit, but during those years of operation, he had never worked so hard and put in so many hours! The same applies to many people who open antiques stores and gift shops.

Far too often people who own antiques stores or gift shops say that they "love gifts" or that they "always loved old things and loved to receive gifts." They might add, "My parents rewarded me and demonstrated love for me via gifts." If you are interested in becoming financially independent, however, that requires profits. I would enjoy asking some of those 105,035 owners of retail gift shops a simple question: "Prior to opening your gift shop, did you have a clear estimate of the profitability that would be expected from such an undertaking?" I already know the answer. Almost all will say *no!* Would they have ever invested their money, intellect, talent, time, and other resources if they had the hard numbers? Probably not, although the compulsion to be involved with things that they love is very strong in many women.

For those who contemplate the gift or antiques business, here are some figures to keep in mind. There are 103,373 small business antiques stores operating in America. Their average net income is only $1,162.00. About 41 percent generated a positive net income. The news is even worse for gift shops. Small business gift shops nationwide had, on average, a net profit margin of only 0.023 percent. So if one of them is fortunate enough to sell $1 million worth of gifts in a year, its net income would be only $230! In terms of profit margin, gift shops rank 146th out of the 153 small business categories studied; only about four in ten (42%) made even one dollar of profit. Finally, here is one more measure of productivity (or lack of it). The average annual net profit generated by the 105,035 small business gift shops operating in America is $7.70. Again, I believe that the majority of people who opened these businesses did not do a thorough job of studying the profitability figures of various business categories. As a group, you might call them members of the 770 Club. If you want to succeed in business, turn down all invitations to join this club. Of course, if you wish to open a gift shop or an antiques store as a hobby, sign up for membership.

CORRELATES OF PROFITABILITY

Even if you select the ideal industry to enter, there are other significant correlates of success. If you examine the financial data from the 17,408,809 small businesses in America, you will find that most are profitable at least in the nominal sense, but the term *profitable* can be misleading when used to describe the productivity or lack of productivity of small businesses.

- About 75 percent of these small businesses had any, even a penny's worth, of net income. Correspondingly, the other 25 percent (the unprofitable) had no positive net income at all.[2]
- The average receipts figure for the segment with net income was $61,389, while that for the segment without net income was only $26,631.
- The average net income for the group with net income was $17,292.

These figures for receipts may seem rather small when contrasted with those of major corporations in America. Before deciding to become a self-employed business owner, you should review those numbers. The profits and ultimately the income earned by a business owner are not a perfect predictor of the owner's net worth. Self-employed business owners are the best overall at minimizing realized net income while maximizing unrealized income or appreciation of wealth without

[2] Source: MRI Database 2002 and Michael Parisi and Therese Cruliano, "Sole Proprietorship Returns, 1998," *Statistics of Income Bulletin,* (Internal Revenue Service), Summer 2000, pp. 8–100.

generating a taxable cash flow. Note that the average and median net worth, respectively, of households headed by a self-employed person ($919,800 and $248,100) are substantially higher than for those who work for someone else ($169,900 and $52,400). Contrast these net worth figures of the self-employed with the average income produced by small businesses. It is not unusual for business owners to realize the equivalent of just a few percentage points, often less than 8 percent of the value of their net worth and even less in cases where the business owner owns income-producing real estate.

Could you live on an income that was the equivalent of just 8 percent of your wealth? The answer is often a function of one's level of discipline and, of course, net worth. When reviewing profitability figures, consider that many successful business owners do not want to generate big profits. They wish to grow their businesses. They do not want to pay the high taxes associated with large amounts of realized income, and that is why criteria other than net income are important. Rankings based on the realized return on receipts and the proportion of businesses that are profitable within each industry are also important measures of profitability. First, it is important to examine and contrast the sales, profits, and expenses associated with the profitable versus the unprofitable businesses.

What factors are significant correlates of profitability? On average, businesses with net income have a substantially higher level of receipts than those without net income ($61,389 versus $26,631). Again, on average, businesses with net income generate about $2.31 in business receipts for every $1.00 generated by those without net income. This variation reveals something about business operations in America: it is easier to put money into your business offerings than it is to sell what you offer. This simple fact is often overlooked by those who open their own businesses. They may have great affection for the products they sell, and they may have enough inventory, often too much inventory. They may also have office furniture, computers, software, fax machines, telephones, employees, business cards and stationery, and everything else they need, with the exception of the most important thing: customers, customers, customers. There is even more to this story than the lack of customers and sales revenues exhibited by the small business group without net income.

Adjusting for differences in receipts, those businesses without net income had expenses that were disproportionately higher than those of businesses with net income. Taken as a percentage of total receipts, what segment has a higher cost of sales and operations? Note that the cost of sales and operations includes cost of labor, cost of inventory, materials, and so on. The without-profit segment has a ratio of 55.3 percent, versus 34.6 percent for the with-profit segment. In other words, the cost of sales and operations for those without profit are the equivalent of 55.3 percent of their total receipts. For the with-profit segment, the equivalent of only 34.6 percent of the receipts was attributed to the cost of sales and operations.

The ratio of these two percentages gives some measure of efficiency (or lack of it) that distinguishes these two groups. Call it the Index of Inefficiency, or IOI. The ratio of the percentages (the without-profit segment over the with-profit segment) regarding the cost of sales and operations is 1.60. Adjusting for differences in receipts, the without-profit segment allocates a disproportionately higher percent of its receipts to the cost of sales and operations than does the with-profit segment (1.6 times or 60.0 percent more).

Several other business deductions are important to consider. For example, the IOI for all of the 4,328,311 businesses without income versus the 13,080,498 with net income in regard to bad debts from sales is 4.81. This indicates that the without-profit group has a problem beyond low sales volume and cost of operations. Most successful business owners know that it is much easier to extend credit to customers than to have them pay in full, and some types of small businesses have a much higher than average IOI. In the without-profit group, dentists had the equivalent of 8.5 percent of their receipts designated as bad debts. Dentists in the without-profit category discovered that it is sometimes more difficult to get full payment for pulling teeth than it is to provide the service. Once the teeth are removed, they are permanently removed, so the true value of repossessed teeth is little or nothing!

Imprudent credit extension is not the only significant correlate that explains lack of profitability. Two others also come under the credit heading, but are on the opposite side of the credit family.

On average, those small businesses without net income allocate more than three times the proportion of their receipts than do those with net income to interest paid on business-related loans (3.36) and business-related mortgages (3.26). It is not unusual for novice business owners to "max out" their business credit cards and mortgage their homes to keep their dreams alive. Far too often, the dream becomes a nightmare.

In summary, what are the correlates of operating a successful business? First, you must have the ability to sell what you offer. Second, you must evaluate the market for your products. Just because you have great affection for them does not mean that your prospective customers will feel the same way. If you lack empathy for the product needs of the market, you will likely fail in business. You are not the market. Two major reasons that small businesses fail within five years of birth are directly related to their lack of understanding of the market and the heavy use of credit.

RACHEL RICH

Those who do succeed in operating productive gift shops usually have had some real work experience in business, especially in retailing. It does help to have industry-specific experience before you opt to start a business. Yet every year countless numbers of inexperienced people attempt to start their own businesses, and most fail within a year or two. Rachel Rich was among those who recently experienced such a business failure.

Rachel opened a gift shop about three years ago in spite of having no experience in merchandising. In the two and a half years that she was in business, Rachel never made one dollar of profit. Her store was well stocked with high-end gift items. They were selected according to the me, me, me method. Rachel carried those items that she herself would enjoy receiving as gifts. Unfortunately, her taste and the preferences of her target audience were not in sync. Rachel did not understand some of the basic marketing theories of successful retailing: consumer preferences for the merchandise offered, pricing patterns, and store location. She had little idea what the consumers in her trade area really wanted, and her store's location was not ideal for many of the high-end gifts she was attempting to sell. It seems that the commercial real estate agent who leased her the store was better at generating commissions than selecting an ideal site for a gift shop.

Why did Rachel open a gift shop without first studying the profit potential of such an operation? Why did she jump headfirst into a business she did not understand? Her judgment was clouded. Simply stated, Rachel loved gifts and she had a compulsion to open a gift shop. She thought that she was the typical consumer, and she believed that the typical local customers would share her love, her obsession, with the gifts she was attempting to merchandise. Of course, Rachel's lust for gifts was anything but commonplace. In fact, it was at best unique, if not abnormal or even perverse. Why did Rachel have a compulsion to surround herself with gifts and more gifts? In order to answer this question, it is important to look into her background.

Rachel's mother was a self-prescribed social butterfly who never devoted much time to her children or to any domestic tasks. Yet she did find time to polish her skills as a hyperconsumer. Rachel's mother was a shopaholic; she was well known by many of the top-producing sales clerks at most of the upscale department and clothing and specialty stores within her shopping area.

Rachel's father, Doug, was a very successful entrepreneur as well as an astute investor. His passion was his business. Monday through Saturday, he left for work before dawn. He rarely had breakfast with his family, and he usually returned from work after the rest of his family had eaten dinner. At night, he spent hours alone studying trade journals, technical reports and periodicals, and investment-related publications, hoping to enhance his business and investments. His efforts bore fruit.

Doug was, as they say, all work and no play. At best, he was a father in the legal sense, but not when it came to allocating any of his precious time to his children. Nor did he spend much time with his wife. Yet Doug, the decamillionaire, was the owner of a very successful business. The business was his obsession, and he worried constantly about time allocation. When he had to allocate more time to activities not directly related to his business, he became gravely concerned.

Doug was more than willing to trade his money for his time. For example, he proactively encouraged his wife over and over again to upgrade her wardrobe and participate in a variety of activities at the tonier clubs in the area. She rarely complained about her husband's long workdays because she was preoccupied with shopping or club-related activities and social events. Doug made a good living. His wife spent a lot of time and money shopping. As a result, neither parent had much time to nurture their children.

Even when Doug was at home, his mind was always preoccupied with business issues. Perhaps he felt a bit guilty for not interacting with Rachel, but not very. You see, Doug thought that all women have a place in the home, in the store, or in the club. While he was never abusive to women, he nevertheless felt that they were inferior to men. In his mind, they were to be tolerated. He had an obligation to support his wife and his children, and did so by doling out large sums of money for products and services. But to him, devoting much time to his family was not part of his obligation. His demeanor in interacting with his wife and daughter ranged from patronizing to cold and aloof.

Doug provided the capital for his wife's and daughter's expensive clothing and luxury automobiles, and felt that he could placate those who might otherwise demand more of his precious time. For Doug, every time-related threat could be solved with money, which was less precious than time. So why not spend money on gifts for Rachel and her mother? The only signs of affection that Rachel ever received from her father were gifts and money, gifts and money, more and more gifts and money. It is no wonder that today Rachel has an obsession with gifts.

She learned to show great affection for herself by buying gifts and more gifts—it was so easy since Dad loaded her up with cash. If she was really clever, she could save lots of money by purchasing gifts wholesale. How is this possible? She opened her own gift shop. Why purchase gifts anywhere else when you can be your own best customer?

Acquiring gifts gives you a burst of satisfaction and seems to enhance your self-esteem, but these feelings of happiness do not last. That is why you must keep acquiring and giving yourself more and more gifts; otherwise, you will sink back into your state of dissatisfaction. Without a fresh supply of gifts, your self-worth and self-esteem are always in jeopardy.

Today, Rachel has a better understanding of her gift-craving behavior. She also now knows why she was not the most popular child in school or in her neighborhood. Rachel often went out of her way to display the many gifts she received from her father. When she got an expensive dollhouse filled with dolls and furniture, Rachel insisted that all her "friends" stop by to look it over.

Of course, those children misread Rachel's motives. She was not really trying to prove her superiority by showing she had more toys. She was not trying to brag or to boast about her possessions, nor did she intend to display the economic superiority of her family. In her mind, the dollhouse and accessories were symbols of her father's affection. They were evidence that her father did, in fact, care a great deal about his daughter. Yet her friends and schoolmates thought that Rachel's real purpose in showing off these gifts was to brag and prove her superiority.

Perhaps if her peers had understood Rachel's real motives, they might have been more accommodating. If her detractors had been offered all the same gifts that Rachel received instead of having a warm, caring, and nurturing father, they might have been transformed into her.

With this greater understanding of Rachel, you may begin to appreciate why she had a compulsion to open a gift shop.

DOUG, RACHEL'S FATHER, DEFLECTS REQUESTS FOR HIS TIME AND ENERGY

Requests by Rachel	Doug's Deflections and Curveballs
Dad, I am having trouble with my math homework. You were a math major in college. Can you help me?	I can't remember much of the math I studied. I will hire a tutor for you. Math has changed a lot since I was in school. How about if I buy you a new calculator or a computer with math software?
Our team made it into the soft-ball league finals. Any chance you could stop by and see me play?	I have to work. I have to earn enough to fund your college education. Perhaps you could have a friend tape your performance. You should have a video cam of your own. Let me take care of that.
Dad, is there any chance that I could work in your office this summer?	I was planning to send you and your mother to Maine for the summer. You need to start shopping for the right clothes—just put it on your credit card.

Why did those who succeeded in business opt for self-employment in the first place, and how different were their motives from Rachel's? Most (61 percent) of the successful self-employed businesswomen had great affection for the product or service they currently offer even before they started their own businesses. Rachel also loved her products; in fact, she was obsessed with them. With this exception, Rachel's motives for opening a business were not congruent with those of most women who are successful business owners.

Rachel received more satisfaction from buying gift merchandise than from selling it, whereas successful business owners derive great satisfaction from correctly anticipating what their prospective customers will purchase and from seeing that their customers are happy with the products offered. Even so, this "affection for product" is not the most significant criterion for selecting the self-employment vocation.

The large majority (84 percent) of the successful women opted for self-employment because they felt, even before making that decision, that it would allow them to fully utilize all their abilities and aptitudes.

In sharp contrast, Rachel never looked at owning a gift shop that way—she was never even sure of what abilities and aptitudes she possessed. Most successful business owners had leadership experiences and aptitudes before they ever became self-employed. Most had demonstrated perseverance and considerable discipline and were always well organized. Almost all successful businesswomen are frugal and get more satisfaction from saving, investing, and building a business than from spending money on expensive gifts earmarked for themselves.

Most millionaire women (74 percent) who are business owners opted for self-employment because they believed that it would give them high self-esteem.

Again, Rachel is a different kind of woman in this regard. Opening a business did not give her high self-esteem, although she did have some foggy idea that being a self-defined gift expert would translate into a higher level of self-worth.

According to most of the successful women I interviewed, self-esteem is enhanced by setting goals and then reaching or exceeding them. Rachel never had any objective standard with which to judge her business-related accomplishments. Of course, if her objective was to surround herself with expensive gifts, then at least she had one short-lived accomplishment.

Rachel used the inheritance she received from her grandmother to open her shop, then asked her dad for an interest-free loan. He did loan her money, but in spite of being a successful entrepreneur, he gave her little advice about how to succeed in business. When the money from these two sources was depleted by her unsuccessful enterprise and her suppliers would no longer extend her credit, Rachel began borrowing money. Rachel had three business credit cards that she used to purchase merchandise and supplies from those who would accept this form of payment. She also kept her business alive for a while by paying bills, including her rent, with the money she received from several home equity loans. Eventually, Rachel's house of gifts collapsed, and she was out of business. But she still owed creditors more than $20,000. At this point, her father saved her from bankruptcy.

Rachel's business failed because its owner had an acute case of me, me, me. "I love it, so the customers will kill for it." She never gave much thought to any of the key vocation-selection criteria previously discussed. Thus, her failure was predictable.

BUSINESS OWNERSHIP: A LIFELONG DREAM?

Did you know exactly what you wanted to do for a living before you were twenty-one? If the answer is no, you are not alone. Before the age of twenty-one, only one in five millionaire women had any idea that they would be running their own businesses one day. Of course, it would make a great story to suggest otherwise. Just think of all the articles that could be written about "women in business from birth." Yes, it was Amy who decided when she was in diapers that she wanted to be an entrepreneur. Yes, it's Amy who majored in accounting in undergraduate school. Yes, it's Amy with an MBA in finance. She got this education with a single goal in mind: Amy always wanted to be a self-employed business owner. Most millionaire women who own businesses were late bloomers in the world of commerce. They did not major in business administration. Most (about 95 percent) are currently married or were married at least once, and 80 percent gave birth to at least one child. They got into business after their children were born and had begun attending school. The median age of these women at the time they became business owners was thirty-six.

Often, women in their thirties and forties tell me they are reluctant to start a business because they are too old. To all of them I say, "Read the cases." Some women profiled herein were in their forties or fifties before they went out on their own. Or as one millionaire woman, Florence, put it so aptly:

> *Follow your dream no matter at what age. . . . I didn't follow mine until I was fifty-two years old (eight years ago).*
> *. . . [I] started my own business because no one would hire me . . . [they said I was] too old!*
> *Now I have two offices and sixty employees. . . . My regret is that I should have started it sooner.*

Perhaps Florence would have been as successful if she'd started her business earlier in life, especially if she was still married to her first husband, whom she eventually divorced. He had to be pampered constantly, but it gave her a lot of training for her business, private home care. Being on her own also gave her a chance to breathe and to use all her abilities.

> *Don't be afraid to go it alone! . . . Don't think you don't know enough to start a business. . . . Most . . . start in a garage or a small building. It only takes an idea, a plan, and an overwhelming desire to make it work.*

YOUR SEARCH, YOUR CHOICE CRITERIA

It's likely that you will make many business-related mistakes early in your adult life. If you are like these women, you will have at least one paying job that you dislike. Your employer may discriminate against you or at least disrespect you as a woman. But in the process of "bouncing around" in the labor market, 40 percent of these women indicated, they "stumbled across a great opportunity," and that opportunity was to own their own businesses. Just over half (51 percent) reported finding their ideal vocation (self-employment) only after much trial and error.

Intuition plays a role in selecting one's vocation. In fact, 56 percent of the millionaire women report that the idea of going out on their own came at least in part from their intuition. Take Tyler, for example. She opted to go it alone as a marketing consultant for corporations with a multinational presence. Here is what she had to say about her decision to start her own firm:

Trust, always trust your own intuition, your inner guide.

The data also suggest that women who are contemplating self-employment need to ask some important questions, the same questions that most millionaire businesswomen once had to answer when selecting their businesses.

Will going into a particular type of business allow me the full use of my best abilities and strongest aptitudes?

As mentioned earlier, fully 84 percent of the millionaire women profiled in this book could answer yes before they started their businesses.

Will owning this business give me high self-esteem?

More than three in four women (76 percent) answered yes to this question before they decided to take the plunge.

Do not be afraid to admit that money has something to do with your choice. Fully 67 percent stated that:

the chance to become financially independent was an important factor in selecting the type of business upon which they decided.

More than six in ten (61 percent) indicated that they had great affection for the type of business they selected even before they made their decision. About one in three (32 percent) mentioned that the selection process was related to their part-time employment experiences.

Be flexible; when one door closes, look for another open one. I thought I had life planned when I got my education degree and began to teach. I quit to raise a family while my husband worked. But layoffs (husband's) and economic woes encouraged me to start part-time work in an unlikely profession (tax preparation—but I was a Spanish teacher who enjoyed math and puzzles). An opportunity availed itself to buy the business. Because we'd always saved, even in our leanest times, we had the down payment. And in our business, flexibility is the key. It is good to have goals, but to be so tied to attaining them via a certain set of steps will likely lead to frustration and ulcers when circumstances change. We have to accept change as part of the plan and be ready to move with it.

Yes, a Spanish teacher became the owner of a tax-preparation business. This is quite a different story from Amy's (she majored in accounting and finance), but necessity and adversity are often the parents of a successful business operation.

It is easy to theorize that "if only" the women profiled herein had started their businesses earlier in life, they would have become successful business owners five, ten, even twenty years sooner. "If only" they had majored in business in college, they would now have a really successful business. And "if only" a relative who owned a business had taught them how to run one like theirs, they would have been successful. In reality, things do not seem to work out that way. Successful business owners will tell you that adversity, trials, failures, fears, and reversals all had to take place as a prerequisite for succeeding.

Only 8 percent of the women reported that the type of business they own had anything whatsoever to do with a business that their parents or other relatives operated. Most of their parents did encourage them to become business owners, but only 16 percent reported that parents ever suggested the type of business they now own. However, 31 percent mentioned that the type of business they chose to own was suggested by one or more of their mentors.

What about the case of the imaginary Amy? Amy, aka "always planning to be in business Amy," is still planning to own her own business one day, but she is uncertain about why. Nor has she ever encountered the set of situations that led most of the successful women profiled herein to pursue the world of business ownership. Amy has never encountered adversity or had to worry about how she would send three children to college on her own income. She's never once bounced off a glass ceiling, either.

Perhaps Amy will one day open a business of her own, and it may eventually become a productive enterprise. But I would not bet money on

Amy. She can plan and plan some more and get straight A's from the top business school in the country, but Amy lacks fire in her belly. And fire in the belly beats all the other things Amy thinks will lead her to success.

How can it be that Amy, the ultimate planner, is unlikely to succeed? Amy even hired a personal coach and human resource counselor to help her plan her way into Business Ownerville. Certainly this alone will enhance her chances of success. Or will it? How many millionaire women business owners sought the counsel of a human resource adviser when they were contemplating self-employment? Only 4 percent did so.

Only 8 percent reported taking an aptitude test to determine if they were entrepreneurial material. Amy loves to fill out those personality profiles, and the administrators keep telling her:

> *Amy, you are a planner, not a doer. Perhaps you should become a professor.*

But Amy is not discouraged. In fact, today she is attending yet another conference, this one called "Discover Your Own Business Opportunity." Last week she attended a franchise fair that was sponsored by more than two hundred franchise marketers. Will Amy find just the right business this way? Only 4 percent of the millionaires surveyed "discovered" their business at either an opportunity or a franchise fair, but to this day, Amy is still planning. Passion and perseverance can't be planned. At the very least, Amy needs to get out of her parents' home and intern with a millionaire business owner. She needs to find out for herself if she has the need and motivation to opt for self-employment. She might wish to apprentice with Marsha, a successful African-American business owner who operates a child-care business. Note Marsha's suggestions to the Amys of this world:

> *Have a passion and develop the determination to make the most of the passion. Do not let a dream die; take risks, operate with a positive, energetic attitude. Surround yourself with a faithful, loving support system, friends, family, business associates, coworkers, and employees. Look at negatives with a sense of learning. Do not let the down times get you—work through each problem and cherish the good times. Keep an open mind for new ideas and experiences. Challenge the way things are done in "the*

profession." Develop a quality component in an operation or a position. Get up each day saying, "It's going to be a great day."

Marsha is a success today in part because she had a lot of experience in various vocations before she discovered her passion. Or, as one of the more vocal respondents recently stated:

It's like finding the right guy to wed. . . . You have got to kiss a lot of frogs before you find the prince. . . . Same with finding what's best for you . . . the ideal [vocation] for you!

CAREER SATISFACTION

Does your career provide you with a great deal of satisfaction? Nearly all of the successful businesswomen profiled herein (95 percent) indicated that their vocation gives them much satisfaction. Fully 90 percent are certain that their success is a direct result of their having a passion for their careers. Look at this another way: only 4 percent suggested that passion for their careers was not a substantial correlate of their success. Another 6 percent were uncertain about this relationship.

In another national survey of millionaire women business owners, respondents were asked to explain their economic success. Nearly all, 93 percent, said that loving their career was an important factor in explaining their high level of economic achievement. Another 6 percent stated that it was somewhat important, and only 1 percent rated this dimension as unimportant.

How do these results compare with the working population in general? Several recent national studies shed light on this and related issues. A recent nationwide Gallup poll found that "more than one-half (55 percent) of employees have no enthusiasm for their work" (D. L. Jones, "There's No Proof Hot Coals or Speeches Motivate the Troops," *USA Today*, May 10, 2001, p. 2A).

These results reflect a nationwide sentiment among America's workers, although certain segments of the working population have a lot of enthusiasm for their vocations. Webster's defines *enthusiasm* as "strong excitement of feeling; something inspiring zeal or fervor." In this case, that translates to passion or absolute zeal for one's job.

Enthusiasm is highly contagious. Women who are business owners are leaders, and good leaders are those who bring out the best in their employees. If a leader is passionate about her job, she can excite others to adopt similar emotions, including employees, suppliers, and customers.

Perhaps we should not criticize workers regarding their lack of job-related enthusiasm. On the contrary, we should spend more time teaching and encouraging them to become leaders who inspire others. Job satisfaction and performance are correlates of passion for one's work. Yes, it is indeed unfortunate that more than half of the workers in America find their jobs uninspiring, generating little or no passion, zeal, or fervor. The business owners profiled in this study repeatedly documented the fact that high levels of productivity in business are a direct result of having high job satisfaction.

The Gallup organization recently surveyed a national sample of 1,028 workers (see Lydia Saad, "American Workers Generally Satisfied, but Indicate Their Jobs Leave Much to Be Desired," *Gallup Poll News Service,* September 3, 1999, pp. 1–5). Respondents were asked about their level of satisfaction with their current jobs, and most workers indicated some level of satisfaction. However, only 39 percent reported being completely satisfied with their jobs. This satisfaction measure is skewed upward by respondents who are self-employed business owners. Nearly six in ten (58 percent) of them reported being "completely satisfied" with their jobs.

These findings are congruent with other studies of job satisfaction. The self-employed tend to have higher levels of it than do other workers. Net out those respondents to the Gallup study of job satisfaction who are employees. What percent of those respondents report complete satisfaction with their job? Only about one in three (35 percent) of those who work for others are in the "completely satisfied" category. These results compare favorably with those generated from my studies of millionaire women business owners who consistently indicated that they are very satisfied with their jobs and that their careers provide them with a "great deal of satisfaction."

How do self-employed women differ in their level of career passion and satisfaction when compared with self-employed men? A large percentage of the women profiled in this book reported greater job satisfaction than men (95 percent versus 90 percent) within the same age, income, and net worth cohorts.

These results are not really surprising. Nearly all (92 percent) of the women profiled were once employees, and women who are employed by others typically earn a smaller income for the same work done by men. They are also significantly more likely to be passed over for promotions, in spite of being well qualified for such advancement. What about women who are employed in the top twenty income-producing occupations in America? On average, they are paid significantly less than men in each and every one of those categories (see *The Millionaire Next Door*, pp. 179–83). In many cases where women are initially given significant promotions and salary increases, something blocks their rise to senior management. Some call it the glass ceiling or the invisible but real barrier to upward occupational mobility. In other cases it is more blatant; call it job discrimination. It is no wonder that nearly all the self-employed women surveyed in this book have very high levels of job satisfaction. They are self-employed and economically successful. They are not overlooked for promotions since they make all the decisions about such matters. They like their employer (all three of them): aka me, myself, and I.

They are self-determined. They make their own job opportunities. They write their own job descriptions. They do their own job evaluations. Their efforts are justly rewarded by the objective realities of the market and its consumers, their clients and customers.

What are some of the other reasons self-employed women as well as self-employed men have higher levels of job satisfaction? In order to answer this question, consider the level of satisfaction workers in general associate with various characteristics of their jobs. According to the Gallup poll of America's workforce, many surveyed are "less than completely satisfied" with the following characteristics of their jobs: on-the-job stress (79 percent); the amount of money that can be earned (77 percent); retirement plan offered (69 percent); opportunities for advancement (68 percent); health insurance benefit provided by employer (67 percent); family or medical leave benefits offered by employer (62 percent); recognition for work-related accomplishments (62 percent); opportunities to learn and grow (57 percent); amount of work required by employer (54 percent); boss or supervisor (53 percent); and job security (52 percent).

Stress seems to be a prime candidate for causing job dissatisfaction, and millionaire women have much less job-related stress than do most workers. Love for one's job provides sort of a halo effect for workers—

certainly this is true for many self-employed millionaire women. Long hours and on-the-job problems seem much less stressful when the task is very much enjoyed.

But there is more to this story. Stress is often the result of incongruent goals. The goals of one's employer may not be at all in sync with one's own aims. Of course, the probability of goal congruency between worker and employer greatly increases when the employer and employee are the same individual.

Workers who are stressed report that they are required to do too much in too little time. Assembly-line workers routinely report that their increasing job-related stress is a direct result of the production line speeding up and up and up again. The individual worker in such cases has little authority to change the speed of an assembly line, but the self-employed design their own time parameters. Every morning while freshening up before work they have a meeting with their supervisor, board, boss, and CEO. Across America these women look into the mirror and ask, "What is the most important task that should be addressed today? When would you like it to be completed? Who should be responsible for completing this work?"

It's amazing! The millionaire women have this meeting of me, myself, and I each day, and there is never an argument. Factions never debate the pros and cons. One very successful woman business owner once said:

> I have never had a single argument, . . . not one, with my boss, and I have had the same boss for more than twenty years!

Of course, being self-employed can be stressful at times. You have only yourself to rely on—or do you? Many women business owners have told me that it is much more stressful working for an employer than for one's own customers. What is riskier: having one source of income as an employee or having many sources of revenue from all your hundreds, even thousands of happy customers?

One of the most successful women who participated in my studies of millionaires explained why she "went solo." She was very talented, more than enough to be hired by one of the preeminent consulting firms in the world, and (later) by a major corporation. She finally figured that she was the very best that the wizards in personnel and their head-hunters could find, and then one morning just before dawn she asked herself the question of questions. What if she was required to go out and find another person with her drive and talent and work habits? Where would she go? It was no contest. She recognized that she would be her very first choice. It took a long time for her to see the light, but then the idea exploded like a comet before her eyes.

Are you good? Really good? Then why do you sell yourself to strangers? Why not sell your talents, your emotion, your drive, your intellect to yourself? Give yourself an exclusive deal on all your skills.

V.

Part-Time Work, Full-Time Wealth and Satisfaction

Prelude

*I*t is true that not everyone is suited to business ownership. Some individuals will always prefer the security of employment in other people's companies. Still others might have a difficult time deciding to make the break from corporate life because of the fear of failure in self-employment. There is another option that a small number of millionaire women have selected: working part-time at their own businesses without "quitting their day jobs." The choice ensures that the women have a reliable paycheck, but it also gives them the opportunity, through hard work and perhaps long hours, to develop their own business. Owning and managing income-producing real estate is an excellent choice of a business that exploits part-time work to achieve full-time financial success. Neither of the two successful business owners profiled in this section, Brian or Ann Lawton Hills, works more than twenty hours a week, but both are financially independent.

These two case studies provide a blueprint for financial success in the real estate field—buying, that is, not selling. Why have I included Brian, a man, among the millionaire women profiled herein? Brian's case is special and irresistible. It represents a triumph that can provide inspiration to many women. Perhaps his story, and that of Ann Lawton Hills, will plant the seed of an idea in the minds of those who are hesitating over the decision to become self-employed.

The business of income-producing real estate is one that highlights the distinction between income and wealth, so a brief discussion of that difference and how many millionaire business owners have achieved financial success through real estate ownership is included in this prelude.

WEALTH AND/OR INCOME?

Imagine the value of having an extraordinary data pool about wealthy people. With this information, one would be able to explain how rich people became wealthy and how they remain wealthy. But how many millionaires would be willing to provide all this information about their income and assets? Few would volunteer. It might take many, many hours to compute all that information. Yet the vast majority of wealthy people provide it to an organization that is the godfather of millionaire research: the IRS. Each year, millionaires submit the ultimate questionnaire in the form of income tax returns. Later, when they pass on, the executors of their estates must also submit federal estate tax returns.

> *Estate tax returns (Form 706) provide a unique source from which to study the nation's wealthiest individuals. The estate tax return contains a complete listing of a decedent's assets and debts, as well as a demographic profile of the decedent.* (Barry W. Johnson and Lisa M. Schreiber, "Personal Wealth, 1998," *Statistics of Income Bulletin* [Internal Revenue Service], Winter 2002–03, pp. 87–115)

What can be learned about wealthy women? The IRS data indicate that as a group, these women have little debt. In fact, for every $1 of debt outstanding, they have $20.27 of wealth. The average net worth of these millionaire women is just under $2.5 million. Of this amount, they had an average outstanding debt of just $123,309. On average, only about 4.5 percent of their total wealth is held in the category entitled "Other Assets" by the IRS. "Other Assets," on average $114,712, does not include: personal residence, investment real estate, closely held stock, other stocks, state and local bonds, federal savings bonds, other federal bonds, corporate and foreign bonds, bond funds, unclassified mutual funds, cash and money market accounts, mortgages and notes, cash value of life insurance, noncorporate business assets, limited partnerships, and retirement assets.

After accounting for the assets listed above, there is not much left. Just how far can $114,712 go in accounting for "Other Assets"? Not far enough to even approach an opulent lifestyle. These women have accumulated more than twenty times the wealth of the typical household in America, but they do not have a large collection of expensive artifacts.

Being frugal is a high correlate of becoming wealthy, but there is something else we can learn about building wealth from examining the asset mix of the wealthy women. Most of their assets appreciate in value without necessarily generating cash flow, aka realized, taxable income. The typical millionaire woman business owner realizes only 8.3 percent of her net worth each year, so only 8.3 percent of her wealth is subject to income tax. Note that this 8.3 percent includes more than realized capital gains derived from her assets. It also includes salary and wages paid to her by her business(es), as well as all other forms of realized income, from royalties to net income from commercial real estate.

Business owners tend to be a productive lot. One of the measures that can be employed to determine the economic productivity of various high-income-producing occupational groups is the ratio of the percentage of Balance Sheet Affluent to Income Statement Affluent within each occupational group. How do business owners compare with senior corporate executives, attorneys, physicians, and stockbrokers? In a recent national survey of 1,001 respondents of those with annual incomes from the low six figures to over $1 million, business owners were found to be the most productive (see *The Millionaire Mind*, p. 79). For every one Income Statement Affluent member among business owners, there were 6.6 in the Balance Sheet Affluent category. The ratio for senior corporate executives was 4.0, followed by physicians (1.7), attorneys (1.3), and stockbrokers (0.5).

Note this very important fact: nearly two-thirds of these millionaire business owners own commercial real estate. And those respondents in the top quartile, ranked according to actual versus expected level of wealth, are three times more likely than those in the bottom quartile to own income-producing real estate. Those millionaires who own commercial real estate are often masters at minimizing their net realized (taxable) income and maximizing their unrealized income (or appreciation of the value of their properties).

A great deal can be learned about building wealth from those millionaires who list their type of business as "farmer," "commercial real estate," "owner/manager of orange groves," "owner/manager of rental property," and the like. Contrast these folks with the others within the millionaire business owner population.

Typically, business owners as a population hold about 30 percent of their wealth in their businesses. They are far more diversified than most people might believe. The other portions of their wealth are held in real estate, stocks, bonds, cash, and personal assets. Those business owners who hold at least 65 percent of their assets in businesses that are labeled "commercial real estate" or "farming" are the masters of masters in regard to minimizing their realized (taxable) income.

> *The greater the percentage of assets which are closely held, the lower the realized rate of return on all assets. Farmers and owners of real estate businesses tend to realize lower rates of return on their total portfolio than other business owners.* (C. Eugene Steuerle, "The Relationship Between Realized Income and Wealth," *Statistics of Income Bulletin* [Internal Revenue Service], Spring 1985)

Examine the income tax returns from a sample of two groups, farmers and owners of real estate businesses. Then match their income with their wealth data, generated from estate data after they pass away. That is what Eugene Steuerle did in his study. For a farmer or an owner of a real estate business to be included in the study, the value of his interest in a closely held business had to exceed 65 percent of his wealth.

For those with assets valued at $840,000 or more, their average realized rate of return from all sources, including their capital assets of all types plus wage income, was only 2.99 percent. Given this finding, what is the expected total annual realized income of an owner of a real estate business who has a net worth of, say, $2 million? The answer is $59,800. With this amount of spendable income, it is unlikely that you will find such a person stocking up on luxury goods or mingling with the members of an exclusive country club. Yet the owner is a millionaire nevertheless. People like this real estate entrepreneur do not dress expensively or drive expensive motor vehicles. Such consumer indulgences do not make one wealthy. In fact, they are substitutes of wealth, not complements.

I once had an interesting experience while presenting these and related facts to a group of fund-raisers from colleges and universities, hospitals, youth groups, and a variety of eleemosynary organizations who were responsible for identifying prospective donors. I explained, "Many wealthy, prospective donors do not look wealthy!" Thus, I suggested, they should prospect successful business owners of the "small hat, lots of cattle" variety, as opposed to the "big hat, no cattle" kind. I further recommended that they study the anatomy or specific type of business wealth that exists within each of their geographic regions, and I noted that most millionaires in America are current or retired business owners. Some were farmers; others were scrap metal dealers or "blue-collar" millionaires who owned real estate businesses. I could tell by the reaction of my audience that most were skeptical. They were used to prospecting for donors among the other variety of millionaires—those who looked the part. I thought that I was not making any headway until a young woman raised her hand and asked if she could present her own case study. Three years earlier, she had given up a career in the corporate world. Now she is very successful in raising money for the Girl Scouts:

> I am responsible for prospecting the northern half of our state . . . apple country. I read what apple farmers read . . . about apple farming and apple farmers. I identify prospective donors from articles about award-winning farmers. My first major success . . . [involved] an elderly farm couple [with] . . . no living heirs . . . [who were] written up in a trade journal. . . . [I] visited with them many times last year. They decided . . . the entire farm will be donated . . . a new Girl Scout camp in the making. . . . The property today is valued conservatively at over $4 million. You would never know that they were millionaires . . . certainly not from the simple farmhouse . . . nor the twenty-year-old rust on the white pickup truck they drive.
>
> Most prospectors are all trying to mine the same vein . . . society people. . . . Personally, I have accomplished much more on the other side of the tracks.

The farm couple, in this case, never generated a net annual realized income of more than $70,000, but they built a net worth conservatively estimated to be near $4 million. How is this possible? The couple's business appreciated over the years. They started out with just a small piece of farmland, and over the years, they purchased more and more. They lived frugally, mostly "off the land." They borrowed money only to purchase more farmland. Note that $70,000 (the couple's income) is only 1.75 percent of their approximate net worth.

231

Is this couple all that unusual among the ranks of successful farmers or owners of real estate businesses? According to the IRS study of estate (wealth) data and income tax returns, this couple is pro forma.

When all nonwage income (from all assets) is treated as capital income, the income for all members of the sample is only 1.88 percent of their assets. (Steuerle, p. 31)

Most millionaire business owners, including farmers and those who own real estate businesses, own commercial real estate in addition to their main vocation. In fact, the higher one is on the scale of actual versus expected net worth (computed via the wealth equation), the more likely one is to report that:

I invest in commercial real estate.

The relationship between wealth and real estate holdings also applies to other occupational groups, such as physicians, attorneys, executives, and accountants. Ask physicians where they are positioned on the net worth scale, and those in the Balance Sheet Affluent category are significantly (three times) more likely than those in the Income Statement Affluent group to say:

I own commercial income-producing real estate and/or I own the medical arts building in which I have my office!

A surgeon can operate on patients twice a day for each working day. In thirty years, that adds up to twelve thousand operations. When the surgeon stops operating, the revenue stream stops, but what if that same physician owns the medical arts building housing twenty tenants? Even while the surgeon is sleeping, the value of the property might be making the surgeon wealthy. And even after he or she retires, the real estate continues to have significant economic value.

CHAPTER 13

Brian's Journey: From Hunter-Gatherer to Cultivator of Wealth

*H*is handwritten letter began with "My name is Brian." His business stationery consisted of three-hole loose-leaf school paper; at the top, he'd "printed" his company's name and address with a rubber stamp.

Perhaps you are thinking along the same lines I did when I first opened his letter, but even before I began to read it, I stopped myself from prejudging Brian. Over the years, I have discovered something about the letters I receive. The quality of the stationery has little or no correlation with the value of the message or the economic status of the writer.

What about the fact that the letter was handwritten, actually printed? What about the fact that the letter had more than a few misspelled words and many missing commas, periods, and question marks? Still, I was not deterred from reading what Brian had to say. It's the thought, the passion, contained in the message that's most important. The second sentence contained a message that caused me to pause.

I saw you on the Oprah Winfrey show then bought your book two days later and read it in one day.

I wondered how this fellow had time to watch TV. Brian had apparently not been working between 4:00 and 5:00 P.M. that weekday.

Could he be out of work with a lot of time on his hands, or perhaps just a slacker? I found out that Brian is not a slacker at all. He, if anything, is at the other end of the productivity scale. He has enough wealth to do just about anything he wants to do. He enjoys watching Oprah because he admires her, and they have something in common: both are successful entrepreneurs. Brian tries to emulate successful people.

Once again, I say, "Don't judge one's financial statement by the pseudoindicators of wealth." So what if Brian writes his business letters on three-ring loose-leaf paper! He is frugal, frugal, frugal. In his mind, expensive business stationery is a waste of money. He will tell you that it's better to invest such dollars in more productive areas of his business.

Before I discuss his financial status in more detail, consider Brian's background and current lifestyle. Actually, his own words can tell one much about who he is and how he thinks:

> *Please forgive my spelling. I have little education. I don't know why I'm so compelled to write you a letter but I will enjoy writing it and I hope you get a kick out of reading it.*

I have great admiration for Brian, especially given some of the challenges he has encountered. Brian took the time and initiative to write to me and was not deterred because of the quality of his spelling and grammar. Perhaps he knew I would not be critical of his composition. On the contrary, I greatly respect his efforts, and I value the three long, very insightful letters he sent me.

Brian took the time and initiative to write for a very unselfish reason. He hoped that his case study would help others succeed.

> *I have learning disabilities but . . . God bless America. If I can do it, anyone can do it . . . become a millionaire. . . . Just follow the rules.*
>
> *I was like you said . . . [I was] a C or D student. . . . Some teachers would give you a D if you would just show up. . . . [In] auto shop and P.E. I would get good grades. . . . Everything else was just . . . C's, D's.*

Brian was not a great student, primarily because he has dyslexia. Webster's defines *dyslexia* as an "impairment of the ability to read."

I had and have dyslexia. I mix up letters and numbers all the time. Growing up I figured I was just a big dummy. [In school] I was always put in the dummy row. I took the G.E.D. test in high school and failed twice.

But as you will discover later in this chapter, Brian is quite good at reading other types of symbols, the clues that define economic success. Not all logic or even intellect is gained or even enhanced by reading printed letters and numbers, as Brian learned on his road to economic independence.

Brian always had a love for motor vehicles. At age fifteen, he began working at a car wash. He enjoyed the work from day one. Not long afterward he began detailing automobiles at the car wash company, and he was very, very good at his work. He was so good that an increasing number of patrons of the car wash insisted that Brian be the one to detail their vehicles.

Brian realized that there was a limit to the number of cars he could detail for his employer. Once it was reached each week, he could not generate any additional income. Through his own insight and the encouragement of many of his customers, Brian made a bold decision. Yes, the dyslexic, self-designated "big dummy" started working for himself. Brian began his own car wash and detailing business.

His plan did not require much capital. Many people think businesses are defined by buildings, parking lots, and other expensive artifacts of a high-cost enterprise, but Brian saw things differently. He reasoned that his customers would pay a premium to have their automobiles detailed at a time and place that was most convenient to them. Brian has empathy for the needs of others, especially his patrons, so he asked them about their detailing preferences.

Most reported that it would be significantly more convenient for the washing and detailing to be done in their own driveways. This would enable the customers to leave their automobiles at home, and they would not have to worry about the time and effort to drive downtown to the traditional car washes. Nor would they have to concern themselves with picking up their cars once the detailing was complete. His customers also begrudged the time they wasted sitting at a "hand car wash" location waiting for their vehicles to be processed. Brian's "at-home detailing" concept was rather innovative when it was first initiated more than twenty years ago.

His business was almost an instant success, but success can generate its share of problems. Brian's was a one-man operation. Within a few weeks of opening, he was booked solid for months in advance. Here again, he demonstrated great insight about his opportunities. How could Brian increase his revenue, given the fact that he was already operating at full capacity? Hiring others to detail did not work. He discovered that no one else had his level of dedication for, as he calls it, "the details." In other words, people recognized the variation in quality between a Brian detailing job and one done by a surrogate.

First, he increased the fees charged for an at-home washing and detailing job. He did this several times, until his prices were at the threshold of the absolute maximum he could charge. Then Brian had another idea. Was it possible that consumer sensitivity to the variations in prices charged for washing and detailing differed by geography? How did the price sensitivity of his current customer base compare with prospective customers in other geographic targets of opportunity? Brian discovered that overall his "hometown market" was way above the norm regarding demand for his services, but he reasoned that demand would be even greater in some other markets. The market for high-priced washing and detailing is a function of the concentration of very expensive or exotic automobiles within specific geographic areas.

Again Brian's logical reasoning, in spite of his dyslexia, served him well. He moved his business from his comfortable hometown surroundings to another market area, one selected because it had the highest concentration per capita of registered high-end motor vehicles in America. This was the market opportunity among market opportunities! In his own words, Brian told me:

I detail high-end cars only.

Among Brian's client base are some of America's wealthiest families who own "stables" of exotic cars ranging from investment-grade vintage Ferraris to Rolls-Royces. All of his clients, by definition, have the desire and means to have their motor vehicles maintained in near-showroom condition.

My detail business does about $60,000 to $70,000 net a year. Not bad, but not a killing either. Trust me, I work my butt off for it.

Until about ten years ago, Brian was in the Income Statement Affluent category. In spite of his hard work, Brian spent almost all of his income and had a low level of net worth. Like most Americans, he had to "hunt and gather" each day just to pay all of his bills. He was living high on the hog, and although he was single with no wife or children to support, he had to fund a hyperconsumption lifestyle.

It's easy to appreciate his orientation at that time. Each day he worked detailing cars at the homes of multimillionaires and billionaires. They owned mansions and fleets of luxury and exotic automobiles. Some of his clients were Income Statement Affluent—big earners and big spenders. This type of atmosphere had an influence on Brian's lifestyle. It's not unusual for people who feel inferior, as Brian did, to overcompensate by displaying expensive artifacts. He wanted to impress his friends with his own so-called status symbols and success. But the unrelenting burden of underwriting these symbols eventually outweighed the short-lived ego boost they gave Brian.

> My friends all thought . . . that Brian has his stuff together. But the car insurance and house payments was getting old. . . . [I] began thinking . . . who was I trying to impress? . . . House payment over $2,200 a month. . . . [I] bought a nice Mercedes and put $40,000 into a Harley . . . owned a Turbo Porsche.

After Brian spent years doing his high-consumption dance, he began questioning his own motives. He was working very hard to support his consumption habits. But he was not accumulating much wealth. Brian began hating the "first day of each month"—the deadline day for his house payments, insurance payments, Mercedes payments, Harley payments, and so on. If this pattern continued, Brian realized, he would be working very hard every day of his life until the day he died.

> I figured . . . it was all about ego, my ego. It's all about letting go of the ego. . . . Who was I trying to impress?

He decided that it was just not worth it, not worth the work-to-spend, work-to-spend, work-to-spend cycle every single month.

Brian has had a mentor who helped him become an economic success. I refer to him as Mr. Frugal. He was an expert at playing great economic defense. In other words, he knew how to "hold on to a dollar." Mr. Frugal was ten years older and "twenty years" smarter about money than Brian.

> *An old friend of mine that always seemed to have his head on straight told me, "If you are tired of it, sell the toys." I had $80,000 equity in my home, $20,000 in the Porsche . . . and from the $40,000 I put into the Harley, I got back another $20,000. . . . [I] sold it all.*

What did Mr. Frugal tell his friend Brian to do with the proceeds? He suggested that Brian do what he, Mr. Frugal, did years ago.

> *Take the $120,000 and make a down payment on a four-plex . . . that way you live for free! Your three tenants will pay for your home.*

That was twelve years ago. Brian took Mr. Frugal's advice, and it was an excellent starting point for Brian to become financially independent.

> *It's my life . . . my freedom and future I was playing with. Paying big bills . . . I was never going to be independently wealthy. . . . [I] sold it all and it was hard initially to give up that lifestyle. But in no time I went from paying $2,200 per month in house payments to living in my very nice four-plex for free!*

Brian made the transition from being a habitual hunter and gatherer of income to a cultivator of wealth, thanks to Mr. Frugal. What if Brian did nothing else but detail cars and live rent-free with low overhead and an annual income of $70,000 from detailing? Brian could have eventually become a millionaire, assuming that he saved and invested wisely. But Mr. Frugal was not an investment expert. His skill was defense, keeping spending to a minimum.

Brian was not interested in waiting for a long time before he became truly independent. Here is where a second group of mentors came into play. They played extraordinary offense as well as good defense, and Brian adopted their abilities to generate substantial wealth. They taught him how to leverage his hard-earned dollars as well as his initial investment in income-producing real estate.

BRIAN CAN READ: THE SYMBOLS OF OPPORTUNITY

Yes, Brian has difficulty reading and writing the English language. However, he has an outstanding ability to recognize and properly interpret a different kind of language. He has the gift of being able to recognize economic opportunities. Part of this gift is his ability to identify and leverage his relationship with mentors.

Ten years ago he was confronted with a set of clues for becoming wealthy.

A very wealthy customer of mine told me to skip the washing/detailing of his cars next week. He and his family were going on vacation to Hawaii for one week. My customer and his family came home not one week later, but three weeks later. I asked my customer, "Where have you been?" [Do] you know what he told me? [He] said, "The weather was so nice we decided to stay an extra two weeks."

How did Brian interpret the true meaning of that statement?

The weather was so nice we decided to stay an extra two weeks.

Would you read the signs in the same way that Brian did?

I could never in my business just decide to take off "another two weeks." I have scheduled commitments . . . impossible. Also, I'm thinking when I was a kid we [Dad, Mom, and children] would load up the camper and go to the beach Friday night. But we always had to come home on Sunday night because my dad had to be back to work Monday. He worked construction.

Brian began to realize that there were two distinctive groups of people in the employment world. Members of the first group, which includes the majority of workers, could not arbitrarily stay at the beach for two more weeks. The second group, the minority segment, was composed of people who could take extra time off. At the time of his revelation, Brian was in the first category, but he believed that he might be able to change groups.

> *I started looking at my customers . . . studying their lifestyles, not their homes and cars. I found that my richest customers . . . owned apartments, lots of apartments. . . . One customer alone owned two thousand apartments in just one county.*

Brian discovered that his customers were, in fact, first-generation millionaires. All had begun with modest amounts invested in prototypical "apartment investor starter kits," but today, they are very wealthy. It's not all about wealth, though. Brian discovered that they did not work those fifty-, sixty-, and seventy-hour weeks that his career required.

The more Brian thought about his experiences with various customers, the clearer the picture became. He recalled many of the encounters he'd had with clients. Often they would think nothing of taking ten or twenty minutes just to talk with him. They were not at an office working hard, because they were cultivators of wealth. They worked planting seeds, studying and investing in income-producing real estate. Then they collected rent. Rents were due on these apartments whether their owners went to work one day or five days a week.

Brian had other types of customers who had nice cars, lovely homes, and very high realized (taxable) incomes. Like Brian, they worked very long hours.

> *Doctors and attorneys had the nice homes and cars, even airplanes, but I never saw them . . . they were never at home. . . . No matter how early I was working or how late in their driveways, they were always at work.*

Brian understood much about the lifestyles of these hunter-gatherers. They had to work each day or earn zero. The doctors and attorneys had something in common with Brian. They could not inventory what they sell. No matter how many operations the surgeon performs, if he stops cutting, he stops making a living. It was the same in Brian's case when he detailed cars.

At this time, Brian was at a crossroads in his life. A lifetime career of detailing translates into more than 11,250 days of hard work. At ten hours per day, Brian could expect to put in 112,500 hours, 6,750,000 minutes, or 405,000,000 seconds of labor.

Brian decided to make a change in his life. He would keep detailing cars because he loved his job, but he would also become more and more involved in the "apartment business," as he calls it. The transition from being a hunter-gatherer of income to becoming a cultivator of income and wealth was not all that difficult for him.

I had no idea how to acquire a sixty-five-unit apartment build- ing but as a start, I learned how to buy and operate four-plexes. My point is that I did not have to reinvent the wheel. I just fol- lowed the leaders. I asked for help only from the [customers] who made it big [in the apartment business].

Not one of Brian's customers turned down his request for advice. Actually, they were delighted and flattered to act as his mentors because most self-made millionaires have great empathy and respect for those who have a strong desire to follow in their footsteps. These millionaires feel that their motives for becoming independently wealthy are misun- derstood. They have a strong desire to tell their side of the story. It's not the money; it's the freedom.

All my customers [in the apartment business] were willing to answer all my stupid questions. Now [after becoming a mil- lionaire through the apartment business] I have tried to tell my family and friends what I have found [that is, the joys of being a cultivator]. No one could see the light.

But don't all of Brian's customer-mentors own very expensive auto- mobiles? Yes, and all live in multimillion-dollar homes. His wealthy mentors all told Brian the same thing.

Buy the toys [expensive artifacts] well after you become wealthy. Not before. If you buy before you become wealthy, you will never reach your goal of becoming financially independent.

Today, Brian the cultivator is able to generate income and wealth. For him to make the transition from hunter-gatherer to cultivator, he had to adopt the same set of values that his mentors adopted early in their working careers.

> *I used to want to be rich just to show off . . . to spend on exotic cars, motorcycles, boats, and my custom homes, and so on. But the more I understand money, the more I realize that people with money don't care so much about having the big-ticket items as being financially independent.*

Brian is right. Self-made millionaires are much more interested in being financially independent. Brian recalls his many conversations with "Mr. Smythe," who owns two thousand apartment units. On average, these units rent for about $850 per month, or a total of $1.7 million gross per month. Every first day of every month, two thousand tenants pay their rent, so in reality, Mr. Smythe has two thousand people working for him.

In a thirty-day month, that $1.7 million gross translates into $56,667 per day, $2,361 per hour, and $39 per minute. Even when he is sleeping, Mr. Smythe is generating income. He is grossing $39 per minute for every hour, every day, every week that he is in the apartment business. Even when Mr. Smythe and his family are on vacation, it's still the same cash flow. Mr. Smythe is the consummate cultivator of income and wealth. He does not have to be at the office every day to make a living, and he does not have to hunt and gather just to stay alive. Neither does Brian.

> *I used to hate the first of the month [before I owned apartments]. . . . My friends don't like the first of the month with all those payments due. . . . But I have to tell you now that I can't wait for the first of each month.*
>
> *My real estate holdings are worth over $5 million. . . . [I have a] net worth of $1.6 million . . . so I don't think I'm a big dummy. I just have a learning disability. God bless America. If I can do it. . . . [I] started [small] with one four-plex, then bought the four-plex next door [and so on]. My apartments don't know I can't spell, and they don't know what color my skin is. Anyone can do it. Just follow the rules.*

Brian is a wonderful role model and mentor for those who wish to become financially independent. He was very smart to select the apartment business, which gave him a great chance to become a multimillionaire. He was also very smart to ask the most successful patrons of his automobile detailing business some very simple, fundamental questions:

1. How did you become successful?
2. Would I have a chance of succeeding in your type of business?
3. Would you be my mentor?

Brian was able to succeed in part because of his ability to get the most out of his circumstances. He very cleverly leveraged the high-quality, dependable service he provided his automobile detailing clients. His high-grade service put him in the good graces of his successful mentors, who appreciated his hard work and ambitions. I have often said:

If you want to catch a cold, hang out with sick people. If you want to lose, associate with losers. But if you want to become successful, go out of your way to associate with successful people.

The advice he received from his mentors was free of charge, and so is the advice he now gives to those who ask him, "Will you be my mentor?" His pride is the direct product of beating the odds, overcoming challenges, and permanently resigning from the Hunters-and-Gatherers Association of America. He still details cars because he loves to do so, but Brian will tell you that much joy and satisfaction in life can be found among the ranks of the cultivators of wealth. In America, we are supposed to be free. But what if you absolutely have to go to work every day just to pay off your bills and credit balances? You have put yourself into economic chains. You must hunt and gather each and every day of your working life. Brian thinks it's time that people in chains wake up, take the initiative, and join the Cultivators Club.

Dear Dr. Stanley:

Today at age forty-one, I still live in the same two bedroom four-plex I started with, and my estate is over $5 million. . . . [I have a] net worth near $2 million. In about two more weeks, I will have about 250 tenants . . . all in four-plexes. . . . [I] started with one then I bought both four-plexes on both sides of mine . . . and so on . . .

Today I could easily buy back all the toys [Porsches and Harleys] and the custom home. . . . One day maybe but not for a few more years. It's money [wealth] . . . money is freedom. I used to want to be rich just to show off my cars and boats. But money, if used right, really represents only freedom. That means the freedom to do whatever turns you on.

I do play hard on the weekends . . . but I never had cable TV until a year ago . . . $25 a month is dumb. . . . My only auto is a 1991 Toyota truck purchased used with 75,000 miles on it. Today it has 170,000 miles on it. . . . But it's real nice. My TV is over ten years old . . . so is my couch. My expensive-looking Christmas sweater with the fancy label? Found it on top of one of my customers' trash cans. Washed it . . . I wear it at Christmastime. Every year people tell me what a nice sweater it is. Can you believe it?

On the other hand, I'm not cheap with the people I love . . . not with my sister and brother and their kids and not with Mom and Dad. In nine out of ten opportunities, I pick up the tabs. Plus I'm a great landlord . . . have a good relationship with all my tenants. I would have to say yes I'm the most cheap with me . . . myself. But not the people I care about.

People often ask me how did you get to own all those apartments? You know what I tell them? Just get one . . . just one . . . then focus on getting the next one. Do you think I'm greedy? No, it's not what gets me out of bed in the morning. . . . I can tell you love what you do . . . and it's funny, I love what I do. . . . You can see I'm no good with putting letters from the alphabet together but I know I'm no dummy! No dummy, even though I was always put in the dummy row in school!

I feel very lucky to be me. For most of my life, I felt that I was less of a person than other people . . . I didn't feel like I fit *in. As I get older and more successful, I don't care as much what people think of me. If you saw me on the street in my 1991 Toyota pickup and didn't know me, you would guess I was a regular guy making $20,000 to $30,000 a year. Life is funny. I live in my two-bedroom apartment and I gotta tell you I have never been happier.*

Sincerely,

Brian

CHAPTER 14

Ann Lawton Hills

*A*nn Lawton Hills is a millionaire. She and her husband, who passed away three years before my interview with her, were fastidious savers and investors. Years ago they'd begun investing heavily in blue-chip winners such as IBM and Philip Morris, and in the shares of selected drug companies. They were long-term investors. They bought and held. They used a focused approach when investing, and they never owned more than eight different stocks in outstanding corporations. Mrs. Hills always felt that it was much easier to research and then select a small number of stock offerings than to own "a mutual fund's variety." This situation paid off handsomely over the years for the Hills.

Mr. and Mrs. Hills enjoyed a frugal yet comfortable lifestyle, and their commitment to becoming financially independent was driven by one major issue: it was uncertain how long Mr. Hills would remain alive. He had been born with a heart abnormality. His father had died at the age of thirty-five from the same condition. Medical experts had advised Mr. Hills that he could pass away at any time. He, in turn, had told Ann Lawton this same glum forecast, but it had not deterred her. Ann Lawton had married "the only man she ever loved" when she was twenty-five and he was thirty-seven, and their marriage was a close bonding of two very unselfish people. Mr. Hills passed away just prior to their thirtieth wedding anniversary.

Mr. Hills's physical abnormality created special problems. According to Mrs. Hills, he was uninsurable. He had zero life insurance. What would you have done if you were confronted with this grim reality? How would you provide for your wife if she became a widow tomorrow? If you were Mrs. Hills, how would you plan for your future?

For nearly twenty years, both Mr. and Mrs. Hills worked. Mr. Hills was a self-employed sales representative and Mrs. Hills was an administrator and bookkeeper. The couple lived on his salary and invested all of hers. As time passed, it became more and more obvious to them that their goal of financial independence was becoming a reality.

Being financially independent did not automatically translate into a solution for impending loneliness, but Mrs. Hills thought about a partial solution to that problem. What if she surrounded herself with surrogate sons and daughters? What if she shared her living space with "mature college students"? This could likely provide Mrs. Hills with both an income and a possible remedy for her anticipated loneliness.

The idea came from her own experiences in college. Mrs. Hills had paid for her college expenses in part by being an aide (or student intern) to a wealthy couple. They provided her with a room in their home as well as with board and a small stipend. Mrs. Hills did "light cleaning," shopping, bookkeeping, and related chores around the home, and became a companion to the wife. The husband often traveled out of town, and they found it comforting to have Ann Lawton in their house.

Mrs. Hills recognized that her experience as an intern could be useful. She and her husband agreed that an intern program would be especially helpful to her if she suddenly became a widow. Even more than hiring an intern, Mrs. Hills wanted to remain active, to always be doing something, to continue earning and investing, but she feared being totally alone someday.

After considerable deliberation, the couple decided to move into a much larger home in order to accommodate more than one intern. The home—some would call it a mansion—was three short blocks from the university. It had been on the market as an estate sale for some time. To most people it probably appeared to be a white elephant, and it needed a lot of work, but Mr. and Mrs. Hills felt it was ideal for what they had in mind.

The couple purchased the mansion at a bargain price, but the property was more than an investment. It represented a vocation for Mrs. Hills. She and her husband occupied the first floor of the mansion, which had more space than the entire home they had previously owned. One separate back bedroom and bath were designed for Mrs. Hills's personal assistant, a student intern. Shortly after moving, Mrs. Hills resigned her full-time position as an administrator and bookkeeper and opted for something different—something that would give her more control of her time and lifestyle. She entered the ranks of the self-employed.

The mansion was ideally suited for Mrs. Hills's purposes. The huge basement contained two "in-law" apartments as well as two studio apartments, and she planned to rent only these four units to students. She calculated that the rent for three units would be sufficient for her to break even. Rent from the fourth unit was "all profit."

Having people . . . young . . . lovely people around . . . [made for] great company. . . . [It] keeps one young in spirit.

So much for Mrs. Hills's initial plan. In short order, demand outpaced and greatly exceeded supply. A number of prospective tenants wanted to rent space from Mrs. Hills, all the apartments were rented, and she had to turn down even the most qualified applicants. This troubled her so much that she decided to increase her supply.

The second and third floors of the home were hardly ever used, so Mrs. Hills decided to rent them out completely. Soon she had a full house of great tenants, and she was once again faced with the problem of demand exceeding supply. She developed so much self-confidence as a landlord that she decided to buy another nearby property, then another, and so forth. Before long, she owned what amounted to half a block of "nice" real estate. Yet, as always, demand for her brand of high-grade housing continues to exceed supply.

Mrs. Hills feels that it's what keeps her going. She misses her husband of thirty years a great deal, but her tenants are more like family to her than customers. It is hard to feel alone when surrounded by all those bright, happy faces. And best of all, she rarely spends more than twenty hours a week managing her properties.

QUESTIONS OFTEN ASKED ABOUT MRS. HILLS

How does Mrs. Hills furnish her apartments?
All of the furniture was purchased at estate sales, which Mrs. Hills

often attends to enhance her collections of antique silver and furniture. In the process, she often encounters good used furniture that is being liquidated. Mrs. Hills never buys junk for her apartments. Most of the appliances were purchased from individual sellers who listed their offerings in the classified section of the newspaper.

What sources does Mrs. Hills employ for house painters, plumbers, heating and air-conditioning servicepeople, carpenters, and such?

Mrs. Hills has never had even one full-time employee, and she rarely hires a conventional service company for her needs. The tradesmen she usually hires are moonlighters recruited from the ranks of tradesmen employed by the university. Mrs. Hills has a unique method of identifying them. She uses the "if you see" approach. She often asks her student tenants:

If you see some fellow doing a good job painting while you're on campus, ask him for his name and phone number. Tell him your landlord is looking for some help on the off-hours he's not working for the university.

Over the years, Mrs. Hills estimates, she has saved many dollars by employing her team of moonlighters, and she often uses a rather interesting compensation system. Mrs. Hills has an "ugly basement room" filled with furniture and an assortment of appliances that she purchases at bargain prices for her future needs. She uses them to barter with her moonlighters. For example, a painter from the university recently painted one of Mrs. Hills's three-room apartments. She paid him half in cash and half with a side-by-side refrigerator and a room air conditioner! Mrs. Hills was delighted with the deal. The color and large size of the refrigerator "just never matched anything I own."

What other types of businesses did Mrs. Hills own or manage before she entered the apartment business?

Mrs. Hills never owned a business before venturing into real estate. She was forty-six years old when she began that career.

Did Mrs. Hills have a difficult time learning how to operate her business?

Mrs. Hills did a lot of planning and market research before she started the business. Her decision to purchase property near the university paid dividends right from the start because the demand for her apartments was always high. Finding suppliers, especially honest tradespersons, was not so easy. Initially Mrs. Hills knew little about the real estate business in terms of hiring painters, carpenters, and such, and several of these people tried to rip her off. For example, she once asked a roofer to come by to fix her leaking gutters. He told her that all her gutters and downspouts had to be replaced because they were completely rusted through. Mrs. Hills was shocked at the estimated cost of the job. She asked several of her tenants what they thought about the estimate and one of them, a law student, told her:

> *Copper does not rust. Your gutters and downspouts are all copper. If they're leaking, it's probably because they're filled with the leaves from all those tall oak trees in your yard.*

The student was correct in his assessment, and Mrs. Hills learned over the years to always get a second opinion or estimate. Today she has a list of outstanding and honest suppliers, but it was not easy to develop; some tradesmen view a woman in this type of business as a babe lost in the wilderness, naive and with lots of money. They soon learned that Mrs. Hills was a strong, very bright woman. Those who judged her as lacking in intellect and resolve soon found out that she was a smiling tiger.

How did Mrs. Hills deal with the loss of her husband?
In spite of planning for this for nearly thirty years of marriage, Mrs. Hills did have some difficulty. She told me that for more than a year after her husband passed away, she never smiled or laughed. But again, her tenants, her business, helped her get over her grief.

Mrs. Hills noted the one particular circumstance when she laughed for the first time after losing her husband. That day she was eating lunch in her kitchen when Mr. Anthony came in with his rent check. He must have noticed that Mrs. Hills had tears in her eyes. Mr. Anthony was a first-year student at the vet school, and was also bold and apparently a "healer of the heart." Mr. Anthony took hold of Mrs. Hills's left hand with his right hand. Then he squatted down, all the time making sounds and gestures like a chimpanzee. He alternatively scratched his head and then under his arm. All the while, he was jumping up and down in classic chimp style. Then he made a wonderful chimp face and put it close to hers while gesturing, chattering, and gyrating. Mr. Anthony was determined to change Mrs. Hills's mood. Within thirty seconds, Mrs. Hills burst out laughing, even while the tears rolled down her face. Mr. Anthony's chimp impersonation broke the spell that had had a hold on Mrs. Hills for more than a year.

During the course of my interview with Mrs. Hills, we were interrupted several times. Ms. Lucy, a Ph.D. student, stopped by and offered to pick up some things from the supermarket. Later another tenant, Mr. James, returned with a rake he had borrowed when he'd taken it upon himself to rake up the leaves in front of his apartment because the regular yardman had the flu. Mrs. Hills particularly admired tenants like Mr. James. He was a West Point graduate and was studying for a Ph.D. in engineering. Men and women with military backgrounds often found that Mrs. Hills just happened to have a vacancy for them. For Mrs. Hills, the real estate business was not just about money. Her tenants were her surrogate family. When one young tenant couple had their first child, Mrs. Hills gave them a brand-new crib, changing table, and high chair. When an older renter had a bad cough, Mrs. Hills sent over her favorite remedy: a "hip-pocket bottle" of Wild Turkey laced with rock candy, lemon, and cloves. The stories go on and on. Mrs. Hills obviously is a strong and very kind person. Her pride and high self-esteem were enhanced each time a tenant said thank you.

THE EXPLOITERS

Not all the people Mrs. Hills met over the years were kind to widows—some actually sought out widows to exploit. The really clever exploiters actually attempted to capitalize on these women when their fears, worries, and concerns were at a peak. If you choose to own and manage income properties, you would be wise to keep a vigilant eye for characters like these.

Not long after Mr. Hills's death, Mrs. Hills received a call from a Mr. S.B., aka Slime Ball. He explained that he was in the furniture business. He said,

I was recently in your area. One of your neighbors suggested I call . . . mentioned that you would be interested in selling some items.

Of course, Mr. S.B. could not recall the name of the neighbor who'd supposedly made that suggestion, and it was highly unlikely that there was ever any suggestion at all. Mr. S.B. prospects widows. Apparently, he'd targeted her the same way he identifies and targets other widows: by reading the obituaries in the local papers. Then he telephones the widows and uses the "your neighbor suggested" theme.

Mr. S.B. figured when he identified Mrs. Hills that he had just found one more vulnerable woman. He probably didn't realize that he was talking to a smiling tiger when he telephoned her. Mrs. Hills informed him that she did have a few items that she wished to sell and invited him over to one of her smaller homes. Mr. S.B. and his two understudies showed up with an old truck. Mrs. Hills escorted them down into the basement and showed them a large breakfront made of oak. It came apart in four or six pieces, and it was so heavy that even a pair of football players would have difficulty lifting it off the ground. The family who'd previously owned the property had left it in the basement.

Without haggling too much, Mr. S.B. and Mrs. Hills agreed on a price. Then he told her that he would go to his bank and get some cash to pay her. During this time, Mr. S.B. had his two junior S.B.s disassemble the piece and move the components from the basement out to the property's driveway.

Mr. S.B. arrived back from the bank. He got out of the truck and began pacing all around the components with a deep frown on his face, shaking his head.

Mr. S.B. then told Mrs. Hills that he'd misjudged the value of the piece. Now that he saw it in the light of day, the breakfront was not as old an antique as he'd first thought, and it had numerous flaws that went undetected while it was in the dimly lit basement. He then informed Mrs. Hills that the piece was worth only about half of the price they had previously agreed upon. But there was more bad news. Mr. S.B. and the apprentice S.B.s were late for another appointment. They would not have enough time to move the components back into the basement and reassemble the breakfront. So the threat was for Mrs. Hills to take half of the agreed price or else have the components rot in her driveway.

Mrs. Hills explained a few things to the S.B.s, pointing to all the homes she owned in the area. She detailed the fact that many strong young men were among her tenant population. Some had played varsity football in college. The S.B.s began to realize that money or lack of it was not a salient motive for Mrs. Hills. Nor would "lack of muscle" be a major impediment to returning the piece to the basement. Mrs. Hills also explained that it would have cost between $100 and $150 an hour for a professional moving company to disassemble and move the components outside, so the breakfront was now worth more outside than it had been in her basement.

Mr. S.B. began looking over the components once again. With a pained look on his face, he began raising the proposed sale price.

Mrs. Hills again emphasized the fact that her asking price was a genuine bargain. Mr. S.B. recognized that he had no choice. He paid the full price in cash.

Mr. S.B. was no match for Mrs. Hills, the smiling tiger of a widow. She had trained for this battle from the very first day of her marriage to Mr. Hills, anticipating that she could be on her own in an instant. Unfortunately, most widows believe their husband's words: "I will always be here to provide for you and care for you." But in more than three of four cases in America, husbands pass away before their wives.

WHO IS READING ABOUT YOU AND YOUR FAMILY?

Mr. S.B. used the newspaper to find Mrs. Hills during a time when he assumed she would be more inclined to fall for his tactics. He and others like him have used the newspaper and other public records to locate potential victims for years. My own mother-in-law once gave me another example of this method of information gathering, and her story should serve as a caution to those who like to "advertise" the locations of personal events.

Just a few days before I was married, my future mother-in-law suggested that someone should stay at home and guard the wedding gifts during the ceremony and reception. Apparently the infamous "newspaper gang" was operating in the area.

These enterprising burglars were heavy readers of newspapers, especially the wedding announcements. They noted the names and sometimes addresses of the brides' parents and the time and date of the wedding, then made their assault during the wedding and reception. First, they would call the home of the bride's parents to see whether anyone was "guarding the gifts." If all cues indicated that the coast was clear, they would break in and remove the gifts and anything else that appealed to them. They were able to raid several homes in one day. The exploits of the newspaper gang show that printed information can be used as market intelligence (Thomas J. Stanley, *Marketing to the Affluent* [Homewood, Illinois: Dow Jones-Irwin, 1988], pp. 104–105).

PROFESSOR WILLIAM AND HIS DH BRAND OF CLOTHING

Countless individuals give testimony to their frugal nature, and I admire some of their behaviors. There is nothing wrong with being frugal as long as you don't damage the health and welfare of yourself and others. However, some people who have contacted me took pride in telling me how they negotiated price-related deals that were unconscionable. These unscrupulous people actually enjoy bragging about how they identify and exploit people who are very vulnerable. It is one thing to be an exploiter of the weak like Mr. S.B., but it is quite another level of unscrupulousness to exploit the weak and then brag about it. Such is the case of Professor William.

Dr. William sought me out one day at a conference because he thought his case study should be published. He fervently believed that his method of obtaining "great deals" on certain categories of consumer products would "help the youth of America become more intelligent about economizing."

After determining my identity and keen interest in profiling frugal millionaires, he told me his story in an interesting, unusual way. I guess that I should not have been surprised about his ability to profile himself in an interesting manner—he has lectured here and abroad and done much consulting for large corporations. Dr. William has written several textbooks and published many articles, and he holds the rank of full professor of economics at a large, well-respected university.

DR. WILLIAM: How much did you pay for that tie you are wearing?
DR. STANLEY: About twenty dollars. It's a Brooks Brothers . . . on sale. They never go out of style.
DR. WILLIAM: Do you know how much I paid for the tie I have on?

DR. STANLEY: Bet it was less than twenty dollars.

DR. WILLIAM: Right! . . . Paid twenty-five cents. . . . I like ties . . . have many, many . . . so many that I could wear a different tie each day for months without repeating.

Then Professor William asked me more and more questions, it was as if he were lecturing to one of his classes.

DR. WILLIAM: How much did you pay for that shirt? Those shoes? That suit?

Given his smile, I could tell that Dr. William felt that he was making his point. Yes, indeed, he paid a lot less than I did for shirts, shoes, and suits. In fact, the entire wardrobe he had on that day cost him less than fifty dollars!

DR. STANLEY: How is it possible that you paid so little for your clothing?

DR. WILLIAM: I call them.

DR. STANLEY: Call? Whom do you call?

DR. WILLIAM: I call them . . . those in need . . . those that have a need to unload.

DR. STANLEY: Define *them*.

DR. WILLIAM: Obits . . . obits. . . . I call and ask, "What do you have . . . what sizes?"

DR. STANLEY: You call whom?

DR. WILLIAM: I call widows . . . ask them what clothes they might wish to sell.

DR. STANLEY: Are you talking about clothing that might be in a closet that's never been worn, or are you talking about used clothing?

DR. WILLIAM: Most of it's in good shape . . . shoes already broken in!

So what if Dr. William is a multimillionaire? He is wearing the DH brand of clothing—that's for Dead Husband. In spite of his notable achievements, Dr. William's shopping methods cast a heavy cloud over him. Dr. William, a professor in daylight, is an exploiter of widows at night. Can you imagine the inability of a recently widowed woman in dire straits to negotiate wisely with Dr. William? But not all the widows that Professor William called were accommodating. Some were widows who were financially independent and possessed the psychological strength of a smiling tiger, like Mrs. Hills. They had a different response to Professor William's proposition, suggesting that he should have his biographical sketch printed in the obit section of the newspaper: "Drop dead immediately!"

Such a response is difficult to generate from those who spent most of their adult lives completely dependent psychologically and economically on their spouses, but women like Mrs. Hills spend much of their adult years preparing themselves for calls like Professor William's. Dr. William and his ilk are not worthy of wearing even the well-worn used clothes of Mrs. Hills's late husband.

VI.

Alternate Routes

CHAPTER 15

The Sales Profession According to Beverly Bishop

*W*hat if you don't want all the responsibilities associated with owning your own business but you still wish to achieve and to be well paid for your efforts? You would probably consider becoming an employee, but what if an employer won't pay you, a woman, what a man receives for the same level of productivity? Certainly, there must be some vocation other than self-employment that rewards productivity on an objective basis. Yes, there is such a vocation, and it's called the profession of selling. Some just call it selling. But for those extraordinary people who generate sales volumes substantially above the norm, selling is, in fact, a profession.

The sales profession has many of the positive qualities that are also associated with being self-employed. If you are compensated via full commission, then you are paid for every dollar of revenue you generate. Of course, there are risks associated with the profession. If you don't produce, you don't get paid. However, if you are willing to work harder and smarter than the next guy, you will be rewarded. You will cultivate a client base, and these people will continue to do business with you. They will recommend that others do the same. As your client base increases, your employer will likely recognize, reward, and respect your abilities. Employers realize that extraordinary sales professionals are a precious minority.

Over the years, I have surveyed and personally interviewed nearly one thousand top-producing sales professionals, and I have written books about them. Selecting just one individual to profile, the most outstanding role model for those who contemplate this career choice, was not easy, but I did, in fact, select Beverly Bishop. You will recall that Beverly's eleemosynary habits were discussed earlier, and obviously, if one is intent on giving many dollars to noble causes, it helps to have the dollars to give. Beverly is 100 percent self-made affluent. She earned every dollar she received as a commission for selling thousands and thousands of motor vehicles. One must be extraordinary to sell that many cars, and in my estimation, Beverly is the most extraordinary of the extraordinary.

However, Beverly is much more than a revenue generator. She does it with style, dignity, humor, and professionalism. How else could one explain her client base of several thousand repeat customers? Beverly has always been an important asset to her employer, to her customers, to her church and other noble causes, and to her profession.

BEVERLY, WHY CAR SALES?

How did Beverly wind up selling automobiles? She wanted a job that paid for performance. Beverly always felt that she could outperform most other people, and she selected the sales profession for this reason. Of course, not all sales positions have the potential to generate six-figure incomes.

It was a good friend of Beverly who suggested that she enter the male-dominated automobile industry. She had some sales experience dating back to high school and later in retailing, but as her friend suggested, "If you sell a lot of cars, you earn a lot of commission dollars . . . it's all on performance." He also assured Beverly that it did not matter if you were tall or short, young or old, male or female. If you perform, you get paid.

There was one problem with this logic. You can't perform or sell cars if no one will hire you. Nearly thirty years ago, Beverly asked more than a dozen dealers to hire her for a sales position, but it was the same old song and dance. They all claimed that they did not have any openings in sales. In reality, there were many openings "for men only." They all told her the same thing, "We have opportunities in the clerical area." Each time she heard this, Beverly recalled what her mother had told her on countless occasions.

Find a job where you compete with men, always men. Never compete against women. Always compete against men . . . it's much easier and you will always get paid more for your efforts.

Beverly heeded her mother's sage advice. She kept on trying to get a job selling automobiles, but she couldn't land one without some kind of assistance from her good friend Gerry. He helped her get her first job selling automobiles. He was also the first person to suggest that Beverly was a natural for this vocation.

Gerry was a superstar in the world of selling automobiles. Dealers all over the metro area coveted this top-producing sales professional. One in particular had an especially strong interest in hiring Gerry, but Gerry kept turning down each and every offer. Eventually, he countered with a proposition. He informed the dealer that he would take the offer, but the dealer would also have to hire Beverly. After much consternation, the man agreed to hire both Gerry and Beverly as a package deal.

The dealer absolutely, positively did not want to hire a woman for a sales position, but he figured that was the only way to attract Gerry. He strongly believed that no woman could be successful at selling automobiles. At the time, most automobile salesmen were hired on a contingency basis. They were usually given ninety days to prove their worth by selling a certain number of vehicles. Beverly was not afforded the same grace period.

She was told that if she did not make at least one sale within two weeks, she would be fired. The dealer reasoned that Beverly would never even come close to making a sale within that period, so she'd be gone in two short weeks.

The dealer soon found out that his plan had a big hole in it. He'd grossly underestimated Beverly's tenacity and her extraordinary potential as a sales professional.

On the first day out [on the job], I will never forget it. It was March 15. It was a Saturday. I sold four cars. My manager thought I would be history in just two weeks, but I surprised him!

Yes, Beverly sold four cars in one day, and without product or sales training. Before she'd ever set foot in the showroom, she did a lot of homework. She read every product and options manual and every credit program for every model and form of credit deal offered.

I slept with the literature. I took it to bed with me. I wanted to be prepared.

Beverly was well prepared from day one, and she was a natural in this field. The product knowledge she acquired gave her a stronger sense of confidence. It is often said that knowledge is power, so Beverly had a lot of power from the first day on the job. She could answer any question about any product or credit package.

Her sense of power and confidence paid off immediately. Here's what happened with the very first prospective customer she greeted outside the showroom on the first day of her sales career.

Early Saturday morning . . . I was walking the lot, studying the inventory . . . before the store opened up. . . . It impresses customers if you have your inventory memorized.

I saw this fellow kicking tires . . . found out later that he was just killing time. His wife was across the street getting her hair done, so he thought that he would just walk around and look over our inventory. . . . [He'd] had no intention of buying a car when he woke up that day.

When I first spoke with him he looked a bit shocked that he was talking to a woman. But I sold him . . . he was my first customer. I sold . . . three more the same day. I remember what he said. He asked, "Are you going to sell me a car?" I said, "I'm going to give it one hell of a college try!"

Then he said, "I always have said that I would rather get screwed by a woman than by a man any day."

After that, I said to myself, "Welcome to the car world, Beverly."

That type of language never stopped Beverly from establishing herself as a top-producing sales professional in the automobile industry.

I never let it get to me. Even in cases when my colleagues would be standing there by me, telling off-color jokes. I just excused myself and walked away.

I often told them, even in sales meetings, "I'm a woman coming into a man's world. I'm not here to change you. I'm here to work . . . produce." Anyway, I'm more interested in talking to my customers . . . I never sold a car to a car salesman!

From day one, I never let it bother me . . . interfere with doing my job. I became the top salesperson [at the dealership] within fifteen days of first starting out. . . . I sold eighteen cars in just fifteen days.

Ever since those first eighteen sales, Beverly has been among America's top-producing sales professionals. The walls in her office are covered with awards and plaques detailing and praising her achievements. During her most productive year, she sold 369 automobiles, and the luxury automobile manufacturer she represented at that time named her "sales professional of the nation."

Beverly has sold more than seven thousand automobiles during her stellar career. That translates into more than $100 million in sales.

Today Beverly receives a lot of recognition, and in many ways, the accolades are much more important to her than "the numbers."

When my manager acknowledges my work it gives me much pride. . . . Recognition . . . it's all about being given credit for your accomplishments and hard work.

Just the other day at our sales meeting, my manager said [to the entire sales force]: "See this hundred-dollar bill? I will give it to the first person that brings me a picture of Beverly holding up the building [standing outside with one hand on the wall, wasting time]. But you know I am never going to give away my hundred-dollar bill . . . you will never catch her holding up the building."

Statements like this one are very important to Beverly. She has come a long way from being turned down by dealers who refused to hire her for a sales position.

THE PROACTIVE BEVERLY:
SELF-ESTEEM, SATISFACTION, AND EMPATHY

How satisfied is Beverly with her career and her life in general? She is at the very top of both the job and the life satisfaction scales. Beverly is a woman with a great deal of pride, self-respect, and self-esteem.

> High self-esteem . . . begins with setting goals and then exceeding them. . . . It begins by being able to do things for yourself, even as a child . . . as a child making your own spending money. If I did not make my own spending money, I could not do things. My folks were of very modest means.

Beverly has been making money since she was eleven years old, when she came up with a novel idea. She started a grass-cutting contracting business. Beverly had no interest in mowing lawns herself, but she realized there was much demand for this service. Beverly did not own a lawn mower or even a gasoline can; however, she knew a lot of boys in the area who had access to their parents' mowers. She reasoned that she could earn a lot of spending money by representing boys with lawn mowers, and she did just that. She took the initiative of knocking on doors and selling her services.

> I contracted to cut lawns. I was smart enough, even then. I would contract a job for ten dollars, then I would hire some boys to push the lawn mower. . . . They got less than half. I did all the contracting and collecting of money.
> Remember, she who sells initiates the deals. The rainmaker gets most of the spoils. . . . Initiative, you have to take the initiative. I just kept knocking on doors. Did the same thing when I sold yearbook ads for my high school. I outsold all the other four [students] combined. But I knocked down most of the doors to do it!

So what if Beverly did not even own any lawn-mowing equipment? She did something more important—she "cut the deals." For Beverly, it's always been brains, not brawn or equipment, that translates into success.

Beverly's parents did encourage her to earn her own spending money, and they often praised her for doing so. But they also encouraged Beverly to be creative in her pursuit of spending money. Her mother was especially impressed with Beverly's ability to leverage the needs of other youngsters.

I did the same thing with babysitting . . . contracted on behalf of girls that wanted to earn spending money. . . . I'd sell, they would sit.

Even at age eleven Beverly took great pride in being able to earn an abundance of spending money, and it's no different today. Beverly is the initiator, the rainmaker, and the proactive sales professional. She likes herself. She loves her job and has considerable satisfaction with her life in general. She also has high self-esteem because she is in control of her life and her career.

How can someone who sells automobiles for a living be so very proud? After all, some people who sell automobiles don't have the same high regard for themselves, or for their colleagues. Beverly understands this full well.

Who is the most distrusted person in the world? A car salesman.

But she is not the typical seller of motor vehicles. She is one of the most productive sales professionals in the industry. How else does she sell between 250 and 275 motor vehicles per year? How else has she sold more than $100 million worth of "iron" during her extraordinary career? She has always worked hard at her craft, but the source of her high sales volume gives her insight into her formula for success. Today, most of her sales come from repeat customers and referrals.

Customers continue to purchase car after car from Beverly, and they go out of their way to make referrals on her behalf. In part, it's because Beverly provides them with added value beyond the core product, but even more important, they respect her. Why else would many of her customers send their sons, daughters, even grandsons and granddaughters "down to see Beverly" when they need to purchase a motor vehicle?

I always call my customers after delivery to make sure there were no problems. Then my last question is . . . "Do you know anyone who might be interested in buying a car?" . . . It's how I built my business . . . from satisfied customers.

Beverly has been especially successful in selling to business owners and high-performing professionals. Often this type of customer is very pressed for time. It's one reason they often postpone purchasing a new motor vehicle. Given the demands of their careers, they don't allocate time to shop for a new car.

Just like this morning, we delivered a car over to the next county to one of my customers. I started selling to this company [the owners] when they had five employees . . . now they are ready to go public. He called me, told me what he wanted, what he had to trade. . . . We picked up the trade, appraised it. Later, we dropped his off [the new car]. The entire deal was done by phone. The customer never had to leave his office.

People like the business owner in this case recognize the benefits of dealing with Beverly, and they often tell their colleagues about her special way of serving her customers' needs.

Beverly's employer recently moved his dealership to a brand-new facility. Since Beverly was the top producer among more than thirty full-time sales professionals, she was given first choice of an office. Most sales professionals in the automobile business prefer to have their offices located near the front door of the showroom, which gives them a better chance to be the first to greet incoming prospective customers. Here, again, Beverly is different.

I did not want my new office near the front door. I wanted it near the switchboard . . . our receptionist. . . . I do it by phone . . . they call me, I call them.

Beverly keeps in contact with her active customer base of more than twenty-five hundred customers.

Selling . . . you have to do it on the phone. I will call. They say I will be ready [to buy] in two months . . . I note it on my calendar. I call back in two months. Too many sales managers say you have to get them [prospective customers] into the store. Not me . . . it's not how I do business.

Good service, including "buy by phone . . . deliver to home or business," is not the only reason that Beverly excels at her craft. Over the years, Beverly's sales managers have always been very liberal in honoring her requests to sell automobiles the best way she sees fit.

Plus, I have enough [power] here to sell cars at a price that I decide upon. I don't run back and forth to a manager to get a better deal for the customer. It's my decision. I will go to bat for a customer to get more for their trade-in . . . and they [the managers] work with me because I have earned their respect.

The managers have to be nice to Beverly. They fully recognize the importance of being conciliatory. After all,

I'm making them a good living.

Beverly has always had leverage in dealing with her employers. Her active customer base of over twenty-five hundred patrons gives them twenty-five hundred reasons why they have to be nice to her. If Beverly moved to another dealership, most of her customers would follow her.

Too many salespeople forget that it's the customer who makes them what they are today . . . it's the customers. . . . Always respect them. Always treat them right. Appreciate them. All of them.

One of the ways Beverly wins much repeat business relates to her philosophy about pricing. She never views a prospect as someone who will buy only one time from her. She looks at the potential of multiple purchases over time and the power of positive referrals.

I make my money . . . commissions . . . on volume. I do not ever do it on one or two people. The problem with a lot of salespeople is that they want to make a killing on each sale . . . it's a problem. When they [the customer] go to trade [the car] in, what happens? They lose a customer because they get so little back on the car that they paid too much for in the first place.

Beverly's frugal lifestyle has something to do with her philosophy of pricing. She has no outstanding debts, and she drives an inexpensive motor vehicle and lives in a modest home. Thus, she never feels financial pressure to maximize the selling price of an automobile and increase her commission.

Beverly worked very hard at developing her customer base. Over the years, it did become easier to generate more and more business from referrals, but the key is Beverly's method of proactively prospecting for new customers. In a way, she is always searching:

> *When I go to a movie on Saturday night, I take my cards and put them all over my demo. . . . [I] park where lots of people would likely walk by . . . get there early so I can park where people will have to pass by . . . the intercept point.*
>
> *When I would come back every one of those cards would be gone. I'd say, "Somebody's been looking at my sharp demo." I sell a lot of cars this way. I do the same thing when I go to dinner or get my hair done. Never without a card, never without a sharp demo . . . still do it today.*

Most retailers, including auto dealers, dislike rainy days—foul weather cuts down the volume of prospective buyers that will be visiting the showroom. Beverly never relies much on showroom traffic, and she looks at rainy days, especially several rainy days in succession, as an opportunity. She knows there are always people out there who have the desire and financial means to purchase automobiles, no matter what the weather may be.

> *On the rainy days I call private businesses . . . any place with a switchboard . . . [and] ask the switchboard operator or the secretary, "Does the owner, senior partner, not have time to shop for cars . . . but might need a car? . . . Would you ask?" . . . [You] can do it by phone. The next thing you know, the guy [prospect] is calling me back. A good secretary knows when the bosses are in the market for a car.*
>
> *You can't believe how many cars I sold this way . . . to people who don't even have enough time to come in and sign papers. Law firms are great places to prospect this way. It is nothing but human psychology!*

270

For some people, giving to noble causes is an important part of their human psychology, their personality, and Beverly also capitalized on this need. She was trained by her mom to be sensitive to the needs of important causes, and among the many causes she has supported over the years are churches. Beverly has been a generous contributor to her own church, but she has also helped many other churches as well.

> The other day a rookie salesman asked me for advice about selling. All he needs to do is think about the needs of others. I just told him about how I write letters. Sit down, write your letter to the churches. Tell the minister that anyone . . . church members, who buys a car from you . . . you're going to make a donation to his church.
>
> And I told this young salesman, who's an African-American, "The black churches are the ones you should contact first . . . members are very much inclined to support their churches. . . . Great people . . . want to donate. I know firsthand. Sold a lot of cars to church members. Members of all kinds of churches, white, black, Baptist, Catholic . . . all have a need to raise money."

Beverly has developed many symbiotic relationships with churches and their ministers, who help her sell cars to their members. Many have purchased their own cars from Beverly, and why not? She does more than just raise money for their respective churches.

> I sell to all the clergy at cost. No commission. I never want to make money on them.
>
> A manager once said, "You could have held back five hundred dollars on that trade you made with that minister." I said, "Not me, I'm not messing with God or any of His representatives."

Beverly also advertises, but not in the typical commercial media.

> I buy ads in everything the churches print!

According to Beverly, success in selling is a complement to doing good deeds, not a substitute. If more people who sell for a living understood this, there would be many more Beverly types in the world of marketing.

BEVERLY'S THOUGHTS ABOUT "ORDER TAKERS"

Beverly believes that there are two types of people in the vocation called selling. There are order takers, and there are sales professionals. Order takers do just that; they wait for a prospective customer to walk into the showroom. Then, if the prospective customer is willing, ready, and able to buy, a sale might be made. The order taking in such cases has little or nothing to do with the prospect's showing up at the dealership. The dealer's location, advertising, and product offerings were key. The order taker by definition is reactive and responds when the prospective customer taps him or her on the shoulder.

Beverly has a different perspective about selling. She is a true sales professional. Sales professionals, according to Beverly's definition, go out and find prospective buyers. They earn their commission. They are proactive. They make things happen.

When Beverly works, she works. If she is not talking to a prospective buyer, she is searching for one. In her many years of selling, Beverly has developed a very good grasp of what separates sales professionals from order takers. She uses her own work habits to illustrate her point.

The biggest difference between the way I sell and most of the others . . . [is] I work every minute I am in my office.

Go by a car dealer on a Saturday morning in America. . . . All the guys . . . the order takers, are standing around talking to one another.

I spend my time even before the dealer opens talking [by phone] to customers . . . prospecting for customers.

Beverly's business is never flat, even when the order takers think the sky is falling. Her sales volume is never really low because she is always busy. She has a large base of loyal customers, and she is also constantly calling, writing, and conducting other forms of prospecting.

That's the time to turn up the fire . . . calling more prospects . . . finding out when they might purchase a car. . . . I'm always working . . . I never look at the clock . . . I put in the hours. . . . If I'm not selling, I'm always prospecting.

Most car salespeople work bankers' hours.

BEVERLY SPEAKS OUT ABOUT MOTIVES

Beverly is analytical and very intelligent, and sees many things that others do not. Take, for example, her hypothesis about sales professionals. Beverly told me that most high-income-producing sales professionals are underaccumulators of wealth. In her mind, they spend for "big hats" but have little or "no cattle"! In other words, these sales professionals are on the earning-and-spending treadmill. They earn to spend, not to save. Often they feel compelled to be very aggressive—most too aggressive—in selling just to pay their creditors. No wonder many have few, if any, repeat customers.

Where are such sales professionals positioned on the "job satisfaction" scale? According to Beverly, many are not happy. They view work as an unpleasant task—a requirement to pay for their excessive spending habits. The problem that often crops up is that their dissatisfaction with their job is telling. Beverly believes these discontented sales professionals give themselves away by overselling. They try to shove the product down the throats of prospective customers, compelled to do so because they have considerable debt to pay off.

Beverly has observed this type of behavior among many sales professionals for nearly thirty years. Yet she believes that none of those in the hyperconsumption group has ever been able to enhance his/her job satisfaction by spending. And if they have low job satisfaction, they have less than high satisfaction with life overall.

Just how accurate are Beverly's hypotheses? According to my empirical studies of sales professionals, her perceptions are quite valid. I have consistently found in my national surveys that sales professionals are at or near the bottom of the wealth-accumulation scale. In other words, within each income and age cohort, those involved in selling are significantly more likely to be found in the Income Statement Affluent category than nearly any other occupational group. As mentioned previously, those in this category have less than one-half the net worth that is expected statistically from those in the same income or age cohort. Sales professionals are among the least likely to be found in the Balance Sheet Affluent category, among those who have a minimum of twice the net worth that is expected from those within the same income and age group.

BEVERLY ON SELF-RESPECT AND COURAGE

How is it possible that Beverly has very high self-esteem and pride? She herself mentioned that overall, those involved in selling automobiles are viewed by the public as having "the worst image . . . second only to lawyers." You wouldn't have much self-esteem if the public viewed those in your profession in that light, but Beverly has a strong and positive self-image.

Beverly is not the prototypical automobile sales professional. Thousands of her customers will tell you they have great respect and admiration for her. You have learned that Beverly is well respected by her customers, that she consistently outperforms the vast majority of her competition, and that she has such high job satisfaction, self-respect, and confidence. But why does someone who earns so much spend so little on herself? In order to answer this and related questions, it is important to profile Beverly and her philosophy about how to succeed, her job description, her place on earth, and her life in general.

Beverly has always been a strong-willed, very determined person. Her mother was her role model in this regard.

My mother was the kindest, most unselfish person I ever met. But she would never take any disrespect from anyone. I adored my mother. I was very close to my mom.

As you have already learned, Beverly is also a very kind person, and she is also like her mother when it comes to demanding respect. Beverly never allows anyone to get away with showing her disrespect. It doesn't matter how big or powerful the person, Beverly will not tolerate disrespect. A senior marketing executive of a luxury car company found this out the hard way. At the time, Beverly was the number two top-producing sales professional for the luxury car manufacturer.

I won an award, a trip to Mexico. It was a recognition trip for the top five sales professionals.

We were all in the bar having cocktails. I was talking to Brian, the number one fellow. Then the senior vice president of sales for America came over to congratulate Brian for being number one. He said to Brian, "I know you're the number one guy, but who's the number two guy?"

How insensitive of the senior executive to overlook Beverly. Had he not been following the sales data associated with Beverly? Beverly quickly sensitized him.

I looked at him and said, "Wrong, it's not a guy, it's me, it's Beverly." But then he yelled out, "Let's initiate our first lady to the million-dollar club . . . let's have her buy drinks for everyone [about twenty-five folks]. She might not be here next year." I said, "You know what? I will be number one at next year's recognition trip." He was incredulous. So I bet him a hundred dollars that I would be top ranked next year. He accepted my offer.

Apparently, this fellow thought that he could humiliate Beverly, that she would back down in front of twenty-five people and not agree to pay for all those drinks. Again he misjudged her. Beverly responded instantly to the fellow's proposal.

I called the waiter over and said, "Take all their orders and charge it to my room."

Hearing this response, the senior vice president of sales began to realize that he was messing with a smiling tiger. So he tried in vain to smooth things over, but once again, he demonstrated a lack of empathy for Beverly's needs and ego.

He said, "Look, honey, if you can't afford this, we will help you pay for it."

How did Beverly interpret this statement? He thought she would never again be able to replicate her high volume of sales.

I looked at him and said, "Let me explain something to you. I'm here because I worked hard selling. . . . I make lots of money. . . . You are here because I'm here. You are a host from Detroit. I will take care of this bar bill. I will be back next year as number one!" He said sarcastically, "Yeah . . . right! A hundred dollars says you won't be back."

Who won the bet? Yes, it was Beverly the Gal, Beverly the Tenacious, Beverly the Bold, Beverly the Courageous, Beverly, Demander of Respect. The next year Beverly sold 369 luxury motor vehicles.

> *Just prior to the official announcements of awards, I received a letter from him . . . congratulating me. . . . It also contained a hundred-dollar bill!*

Beverly understands the power of being productive. If you have an outstanding sales record, you can tell all those who disrespect you when to jump and how high!

COFFEE BREAKS

Early in her career, Beverly changed employers. She worked for a sales manager who was a self-described male chauvinist, but Beverly did an effective job of challenging his orientation. The owner of the dealership had hired Beverly over his objections, and he did not like the idea that his boss had forced a saleswoman on him. Shortly after she was hired, the sales manager told her, "Women can't do anything!" Even worse, he tried to get Beverly to act as his "gofer."

> *I'd walk by his office and just to bug me he would say, "Beverly, could you bring me a cup of coffee?"*

How many cups of coffee did Beverly go for? Zero. No matter how many times the sales manager asked, Beverly's reply was always the same.

> *I would say, "Mr. Carol, I don't have the time. Sorry! You want me to do coffee or sell cars . . . your choice. I was not hired to serve coffee."*

Mr. Carol eventually took note of the large number of cars Beverly, the sales professional, was moving off the lot. Beverly took great pride whenever he praised her outstanding productivity, but she noted that it always seemed to be very painful for Mr. Carol to tell his audience of sales professionals about the performance of his top producer.

What does Beverly tell young women who seek her advice about a career in sales?

Work hard . . . become a top producer. Then you will never have to serve coffee! You have to earn their respect. Sell but don't become a sales manager. They wanted to make me a manager. I said, "What, me be dependent on male sales professionals for a living?" . . . Excuse me, this is funny. Oh, I would starve to death.

Sell. Then they will never mess with you. Forget about what the supposed rules are for women . . . do your own thing. Go out and find your own customers.

Beverly followed her own sage advice. That's why she is very successful as well as being a proud and satisfied woman.

Respect yourself and others. Have a positive attitude. Believe in yourself. Have faith. Never let anyone tell you that you can't do a job. You can do anything you set your mind to do. And know that the work does not owe you a living. Have this and good work habits and success will follow. But always remember to give something back . . . help others. Be generous.

Beverly loves her job, and it shows. Prospective customers are good at reading the character of salespeople they patronize. Anyone who talks to Beverly for five minutes will be very impressed by her product knowledge, positive attitude, and candor.

I love my job . . . I bounce out of bed every morning. I can't wait to get to work. I'm at work by 8:00 A.M. The store opens officially at 9:00 A.M.

Beverly also suggests that salespeople should give more of their time and money to noble causes. As mentioned earlier, Beverly donates 30 percent or more of her income each year, and it was her parents who taught her to do so. Her charitable orientation has also helped her to become a top sales professional. She was trained from her early childhood to have a lot of empathy for the needs of others, and that empathy helped Beverly relate well to others, including her customers.

*It's more than money . . . it's my job. I enjoy what I do. I get
great satisfaction. Doing for people makes me happy. Not only
for customers, but also for those in need.*

Today Beverly gives much of her earnings to noble causes, but what
about tomorrow? Beverly's estate plan mentions her intention to donate
substantial contributions to her favorite causes. Why does Beverly give
so much?

*You will never see a money truck following a hearse down the
street! Never! Those people who think money makes happiness . . .
wrong! They never give, never donate. They don't get it.*

*I am amazed that some will spend hundreds of dollars
drinking all night at a nudie bar. Never give a dollar . . . not a
single dollar to help someone in need. I'll bet they don't like
their jobs. Have to mask the pain with self-indulgence, alcohol,
or worse!*

Beverly works hard for more than the income per se, and it's even
more than having the means to help others.

*I made two promises to myself when I was young. First, I
would not have to eat potato soup again, because I ate a lot of
it growing up . . . because I came from a poor family. . . . [It
was also a] loving family . . . the cleanest house . . . we did not
have a lot of material things.*

*Secondly, I will have my independence. I will have it no
matter what and how much work it takes. No matter what I
have to do. Someday I will be able to give my mom anything
she asks for . . . which I did. My first big paycheck I bought her
a diamond watch. She always wanted a diamond watch. She
was so happy. She always worked hard for me. She came up so
poor . . . made so many sacrifices for us.*

Automobile sales gave Beverly the path to fulfill her goals. She only
asked to be paid for her objective performance, and commission sales
gave her that opportunity. She has an uncanny ability to leverage her
position as a top producer for noble ends.

A married couple with very modest means . . . three of their own kids, then they adopted four kids . . . all with Down's syndrome. I always help out . . . give all the kids Christmas gifts.

The family had this old van, fifteen years old, falling apart. So I kept on the lookout for a later-model used van for them. I was determined I was going to get them a good van.

We had this really, really nice van come in on a trade. I went to my manager and told him that we needed to sell the van to the family at our cost without any commissions and we did.

Months later, a mechanical problem [beyond the thirty-day warranty deadline] came up. It was going to cost $1,800 to fix the van. I went to the general manager and our bean counter [accountant] and said, "We need to fix this, and we need to swallow it [no charge to the family for the repairs]." They said okay, called the service manager, and he had it repaired at no charge.

They are still driving that van . . . a wonderful family. They have nothing but love and faith. But they are happy, very, very happy with life.

According to Beverly, success in selling is a complement to doing good deeds, not a substitute. If more people who sell for a living understood this relationship, there would be many more Beverly types in the world.

CHAPTER 16

Wealthy Educators?

*S*o you say that you have no interest in owning your own business and you are not cut out to be a sales professional, but you still want to become financially independent. Is there any hope for you ever becoming a millionaire in America?

Do not worry. You can still become wealthy by selecting another occupation. You do not have to earn hundreds of thousands of dollars annually in order to become rich. You can make much less yet still join the multimillionaire club.

One such occupation does not usually pay six-figure salaries. Yet, many of those within its domain become wealthy. Try a career in teaching. Become an educator. You shout out loud, "But teachers are never rich!" A client of mine once said it best when describing those who are rich and those who are not supposed to be rich.

> *These people cannot be millionaires! They don't look like millionaires, they don't dress like millionaires, they don't eat like millionaires, they don't act like millionaires—they don't even have millionaire names. Where are the millionaires who look like millionaires?*

Guess what? If you look like, dress like, and drive like you have money to burn, it is unlikely that you are wealthy. Most wealthy educators shun the indulgent lifestyle associated with the Income Statement Affluent.

Many people believe that educators do not have the money or income needed to spend lavishly upon themselves or become rich. Income is a correlate of wealth, but it is not wealth. While it is true that most teachers do not earn six-figure annual incomes, annual income is nowhere near a perfect predictor of wealth. In many ways, it is not how much one earns annually that counts; it is how one lives each year. It is how much one saves and invests annually that really matters. Accumulating wealth is a long-distance marathon! It takes years and years of frugality and wise investing to accumulate wealth. If you do not earn a six- or seven-figure income today, you can still become wealthy tomorrow if you are financially disciplined and strongly motivated. And many educators possess these very characteristics.

What proof is there that educators have a proclivity to accumulate wealth? First, consider the following statement as anecdotal evidence. It is followed by the rock-solid empirical data.

> *My mother is a classic PAW [Prodigious Accumulator of Wealth, or Balance Sheet Affluent] . . . never made much money (college professor—you should know about that—at a small women's college). But [she] always saved religiously, and is going to retire a multimillionaire (if she ever retires). Even now that she has the money, she refuses to spend it. Typical example is the Miata. She lusted after one for ten years, but refused to buy such a frivolous car. All of that angst, over a $20,000 car, in a world of $50,000 SUVs! She finally gave in and got one six months ago—but only because she found a great deal on a used one.*
> *Sincerely,*
> *Laura M.*

Laura's mom, the underpaid professor at the small college, is actually a multimillionaire. Is she just a rare occurrence within the world of the wealthy? The average annual salary of a full-time college faculty member in the year 2000 was only $57,700 for those employed by public colleges or universities, versus $66,300 for those working in private institutions. In 1995, the average was only $49,100 for public and $55,600 for private institutions. Full professors earned more—$62,000 at public and $73,200 at private institutions. By 2000, the average had increased for full professors. They earned $74,400 at public and $88,400 at private institutions.

Many elementary and secondary educators are also prone to accumulate wealth. Yet they are not in the high-income brackets. The average salary for those who teach in secondary schools was only $41,200 in 2000. Elementary school teachers received $40,300 on average, and the overall average for all teachers was $41,700. However, teachers' salaries have increased over the years. Note that in 1970 the overall average annual salary was only $8,600; it was $16,000 in 1980; $31,400 in 1990; and $36,700 in 1995. This discussion of current and past income statistics for educators is significant in order to appreciate the fact that income is not the only significant correlate of wealth.

There is also another form of compelling data that can assist in illustrating that fact: the estate data of recently deceased Americans from our very own Internal Revenue Service. Its data profiled those decedents who had a gross estate of at least $625,000. Fewer than one in twenty (4.5 percent), or only 103,983 of the 2,337,000 people who passed away during 1998, had an estate in that category.

About one in five (20.6 percent) of the wealthy female decedents were once educators. Given the proportion of the female working population, only about 7.4 percent is the expected concentration. In other words, educators are overrepresented by a multiple of nearly 2.8 times the expectation given their overall representation in the female working population.

Male educators were also found to be overrepresented within the wealthy decedent population by a multiple of nearly 1.5 times the expected proportion.

Women decedents with sizable estates were on average older than their male counterparts (81.4 years versus 76.6 years). Given these age statistics, it is likely that many of the educators retired ten, fifteen, even twenty years before they died. Remember how modest the average salaries were for educators. Obviously something other than income accounts for the presence of so many educators among decedents with sizable estates.

Why is it that such a high proportion of the wealthy population is educators? They are not perceived as a high-income-producing group, but income is only one factor that explains the wealth accumulation. Teachers tend to be a frugal group. They are savers and investors more than they are spenders. In fact, it is considered bad taste among most educators to overdress or to overspend on cars, homes, or so-called appearance-enhancing products and services.

Look at the high-income-producing (those with annual household incomes in excess of $100,000) population of two-career couples where at least one partner is an educator. Contrast them with those in the so-called high-income-producing group that includes doctors, attorneys, and senior corporate executives. Who is the least likely to have no consumer debt other than a mortgage balance? Nearly 70 percent of the educator group has zero consumer debt. Fewer than half of those in the high-income occupational categories can say the same.

Most educators work in an environment with certain characteristics that are, in fact, correlates of wealth accumulation. Pension planning, investment seminars, and tax-advantage supplemental investment plans are part of an educator's "on campus" socialization process. Adopting a frugal consumption lifestyle and developing good financial and investing skills are all akin to catching a cold. What happens when you consistently come into contact with sick people? You get sick. Work with frugal people, and you may become frugal. Associate with colleagues who are astute investors, and you may become wealthy one day. Many educators become good investors because their jobs require them to research, study, and learn new material on a continuous basis. These processes are easily applied to making investment decisions.

WEALTH AND NOBLE DEEDS

Educators have a higher than normal propensity to accumulate wealth than others in their income and age cohort. They also tend to donate more of their money to noble causes. Perhaps charitable giving is stimulated within the school or college environment. *Noble deeds, charitable giving, fund-raising drives, the needs of others less fortunate, support of eleemosynary organizations,* and *dollars for scholarships* are commonly heard phrases among those who work on campuses.

The data clearly show that educators as a group are a charitable segment of our society. They give a greater percentage of their income to noble causes than the norm for our nation's adult working population. Educators are also significantly more likely to indicate that they intend to give even more of their money in the future. The data on decedents with sizable estates suggest that such intentions often do, in fact, bear fruit for various noble causes.

The average American household donates just over 2 percent of its annual realized income. On an annual basis, educators donate more: 3.69 percent (see Table 16-1). How does the eleemosynary behavior of educators compare with that of the so-called status professions—attorneys, corporate executives, physicians, and such? Once again, on average, educators rank first, while physicians rank eighth. As a percentage of income, physicians donate, on average, the equivalent of only 70 percent of what educators donate.

Why do many of those in status positions donate less than educators? They tend to be income rich and net worth poor. In other words, many

TABLE 16-1

CONTRASTS IN THE PROPENSITY TO GIVE TO NOBLE CAUSES: EDUCATORS VS. HIGH-INCOME-PRODUCING OCCUPATIONAL GROUPS

Occupational Group	Average percent of annual income donated	% given/% given by educators	Rank by % given
Educator	3.69[1]	—	1
Entrepreneur	3.36	91[3]	2
Attorney	3.28	89	3
Senior Corporate Executive	3.26	88	4
Sales/Marketing/Advertising Professional	3.11	84	5
Engineer/Architect/Scientist	2.73	74	6
Corporate Director/Middle Manager	2.71	73	7
Physician	2.59	70	8
All Households	2.01[2]	55	—

[1] For example, educators on average donate 3.69% of their households' total annual realized income to noble causes.
[2] Computed from federal individual income tax returns for 1998.
[3] For example, households headed by entrepreneurs on average donate 3.36% of their total annual realized income. That is 91% of the portion given by educators. The educator group contained more than twice the proportion of female respondents than did the entrepreneur category. Generally, females give a significantly higher proportion of their income to noble causes than do males. What if gender differences were adjusted for within the context of educators versus entrepreneurs? Then these two occupational categories would be in a statistical dead heat for first position in terms of payments to noble causes.

are in the Income Statement Affluent category. Society dictates that they must display artifacts of the successful, well-compensated professional, and many young professionals are socialized by their more mature colleagues in the art of "looking the part." Educators, however, are not expected to spend as much for their homes, clothes, or automobiles.

There is an interesting piece of evidence that supports this conclusion. About one in five of those professionals listed in Table 16-1 receives annual cash gifts from their parents or grandparents. The same holds true for educators.

How do they differ? The majority of those who receive cash gifts have significantly lower levels of wealth than those who do not receive "economic outpatient care." This is the case even when age and income variations are taken into account. Overall, those who receive economic outpatient care have only 80 percent of the net worth of those who receive nothing, but there is an exception to this rule. Educators who receive cash gifts actually have significantly higher levels of wealth than those who do not because they tend to invest these economic supplements. For many in the status professions who receive economic outpatient care, the effect is just the opposite. Such gifts actually precipitate additional spending and borrowing. Educators who receive economic supplements have on average a net worth that is more than one and a half times greater than those educators who do not receive these economic gifts.

ADDENDUM TO PROFILING
THOSE WITH SIZABLE ESTATES

HEADLINE: EVEN AFTER, WOMEN ARE MORE CHARITABLE

- Females accounted for 46.6 percent of those 1998 decedents who had sizable estates. The average size of their estates was $1.7 million, with a median value just below $1.0 million. Male decedents in this category had a somewhat higher average estate value, exceeding $2.0 million, and a higher median value, nearly $1.1 million.
- Of those 103,983 decedents with sizable estates, what percentage had an estate plan that specified that a bequest be made to charity? Only 17,587, or 16.9 percent, provided such a bequest.

- A larger percent of female decedents (21.0 percent) than male decedents (13.4 percent) earmarked charitable bequests to be distributed from their estates.
- Of those female decedents who made charitable bequests, such donations accounted for 29.2 of the total gross value of their estates; for males, the percentage was 28.2.
- The average net worth of a wealthy female decedent who made a charitable bequest was $2,603,260, versus $3,419,456 for her male counterpart.
- The average charitable bequest made by those 10,175 wealthy female decedents was $762,155, or about 29.3 percent of their net worth.
- The average charitable bequest made by those 7,412 wealthy male decedents who did so was $973,907, or about 28.5 percent of their net worth.

What recipient category received the largest proportion of dollars bequeathed by these wealthy female decedents? The educational, medical, and scientific category ranks first. About one in three (34.0 percent) of those dollars was so earmarked. Private foundations (including their own) was the category that ranked first among the wealthy male decedent population. More than one-half (55 percent) was so earmarked by these wealthy male decedents.

BIG HEART, SMALL HOME: PROFESSOR WERTBERG'S TRIBUTE TO HIS LATE WIFE; OR, WHAT CAN HAPPEN WHEN A HOUSEHOLD CONTAINS TWO GENEROUS EDUCATORS?

She never owned a Mercedes, a BMW, or even a Lincoln. Nor did she own a Rolex watch. What, no Jacuzzi? No country club membership? No Marmot jacket? No, never a single pedicure, not even once. Not even a facial. No, not her. Not a platinum card, no granite countertops, no tanning bed. Never hired a nanny. Never a face-lift or a lip enlargement, no breast augmentation, never set foot in Palm Springs or a Ritz or Four Seasons. Never owned a fur or a home theater. Never owned even a stick of designer furniture; never hired an interior decorator.

Never purchased even one silk wrap. Never had a private banker. But she and her husband had a net worth of nearly $6 million. She loved to sew, read, write, and garden, and she loved to support her favorite noble causes.

Just who is, or was, this woman? She was an outstanding and distinguished professor for most of her adult life. She was admired by her colleagues and her students; she had a close and loving family. She loved her job teaching, researching, and publishing her research. According to her husband, Professor Wertberg, she was in love with life and everyone close to her. Until her untimely death, Mrs. Wertberg always had a smile on her face.

VISITING WITH PROFESSOR WERTBERG

Sometime in the not so distant future, a new type of show may be broadcast on viewer-sponsored television. It will likely be given the title of *The Generous Millionaire Next Door*. The slogan will aptly be something along the lines of "And you think you're frugal." Guests on the show will all be self-made millionaires. Equally important, each will have a low profile. Each will have a history of giving generously to noble causes. The first person that I will invite on the show will not be a woman, but he will pay tribute to his late wife for her generosity in supporting noble causes.

The host and her camera and sound crew take you the viewing audience up to the front door of his home. You note the clean, freshly painted porch. The host knocks on the door, but no one answers. Then a fellow wearing gardening clothes walks around from the right side of the home. He is Professor John Wertberg, the first guest on the very first airing of *The Generous Millionaire Next Door*. Professor Wertberg is holding a rake in one hand and a flowerpot in the other. He apologizes for not shaking hands since he has just been spraying fertilizer. The professor teaches agronomy and knows how to make things grow, and as the viewing audience is about to find out, Professor Wertberg and his wife had a great track record of making money grow as well.

The professor is accompanied by his accountant, Mrs. T. Miller. Mrs. Miller has all the figures printed out for the viewers to see. She has examined the pertinent documents to certify Professor Wertberg's financial position.

Now it's time for the whole entourage to move inside. You and the other viewers head inside Professor Wertberg's home. It's clean, it's neat, it's well kept. It is just like it was when Mrs. Wertberg lived there. But what would your interior decorator think? It's old, it's outdated, it's not at all chic, not fashionable, and certainly totally void of any Martha-approved artifacts. It's comfortable, but the kitchen has not been upgraded in thirty years. Neither has the bathroom or half bath.

You and your fellow viewers are in disbelief! How can this guy be a millionaire? But just then, the CPA lays it all out for the audience to examine. Professor Wertberg has a net worth of $5,813,671. This figure excludes the value of his home.

I know what you and some members of the audience are thinking. You might predict that Professor Wertberg is a tormented miser, a modern-day Scrooge, the penny pincher of penny pinchers. Perhaps he and his wife were so uptight about money that it pained them to throw away even a used tea bag. Or perhaps you think they inherited a lot of money from a rich relative. Some of you may think that Professor Wertberg runs his own highly profitable consulting business on the side, staffed with his graduate students, who earn the minimum wage. How else could this fellow and his wife have accumulated nearly $6 million?

But Professor Wertberg is not only wealthy, he is also a kind, generous patron of noble causes. He is much like his late wife. He is filled with life and love for his vocation and his family and extended family. Professor Wertberg turns out to be a very pleasant fellow, a warm and caring multimillionaire. To be a guest on this show, one must be more than wealthy. One must:

1. Be self-made affluent.
2. Have a frugal lifestyle.
3. Be very happy and satisfied with life.
4. Have very high job satisfaction.
5. Possess high self-esteem.
6. Have a loving, caring family.
7. Have given a significant portion of his or her income to noble causes.

For most of their lives, Professor Wertberg and his wife met all these criteria. Mrs. Wertberg's death certainly had some negative influence on the happiness scale, as well as on the family life criterion. Yet he still gets much satisfaction from life, as well as from his children and his extended family.

Professor Wertberg and his wife came from very humble backgrounds, but both were raised by loving parents. Their parents were generous although they were, in fact, a hair away from requesting public assistance. Or in the words of Dr. Wertberg:

[We were] driven to succeed by desperate poverty as children.

Both Professor Wertberg and his wife earned scholarships to college, and they attended graduate school together. Later they accepted teaching positions at a high-caliber college. Both loved and excelled in teaching and research. Both had many of their papers published and were quickly promoted through the academic hierarchy. Mrs. Wertberg was a particularly gifted scholar.

The couple set goals for themselves early in their marriage. Both wanted to succeed as academicians. They wanted to enjoy life and their vocations and to have pride and self-esteem. Both accomplished these goals. They also wanted to have children, to become financially independent, and to support their favorite causes. These goals in turn were also achieved.

How did this couple accumulate wealth and still make generous contributions? According to Mr. Wertberg, they were always frugal. Big homes, high-status neighborhoods, and expensive products never interested them. For them, pride and status were the result of being respected professors and research scholars. It was not at all difficult for them to live a low-consumption lifestyle. As a result, they were able to save and invest most of their income.

Professor Wertberg will tell his audience what he recently told me:

I had a wonderful wife . . . also a professor . . . very successful.

But Mrs. Wertberg was proficient in other arenas. She was even more frugal than her husband, and she had several money-saving hobbies.

She was a fine seamstress . . . had to be. . . . She was five feet tall . . . [with] very short arms. She was like your examples in The Millionaire Mind *. . . well-made clothes, but homemade clothes.*

Professor Wertberg will also recount numerous instances in which his wife demonstrated other forms of frugal behavior. He will mention to the audience that his wife never liked to spend money for repair services when "down-home" repairs would "make do."

Years ago . . . we bought our first clothes dryer. Later the latch broke . . . [but] the drum turned only when the door was closed. So she propped it shut during use with a two-by-four braced against a basement post. Used it that way for another ten years!

There will be many more components to Professor Wertberg's tribute. Mrs. Wertberg always enjoyed living in her modest home. To her, anything larger or more expensive would have been a gross waste of resources. Resources should be leveraged or used for important purposes, but never wasted. She felt comfortable residing in a neighborhood that was filled with her colleagues and other unpretentious people.

Professor Wertberg still lives in the same house that he and his wife shared for many years. Along these lines, he will likely tell the audience the same thing he told me:

Still live in a "cheap" home, $70,000. But one reason I will stay . . . what if someday I can no longer drive? [I am now] within four blocks of grocery stores, banks, the post office, hardware store, drugstores, and eating places . . . [and] two bus lines.

Yes, Professor Wertberg the multimillionaire still lives in a $70,000 home. He could easily afford to live at a much higher level on the consumption scale, but he rejects that notion. According to him:

A million-dollar house would isolate me out in the suburban boonies.

Also, large homes are more expensive and more difficult to maintain by the home owner.

I also . . . always repaired and painted my own home . . . these are my contemplation periods.

Often while Mrs. Wertberg sewed, her husband painted and made repairs to their home. These things were not done just to save money. The couple received much enjoyment from these simple, inexpensive, but productive activities.

The Wertbergs not only were frugal; they also saved and invested regularly and, apparently, wisely. Professor Wertberg was the senior "investment research partner"; his wife, the junior partner of their investment team. In other words, Professor Wertberg did the lion's share of the investment-related research.

I saved and invested . . . studied . . . like your bus driver [Mr. Benjamin].

Here Professor Wertberg refers to a case that I profiled in *The Millionaire Mind.*

MR. BENJAMIN

Mr. Benjamin paid all of his children's tuition. His daughter and sons all attended private elementary and high schools and prestigious private colleges, medical colleges, and graduate schools. Mr. Benjamin paid for all of it—room, board, tuition, books, and related expenses. Who is this man who demonstrated the ability to fund these enormous tuition bills—a highly paid physician or perhaps CEO of a major public corporation?

Before he retired, Mr. Benjamin was a school-bus driver, a school-bus driver who generated enough income to send his children to private colleges, medical school, and graduate school. He was frugal, but being frugal is not enough to pay for six-figure tuition bills.

When they were very young, Mr. Benjamin realized that his children were extremely bright. He realized that each would greatly benefit from a top-quality education, so he constantly worried about funding that education with his low-paying job. Consequently, Mr. Benjamin began a "self-improvement" reading program. The central topic of it was investing.

Being a bus driver had one side benefit. It gave Mr. Benjamin several hours of free time each day. His fellow drivers often used this time for snoozing, reading newspapers and magazines, drinking coffee, or chatting. Mr. Benjamin used his downtime more wisely. He read about various types of investments. Early in his self-study program, he discovered the truth about the long-run returns generated by corporate bonds, passbook savings accounts, treasury bills, municipal bonds, CDs, stocks, precious metals, and real estate.

Mr. Benjamin concluded that after adjusting for inflation and taxes, only stocks paid a real return on one's investment dollars. But his mother had always told him never to invest in the stock market. She was around during the stock market crash in 1929. But the 1929 downturn was included in Mr. Benjamin's calculations, and he knew that in spite of the crash, in the long run stocks outperformed all other investment alternatives.

Mr. Benjamin eventually became a serious investor in the stock market. Every extra dollar he and his wife could muster was earmarked for stocks, but not just any stocks. Mr. Benjamin spent much of his free time studying specific corporations and their stock offerings. Over the years, he became an expert in his chosen avocation.

The result of Mr. Benjamin's self-improvement reading and investing program was that when he recently retired, the former bus driver had a net worth in excess of $3 million. Remember, that is $3 million after sending his children to the finest, most expensive schools in America.

What is the point? Mr. Benjamin became financially independent because he had courage. It takes courage to invest in the stock market. The market guarantees nothing. It goes up and it goes down! Often, people get in the market late and get out early and they lose a lot of money. Mr. Benjamin was always a long-term investor. He never let fear outweigh the knowledge he obtained from his reading program. When Mr. Benjamin bought a stock, he rarely sold it within ten years of his initial investment. In good times and bad times, he held on to his picks. He frequently had some fears and concerns, but dealing with fear in a positive manner is a foundation stone of becoming wealthy in America.

It takes courage to invest in public corporations as well as in one's own business enterprise, but often it takes even more courage to hold on to one's investments when the public mood is full of fear and panic. Without courage Mr. Benjamin's children would not be doctors today. (Thomas J. Stanley, *The Millionaire Mind* [Kansas City: Andrews McMeel, 2000], pp. 136–37,139)

Professor Wertberg and his wife, like Mr. Benjamin, were always long-term investors. They bought the stocks of blue-chip companies and only sold them for "special purposes." They also took advantage of the IRS mandates by contributing the maximum allowable to their pension plans and 403(b) supplemental retirement annuities.

But their investment strategy was not at all unique. They avoided high-technology and high-risk stocks. Their system worked because they started investing early in their adult lives. They saved and invested on a regular basis, and they reinvested their dividends. The impact of more than thirty-five years of investing this way resulted in the Wertbergs becoming multimillionaires.

Now, whose case study, the Wertbergs' or Mr. Benjamin's, is more compelling? You might guess that it is Mr. Benjamin's, the bus driver with a net worth of more than $3 million. After all, bus drivers don't earn as much as professors. And he sent his kids to expensive schools, graduate colleges, and medical schools.

Before you make your selection, consider something else about the Wertbergs. While Mrs. Wertberg was alive, she was "the senior partner of philanthropic activities" for the family. She initiated a program of giving. Professor Wertberg was the junior partner of this team.

In addition to funding the educations of their own children, as did Mr. Benjamin, the couple also provided funding for other people's children. The Wertbergs eventually realized that they were well on the road to accumulating more than enough money to erase the memories of poverty that haunted them since childhood. After they exceeded their goals of becoming financially independent and educating their own children, led by Mrs. Wertberg, they decided to fund the college educations for worthy students who had much in common with them. All were outstanding students, but they had little or no money with which to pay for their college educations.

What began as one college scholarship then became two, then three simultaneously, and so on. Eventually, as it is today, ten students are currently recipients of the Wertbergs' generosity. Several of these scholarships cover all expenses—tuition, fees, room, and board. How much does the Wertberg Scholarship Fund distribute each year? The figure varies from year to year, but on average, it amounts to approximately $250,000. Look at it another way: for every one dollar of value for their home, the Wertberg Scholarship Fund distributes more than three dollars annually to others—specifically, a $70,000 home versus $250,000 in scholarships.

The Wertbergs never broadcasted these or related good deeds. That would be very much out of character for this couple. The reward was the satisfaction they received from seeing youngsters in need succeed. One has to wonder how many students who attended the lectures given by Mr. and Mrs. Wertberg criticized their homemade wardrobes. They snubbed the Wertbergs via the cloth, not the heart. Dr. Martin Luther King Jr. often said that people should be judged by their character and not by the color of their skin. Similarly, the Wertbergs and other people like them should be judged by their character and not by what they wear or the type of home they occupy.

After Mrs. Wertberg passed away, the scholarship fund took on an additional meaning for her husband. To him it's a wonderful way to keep her memory alive. In a way, she lives in the minds and spirits of all those worthy recipients of the Wertberg Scholarship. Professor Wertberg paid tribute to his wife in this context:

> At present ten . . . [have] college scholarships. . . . They provide the chief reason to keep going. . . . I miss her a lot. And I wear shirts she made for me . . . five winter wool shirts and five cotton summer shirts, and six knitted sweaters. I will mend them and wear them until the day I die.

CHAPTER 17

Why Not Run the Family Office?

JUDY O: What else do you do other than play tennis?

SUSAN J: Ah, the duties of a wife and mother. I run the family office.

JUDY O: I didn't know that your husband owned a family business.

SUSAN J: He doesn't.

JUDY O: So when you say you run the family office, does that mean that you are sort of a domestic engineer who pays the bills?

SUSAN J: It's a bit more involved than that, but you're on the right track.

*T*his discussion took place shortly after Judy and Susan met for the first time. At that time, Susan was captain of the tennis team that Judy had just joined. Judy had some resentment for Susan and all those women she referred to as "don't work outside the home types."

Ironically, up until five years ago, Judy had never worked, as she calls it, outside the home. But five years ago, Judy's husband of twenty years divorced her and married his paralegal, who was half his age.

Judy's former husband never made the big income that some lawyers generate, and when they were still married, the couple never saved much money. Thus, Judy should not have been surprised that the dollar terms specified in her divorce settlement were not nearly enough to support her high-consumption lifestyle. As a result, Judy felt that she was forced to work outside the home.

Judy just can't help it. She has some envy and hostility toward all those women on her tennis team. Not even one works outside the home. In Judy's mind, all the women just play tennis and hang around the house or shopping mall all day. She also thought there was another related issue involved. She made an assumption after she got to know Susan and her other teammates that Susan or her husband had inherited a pile of money. How unfair. Judy's folks never left their daughter anything.

She speculated that it must be inherited wealth. How else could Susan and her husband pay all those tuition bills for their three children who attended expensive colleges back East? And now, one of the kids is in medical school, and another is in law school. The third is involved in a top MBA program. Judy asked Susan about her and her husband's backgrounds and discovered that both of them were from blue-collar backgrounds. Do Susan and her husband live in a fine home that is nicely furnished? Yes, they do. They also own a vacation home in the mountains. They drive late-model automobiles of the midpriced variety.

Initially, Judy figured Susan's husband must earn a lot of money in order to afford all those tuition bills, homes, and related items. So Judy just had to ask:

JUDY O: Susan, what line of work is your husband in?

SUSAN J: He works for a nonprofit regional charity . . . in charge of fund-raising.

JUDY O: Oh, is he one of those who gets a piece of the action . . . a percentage of all that is raised?

SUSAN J: Not at all. He is strictly on salary, a lot less than if he were in the private sector . . . no incentives. . . . But it's an unwritten rule that those who are employed by the organization should give back at least ten percent of their income as a gift.

When Judy heard these words, she nearly went into shock. She could not explain or understand it. Yes, Susan does it all without generating one dollar of earned income. But it's even worse than Judy imagined. Susan and her husband not only live a comfortable lifestyle, they are also financially independent. The couple could retire today and never have to worry about generating an earned income. How is this possible? In the past year, Susan's husband earned an annual income of only $108,000. At his current age of fifty-seven, how much should

Susan and her husband have accumulated in terms of their household worth? According to the wealth equation, the couple should be worth $615,600. In fact, they are worth more than $5 million. How, oh how, did they do it? Actually, it had much more to do with Susan's contributions to the net worth equation than her husband's.

Susan revealed the key to the couple's financial success when she first spoke with Judy. Recall what she told Judy:

I run the family office.

What is a family office? Well, most billionaire families do have family offices. In essence, they set up their own investment and financial-management organizations. Evidently, these billionaires believe they can do a better job for less cost. By doing all or much of this work in their own proprietary family offices, they achieve higher returns on their assets, often with less risk.

But these billionaires have tremendous resources to be managed. Can there be any benefit to setting up a family office if you are not yet even a millionaire? Susan did initially set up, operate, and manage a family office early in her marriage. She never worked at this task for more than twenty hours a week.

In high school and college, Susan was always an excellent student. So she applied her aptitude and lust for learning to the task at hand, operating a productive family office. Her husband had zero input into the investment decisions she made. Actually, he had absolutely no interest in dealing with issues of budgeting, forecasting, cash flow, or wealth. Nor did he wish to involve himself in researching investment opportunities. Susan did it all, and made all the investment decisions. Yet, neither Susan nor her husband had any interest in living a hyper-consumption lifestyle.

So why are Susan and her husband worth eight times their expected level of net worth? Susan's efforts as a budgeter and investment decision maker translated into more than $4 million in net worth for her and her family.

Would Susan have more self-esteem, more pride, more wealth, if she had worked outside the home for the past thirty-five years? Absolutely not. She bubbles with pride and overflows with high self-esteem. She knows full well that she transformed her family into the financially independent household that it is today. But she will tell you with great emphasis that she never would have been able to establish and operate her family's highly productive office if she'd worked outside the home.

Judy could have been doing the "family office act" all during her married years too. But she did not. Nor did her former husband. All during their marriage, Judy never felt the need to budget or do any type of financial or investment planning. So today, she seeks answers about why she has to work outside the home. She thinks that all those, including Susan, who do otherwise are just lucky. They either married Mr. Moneybags or inherited their wealth. There are, in fact, many women, wives and mothers just like Susan, who became wealthy by running the family office.

MRS. A. READER

Imagine that years ago you cut your household's income nearly in half. Yet your family's net worth has increased every year since then. How is this possible? Again, it has much to do with the family office concept, as detailed in the following letter:

Dear Dr. Stanley:

I read your book. . . . You confirmed so many things that I have often thought but have never seen expressed, and my copy of your book is well marked up and well thumbed.

I would like, though, to gently make a case for the non-working housewife, who in your book comes off as a bit of a drone. As I read your book, I found myself wanting to justify myself to you.

When I got married over twenty years ago, I was working and I assumed I would always work. The problem was that my husband had the personality structure (though not the income) of the high-earning self-employed men you describe. He worked long and intense hours. He believed he had no time to study investments and said we had no money to save. He could not find the time to participate in household chores and would not involve himself in any home maintenance. When we took vacations, we went on expensive trips to fancy places; we would spend most of the entire next year paying for these trips. He loved our children but did not want to be involved in their time-consuming care.

When our first child was born, I realized that things had to change. I stopped working, which ended the expensive vacations and his plans for a second home. We lowered our standard of living to what we could afford. I don't need to tell you he was pretty upset with me about this, and if looks could kill, I'd be dead.

But twenty years later, here is where we are. Since I have not been working, I have been able to care for my children myself. My children have never gone to a child-care provider I wasn't happy with or come home to an empty house, as so many do. Because we have lived below our means, we have saved a great deal more money than have many two-paycheck couples whose income exceeds ours. Our house is well maintained—by me alone. My ledger book and files are well organized, and I have a clear picture of our finances; I can instantly put my hands on any necessary information. I could not have taken care of these things if I had had to go to a full-time job.

I think that women who marry men like my husband have several choices. They can get divorced and try to find men more willing to do the heavy lifting of marriage. Since men are pretty much alike, this choice often results in either multiple divorces or in single parenthood. Women can also choose to continue to work and spend most of their salary on child care and other support services while frantically juggling everyone's schedules. Or they can decide that having a home in good order is their first priority and that things that are a lower priority will have to be let go.

Thank you for letting me express these thoughts. I am not including a return address because my husband would be upset if he found out I wrote this letter. The official story is that our family's financial successes are his, while I have just been puttering around at the playground with the kids. I think he really believes this.

Sincerely,

Mrs. A. Reader

What does Mrs. A. Reader have in common with most of the women who head up their households' family office? As a rule, they are well disciplined, resourceful, and unselfish. They let their husbands take much of the credit for the household's financial achievements. More often than not, these women were outstanding students in college. Typically, they had grade point averages a full letter higher than their husbands'. Also, most learned how to budget, account for all household expenses, and invest on their own effectively. They did not learn these skills in college; they learned by reading and by trial and error.

Would you like to bump into some of these women, those who run their family office? Then stop by your local library. Go to the reference section, which houses financial research data and publications like *Value Line*. Often, you will find these women taking notes. If you don't see them there, you might find them at the desk checking out books written by or about Benjamin Graham, Peter Lynch, Warren Buffett, and others. Most of these women don't buy books. They say it is too expensive: "Better to stop by the library and borrow!"

ENDNOTE

What type of a woman would take the time and effort to write me a letter that contained 1,422 words—7,552 keystrokes? Obviously, a woman who felt that her ideas were important. Janie is like most of the women profiled in this book. She wants to share her ideas unselfishly in order to help others enhance the productivity of their households. But one might speculate that a woman who makes a major financial contribution to her household would not have the time to produce such a long letter.

Janie had the time. As head of the family office, she had both the time and the money. She planned it that way. Portions of her letter are included below:

Dear Dr. Stanley:

Having recently read The Millionaire Mind, *I am accepting your invitation to tell you my story. First, however, I want to thank you for setting my mind at ease, as I have wondered for some time if I am just overly compulsive about our financial situation. If that is the case, I have learned from reading both* The Millionaire Next Door *and* The Millionaire Mind *that I am in good company.*

I grew up as an only child in a second-generation immigrant neighborhood in a family that was never economically successful and with a father who had debilitating health problems from the time I was nine years old. I always dreamed of being financially successful but was well aware that having money alone was not what really mattered in life. In fact, I was more determined to marry someone who was healthy rather than rich. Never did I want to buy things. To me being financially successful meant possessing the freedom to make choices that I might not otherwise have.

I'm a saver out of necessity. After all, my family was never in a position to give me economic outpatient care, and it was drummed into me, particularly by my own father, from a very early age that I would have to make it on my own. While I realize now that I probably could have gone to the best among colleges, my parents were unaware that their meager circumstances might have afforded me a full scholarship at one of the better schools. Having graduated in three years and with the guarantee of graduate school education at that same institution, I felt it was time to take a chance and go to a large northeastern city to find opportunity.

Facing large graduate school tuition at a private university, I immediately got a job to support myself and both worked and went to school. Having graduated with a degree in French, my first full-time job was with a brokerage firm because I could easily get there by public transportation. I didn't have the down payment to purchase a car that would have been required to even get me to a teaching job. The pay at the brokerage firm wasn't great, but the education was tremendous. While only a secretary, I learned about the pitfalls of hypertrading stocks. Soon after being fired from the aforementioned job, I married. The opportunity to begin acquiring wealth began. . . .

. . . We are "two peas in a pod." Both of us are savers and not at all interested in buying our way to success. We do not fit your profile of millionaire status in that my husband is a civil servant and definitely not entrepreneurial.

When pregnant with our first child and not working, I needed a new project. So, I began "the book," and started keeping track of all our expenses. This was never intended to be a budget technique, but merely done for information purposes. Could we eventually afford to purchase a home? Could we live on one income? The system of tracking expenses has not changed in twenty-seven years, and at the end of every calendar year, I have tabulated the year's expenses, total assets, and change in financial position. When our second child entered kindergarten, I began the process of fulfilling the requirements to sit for the CPA exam. Wasn't I surprised to find that at the end of each fiscal year, corporations basically perform the same tasks that I had been doing!

As far as the children are concerned—two sons, now age twenty-six and twenty-three—we have never denied them anything based on cost. Just the same, we have been a family of "cheap dates." That doesn't mean that they didn't attend expensive colleges (the $30,000-a-year variety) and enjoy that grand tour of Europe. You might be interested to know that neither one ever had an allowance or was paid for things done around the house, such as mowing the lawn. In fact, they always knew that there was an envelope of cash, often several hundred dollars, in a kitchen drawer, should they ever need the money. When one day I saw our younger son going into my wallet for cash, I went a little nuts. He said he needed five dollars, and the envelope in the drawer only had tens. I then explained that I had already accounted for the cash in the drawer in "the book," and that if I hadn't seen his getting the money out of my wallet I wouldn't have known to account for it. That was the first time he had ever heard of "the book," and from that time on only took money from the drawer, even if it meant having to bring back change. What we didn't realize was that the kids now thought that every family keeps a "book." That resulted in a big chuckle for my husband and me when we found out.

Twenty-seven years have passed since "the book" was born, and through all those years of saving and investing, we have passed through the millionaire threshold a couple of times. When I went back to work four years prior to our older son's entering college, it was with the idea that what I earned would pay our boys' college expenses even though we could easily have afforded it. The purpose was not to dilute the funds we were using for investing. Obviously, given the fact that my husband is a federal employee and I am currently unemployed, we are not high wage earners. Nevertheless, even the boys are almost half-millionaires, as the cash gifts we gave them when they were very young have increased exponentially. That could be a cause for concern, but I'm happy to report that they are both gainfully employed and living and saving on their earned incomes alone. In fact, they are, in our opinion, financially frugal and ambitious. It is understood that the investments we have afforded them will just be tucked aside. Their homes, cars, vacations will be paid for through their own work efforts. While there is never a guarantee that this way of thinking will continue, both my husband and I have great confidence in their ability to be responsible, financially self-sufficient adults. They are truly our most valuable and lovable assets.

We are not yet decamillionaires but feel confident that that day will arrive without inflation totally gobbling up our riches. We live in a comfortable suburban neighborhood with good schools, but hardly one in which anyone would think a multi-millionaire might live.

Again, thank you for affording me the calming effect of knowing that my years of keeping "the book," pounding away on a calculator, and formatting those spreadsheets weren't totally crazed. I must go now, as The Millionaire Mind is due back today at the library, and I just hate to have to pay a fine.

Sincerely,
Mrs. Janie M.

Appendixes

Technical Appendix

SOURCES OF DATA AND SAMPLING METHODS

THE PRIMARY DATA SOURCE

I have been studying America's wealthy since 1973, and the research for *Millionaire Women Next Door* is the most comprehensive I have conducted on the topic, including their many journeys, who they are, their habits, and how they succeeded. The most important source of data for this book was generated from my national survey of economically successful women who are self-employed business owners. Potential respondents were selected from a list of women who own businesses.

A commercial list organization provided a nationwide list of private businesses owned by women. Only those who were deemed to be successful—defined as those who owned businesses that generated a minimum annual net revenue of $100,000—were included in the sample population. From this list of successful businesswomen in America, 2,500 were selected at random for use in this survey.

The national business-based survey was conducted from May 2001 to July 2001. The survey data were collected and tabulated by the Survey Research Center, Institute for Behavioral Research, University of Georgia, in Athens.[1] The center also did the bulk of the univariate and multivariate computer analyses of these and related data from my existing data bank.

---

[1] Neither the Survey Research Center nor the University of Georgia bears any responsibility for the analyses or interpretations presented herein.

Each of the 2,500 women business owners received a nine-page questionnaire, a form letter asking for her participation and guaranteeing the anonymity and confidentiality of the data collected, and a one-dollar bill as a response incentive. Also included was a business reply envelope in which to return the completed questionnaire. A total of 589 surveys were completed in time to be included in the analysis. Overall, the response rate was 23.6 percent. However, it was determined that approximately one in four of the respondents did not fully fit the parameters of the study. In order for a respondent to be included in this study, she had to be a business owner who was also the manager of her respective business. It was determined by analyzing several screening questions contained in the questionnaire that not all of the owners were in fact the "head," "boss," or "CEO" of their respective businesses.

Overall 439 of the 589 women who responded did, in fact, fit the parameters of the study. The others were essentially figureheads who only in a legal or nominal sense managed and owned the businesses. Yes, they did hold the title of CEO or president, but in reality, the husbands of these women were in charge. Why did these husbands insist that their wives assume ownership? Many were motivated by legal or tax-related issues. Some thought it wise to shelter assets from possible legal liabilities by having their wives act as owners.

Of the 439 women who responded and were truly managers as well as owners, 233, or 53.1 percent, were millionaires. All 233 had a personal net worth of $1 million or more.

Each of the 439 respondents revealed her attitudes and behaviors concerning an array of lifestyle and financial or success-oriented dimensions. Questions dealt with financial risk taking, leadership, budgeting, happiness and satisfaction, investment habits, academic achievements (including grade point averages and SAT scores), goals, planning habits, income-allocation patterns, time-allocation habits, and eleemosynary habits and attitudes. Respondents also profiled the parental environment in which they were raised and their ancestry or country of origin.

In addition, respondents were asked about their perceptions concerning the benefits of being financially independent. Accordingly, each respondent indicated the most they had ever actually spent (the actual sales price) for a variety of consumer products, including wristwatches, suits, shoes, and the like. These women also revealed the types of "economic acts of kindness" that they have provided their adult children and grandchildren.

Most (313) of the 439 women who participated in the national survey wrote a "success" essay describing the factors that underlie their respective success formulas. A detailed content analysis was conducted in an effort to answer this question.

CONTRASTS

Much of the data that I have collected in the past proved to be extremely useful in terms of contrasting women and men. The contrasts were generated by comparing the national survey of 439 (233 who were millionaires) self-employed women with those responses from men who were already part of my existing database. While these contrasts are valuable, they are not the main focus of this book. The main focus is on economically successful women who are self-employed business owners. In terms of total survey data, the inputs from 1,165 women respondents (439 from the primary sample and 726 from my existing data) contributed to this work.

THE EXISTING DATABASE

Much of the foundation and many of the hypotheses developed for the national survey of successful businesswomen, as described above, were generated from my early research. These data were derived from the studies of high-income and high-net-worth individuals I have conducted over the past twenty years.

Also included in my existing database are personal and focus-group interviews with more than 700 high-income or high-net-worth respondents. Responses from more than 14,000 individuals are contained in my database.

One might logically ask, given the existence of so much data, why was it necessary to conduct yet another survey. Nearly two-thirds of the respondents in my existing survey database are business owners. However, within this segment of business owners only 726 respondents, or about eight in one hundred, are women. This "existing" data was culled from national samples of high-income and high-net-worth respondents. For a detailed discussion of the sampling methods employed in these studies and a profile of the respondents see, for example, my earlier publications, including:

- *The Millionaire Mind* (2000), pp. 4–9, and Appendix 1, "In Search of the Balance Sheet Affluent," pp. 395–97
- *The Millionaire Next Door* (1996), pp. 4–5, and Appendix 1, under "Targeting by Neighborhood" and "Targeting by Occupation," pp. 249–50
- "Why You're Not as Wealthy as You Should Be," *Medical Economics* (July 1992, pp. 38–42)
- *Marketing to the Affluent* (1988), Technical Appendix 2, "The Financial Lifestyles of American Millionaires," pp. 260–84, and Technical Appendix 4, "A Strategy for Targeting by Geodemography," pp. 297–318
- "The Response of Affluent Consumers to Mail Surveys," *Journal of Advertising Research* (June-July 1986, pp. 55–58)

Not one of the existing samples taken separately contained more than 200 respondents who were high-income/high-net-worth women. Thus, a larger sample was deemed necessary in order to project these results on a national basis. Also, I wanted to break new ground in terms of adding to the growing base of knowledge concerning these self-made successful women.

QUALITATIVE DATA

In addition to the quantitative-survey-based data, I gained considerable insight from the qualitative research gathered specifically for this book. I spent hundreds of hours analyzing the 201 in-depth case studies and the 313 "success" essays provided by economically successful women. In turn, I also reviewed much of the qualitative data derived from wealthy men. This was done in an effort to understand better the key differences between wealthy women and men. In turn, this effort provided a base from which questions were generated for my national survey of wealthy women who were business owners.

SECONDARY DATA SOURCES

Why are some self-employed women more successful than others? More often than not, success follows those who selected a category of business that tends to generate high profits. What types of businesses tend to be profitable? In order to answer this and related questions, I supplemented my own survey data concerning the types of businesses wealthy women own and manage. The profitability (measured five different ways) of 153 categories of the 17 million small businesses in America was estimated by analyzing data from the Internal Revenue Service.

Data from the IRS was also used to estimate the difference between women and men in terms of both income and wealth. Also, estate data provided by the IRS was invaluable in determining the propensity of women versus men to give (provide bequests) to noble causes as well as in determining the occupations of those in the high-net-worth category. Data concerning income, net worth, and occupational categories of business-related correlates of these measures were also culled from surveys conducted by the U.S. Census Bureau.

APPENDIX 1

CONTENT ANALYSIS OF 313 ESSAYS WRITTEN BY WOMEN WHO OWN AND OPERATE SUCCESSFUL BUSINESSES

Essay Topic: "Suggestions About How Young People Might Become Successful Adults," aka "How I Became a Successful Business Owner Myself"

Theme and/or Component	%	Webster's Definition and Researcher's Comments
1. Perseverance	51.0%	The act of persevering; continued, patient effort.
		Most respondents reported success only after initial failure and after strong discouragement from family and friends. There is a sense in which these individuals seem "driven" to overcome obstacles and to prove their critics wrong. Most felt that a key subcomponent of perseverance was having strong aspirations, a strong desire or ambition as for advancement, honor, etc. Respondents stressed that staying focused on the desired result (persevering) over extended periods of time is the key to success.
2. Education and Training	34.0%	Education: The process of training and developing the knowledge, skill, mind, character, etc., especially by formal schooling; teaching; training. Training: The process or experience of being instructed or taught.
		The respondents emphasized the importance of pursuing and completing formal education at institutions of learning. Equally as important was training related to specific job (career) skills through seminars, technical publications, on-the-job training, and learning from other successful individuals in their chosen job or career.
3. Self-Reliance	23.0%	Reliance on one's own judgment, abilities, etc.
		Although the respondents encouraged seeking assistance in various ways, they strongly urged relying on one's own beliefs and strategies as ultimately being a key to success.
4. Caring/Helping	22.0%	Feeling concern about or interest in others.
		Respondents stressed that in order to be successful one must have a caring attitude toward employees and customers.
5. Enjoyment	16.0%	The act or experience of enjoying; the pleasurable experiencing of something.
		Respondents stressed the importance of doing something one truly enjoys in order to stay fresh and motivated.

APPENDIX 1, CONTINUED

Theme and/or Component	%	Webster's Definition and Researcher's Comments
6. Saving/Investing	15.0%	Saving: The act or interest of economizing. Investing: Putting money into business, real estate, stocks, bonds, etc., for the purpose of obtaining income or profit.
		Specific saving and investing advice was varied among respondents. However, the common theme emphasized setting aside funds to weather personal and business economic difficulties.
7. Goals	14.0%	Objects or ends that one strives to attain.
		Respondents stressed setting clearly defined, realistic goals and measuring progress periodically against these goals. Also, many pointed out the importance of regularly reevaluating goals in order to make changes consistent with changes in business conditions.
7. Responsibility	14.0%	Condition, quality, fact, or instance of being responsible; obligation, accountability, dependability, etc.
		Respondents stressed the importance of behaving responsibly in the process of maturing to adulthood, particularly with respect to part-time jobs and assigned family tasks. Also stressed was the importance of owning up to responsibilities rather than blaming circumstances or others when difficulties are encountered.
9. Integrity	13.0%	The quality or state of being of sound moral principle; uprightness, honesty, and sincerity.
		Respondents stressed that integrity is essential to the health and continuance of any business.
10. Spiritual	12.0%	Relating to the spirit or the soul, as distinguished from the body or material matters.
		Respondents stressed the importance of finding and maintaining a spiritual part in life in order to enjoy fully day-to-day business and family experiences.
11. Advisers	11.0%	Persons counseling and recommending courses of action based on knowledge or experience.
		Respondents stressed the importance of seeking the advice of others who are successful in the specific business. They also stressed seeking good advisers in technical areas, such as law and accounting.
12. Nurturing	7.0%	Promoting the development of; raising by educating, training, etc.
		Respondents stressed that the nurturing of employees increases productivity and fosters a "family" business culture.
13. Ethics	6.0%	The standards of conduct of a given profession or group.
		Respondents urged the development of a clear understanding of ethics for the business and adherence without exception to these standards.

Theme and/or Component	%	Webster's Definition and Researcher's Comments
14. Health	5.0%	Physical and mental well-being; freedom from disease, pain, or defect.
		Respondents recommended living a healthy lifestyle, avoiding unhealthy habits, and engaging in health-promoting activities. They suggested that success is not possible absent good health.
15. Opportunistic	4.0%	Of or pertaining to the practice or policy of adapting one's actions, judgments, etc., to circumstances.
		Respondents stressed the importance of evaluating and acting upon favorable opportunities in the business environment.
15. Conservative	4.0%	Conserving or tending to conserve; preservative.
		Respondents stressed being cautious as to expanding too quickly in business; first ensure that fundamental goals and business health are not at risk.
15. Optimistic	4.0%	The tendency to take the most hopeful or cheerful view of matters or to expect the best outcome.
		Respondents stressed that not worrying about what cannot be controlled and always expecting the future to be bright breeds success.
18. Analytical	3.0%	Skilled in using analysis (an analytical mind).
		Respondents stressed developing analytical thinking so that issues are separated into component parts and acted upon carefully. Many differentiated between thinking analytically and acting emotionally.
18. Flexibility	3.0%	Ability to adjust to change; state or being capable of modification.
		Respondents stressed that being able to adjust planning and goal setting to changing circumstances is important to success. Some stated, "Do not be set in your ways."
18. Leadership	3.0%	The capacity to lead or direct action.
		Respondents advised developing leadership skills through formal training and/or seeking leadership positions in school or civic organizations in order to be respected by employees and others for leadership in the business.
18. Creative	3.0%	Having or showing imagination and artistic or intellectual inventiveness.
		Respondents recommended acquiring through formal or informal training the ability to think creatively in problem solving. "Learn to think outside the lines."

APPENDIX 1, CONTINUED

Theme and/or Component	%	Webster's Definition and Researcher's Comments
22. Talents	2.0%	Superior, apparently natural abilities in the arts or sciences or in learning to do anything.
		Respondents stressed recognizing and developing talents, as these may ultimately lead not only to financial pursuits but also to overall life enjoyment.
22. Realistic	2.0%	Tending to face facts and be practical rather than imaginative or visionary.
		The respondents stressed the importance of tempering aspirations with realism; for example, making sure that aspirations are commensurate with talents, skills, and abilities.
24. Liability	1.0%	The state of being subject to an adverse contingency or action.
		Respondents advised against involvement in activities that may expose you to more liability than profit potential justifies.
24. Reasoning	1.0%	The drawing of inferences or conclusions from known or assumed facts; the use of reason.
		Respondents urged making decisions using sound reasoning, not affected by emotion.
24. Forgiving	1.0%	Willing to give up resentment against or the desire to punish another; able to stop being angry with or to pardon others.
		Respondents stressed the importance of being forgiving, in particular toward employees, as a resentful environment does not support success.
24. Introspection	1.0%	Looking into one's own mind, feelings, etc.; observation and analysis of oneself.
		Respondents recommended continuing introspection to help you stay on track with goals and with problem solving.
24. Humility	1.0%	The state or quality of being humble; absence of pride or self-assertion.
		Respondents stressed the importance of humility in making unclouded judgments and decisions.
29. Reputation	0.3%	Estimation in which a person or thing is commonly held; character in the view of the public, the community, etc.
		Respondents stressed that a good reputation is one's most important asset.

APPENDIX 2

THE PROFITABILITY OF SMALL BUSINESSES: NET INCOME

Category of Small Business	Number of Businesses	Average Net Income ($)	Rank According to Average Net Income
Dentists' Offices	91,998	98,417	1
Physicians' Offices	192,236	78,430	2
Podiatrists' Offices	6,296	48,669	3
Optometrists' Offices	12,810	46,672	4
Veterinary Services	20,635	43,670	5
Chiropractors' Offices	31,285	43,174	6
Legal Services	318,005	40,195	7
Brokers and Dealers of Securities	20,838	33,818	8
Insurance Agents or Brokers	294,680	27,401	9
Drugstores	11,213	26,770	10
Lumber and Building Materials Stores	16,066	25,342	11
Paper and Allied Products Manufacturing	1,476	24,516	12
Funeral Services	9,272	23,985	13
Machinery Manufacturing, Except Electric	32,967	23,279	14
Medical and Dental Laboratories	19,427	22,401	15
Real Estate Agents and Brokers	686,323	22,226	16
Commodity Contracts Brokers	9,060	21,960	17
Engineering Services	86,090	21,645	18
Consulting Services	591,665	21,288	19
Architectural Services	70,786	20,734	20
Shoe Stores	5,875	20,140	21
Stationery Stores	7,699	18,683	22
Men's and Boys' Clothing	2,417	18,524	23
Real Estate Property Managers	93,776	18,058	24
Fuel Oil Dealers	3,573	17,707	25

APPENDIX 2, CONTINUED

THE PROFITABILITY OF SMALL BUSINESSES: NET INCOME

Category of Small Business	Number of Businesses	Average Net Income ($)	Rank According to Average Net Income
Surveying Services	15,598	16,990	26
Textile Mill Products Manufacturing	5,668	16,904	27
Other Financial Services	151,731	16,701	28
Electrical Equipment Manufacturing	20,873	16,605	29
Fabricated Metal Products Manufacturing	29,319	15,925	30
TV, Audio, and Electronics Stores	16,239	15,471	31
Wholesale Durable Goods	212,735	15,420	32
Electrical Work	119,468	14,680	33
Mobile Home Dealers	5,038	13,985	34
Advertising, Except Direct Mail	86,337	13,935	35
Subdividers and Developers	14,451	13,632	36
Operators and Lessors of Buildings	16,372	13,615	37
Building Materials Dealers	45,661	13,567	38
Grocery Stores	65,192	13,528	39
Other Medical and Health Services	295,462	13,428	40
Credit Institutions and Mortgage Bankers	27,309	13,206	41
Gasoline Service Stations	37,767	13,103	42
Printing and Publishing	36,786	13,087	43
Registered and Practical Nurses	114,516	12,532	44
Automotive Parts and Accessories Stores	33,627	12,528	45
General Building Contractor	383,626	12,524	46
Water Transportation	4,700	12,379	47
Carpentering and Flooring	478,025	12,244	48
Masonry, Dry Wall, Stone, and Tile	190,962	12,189	49
Barbershops	94,308	11,770	50

APPENDIX 2, CONTINUED

THE PROFITABILITY OF SMALL BUSINESSES: NET INCOME

Category of Small Business	Number of Businesses	Average Net Income ($)	Rank According to Average Net Income
Forestry, Except Logging	55,733	11,691	51
Accounting, Auditing, Bookkeeping Services	393,993	11,557	52
Painting and Paper Hanging	214,214	11,537	53
Jewelry Stores	32,444	11,510	54
Insurance Services	93,095	11,477	55
Home Furnishings and Equipment Stores	49,272	11,448	56
Wholesale Nondurable Goods	163,843	11,393	57
Miscellaneous Food Stores	42,649	11,337	58
Highway and Street Construction	7,799	11,323	59
Roofing, Siding, and Sheet Metal	102,409	11,318	60
Plumbing, Heating, and Air-Conditioning	154,779	11,235	61
Trucking, Local and Long-Distance	419,433	11,227	62
Other Business Services	1,084,937	11,193	63
Investment Advisers and Services	2,246	11,116	64
Miscellaneous Automotive Dealers	21,305	11,022	65
Furniture and Fixtures Manufacturing	31,772	10,920	66
Quarrying and Nonmetallic Mineral Mining	4,315	10,909	67
Management Services	111,893	10,850	68
Other Cleaning Services	68,121	10,543	69
Camera and Photo Supply Stores	3,197	10,305	70
Eating Places	146,470	10,191	71
Concrete Work	44,023	10,080	72
Miscellaneous Specialty Trade Contractors	485,845	9,948	73
Automotive Repairs	138,276	9,827	74
Liquor Stores	20,012	9,597	75

APPENDIX 2, CONTINUED

THE PROFITABILITY OF SMALL BUSINESSES: NET INCOME

Category of Small Business	Number of Businesses	Average Net Income ($)	Rank According to Average Net Income
Utilities (Dumps, Snowplowing, Road Cleaning)	7,147	9,350	76
Bus and Limousine Transportation	9,777	9,000	77
Automotive Service, No Repair	168,094	8,821	78
Motion Picture and Video Production	54,643	8,809	79
Other Equipment Repair	263,441	8,500	80
Coin-Operated Laundries and Dry Cleaning	15,920	8,344	81
Photographic Studios	91,058	8,255	82
Other Manufacturing Industries	92,717	8,193	83
Nursing and Personal-Care Facilities	48,026	8,121	84
Apparel, Other Textile Products Manufacturing	23,213	8,116	85
Counseling, Except Health Practitioners	75,876	8,074	86
Furniture Stores	20,622	7,944	87
Paint, Glass, and Wallpaper Stores	1,682	7,901	88
Equipment Rental	44,061	7,791	89
Beauty Shops	449,286	7,787	90
Computer and Data-Processing Services	48,898	7,627	91
Communications Services	33,637	7,382	92
Commercial Fishing	78,244	7,082	93
Other Heavy Construction	47,443	7,034	94
Air Transportation	11,132	6,916	95
Other Apparel and Accessories Stores	41,709	6,864	96
Hardware Stores	8,945	6,860	97
Leather and Leather Products Manufacturing	3,619	6,855	98
Variety Stores	27,061	6,771	99
Ministers and Chaplains	212,939	6,671	100

APPENDIX 2, CONTINUED

THE PROFITABILITY OF SMALL BUSINESSES: NET INCOME

Category of Small Business	Number of Businesses	Average Net Income ($)	Rank According to Average Net Income
Horticulture, Gardening, and Landscaping	241,480	6,665	101
Hotels and Motels	30,411	6,598	102
Lumber and Wood Products Manufacturing	38,416	6,538	103
Used Car Dealers	56,845	6,501	104
Electrical Repair	43,663	6,370	105
Highway Passenger Transportation	21,637	6,300	106
Taxicabs	98,145	6,257	107
Professional Sports and Racing	104,807	6,098	108
Sporting Goods and Bicycle Shops	32,607	6,043	109
Bookstores	10,338	5,934	110
Farm Labor and Management Services	42,161	5,929	111
Automotive Rental	17,803	5,898	112
Food and Beverage Production	20,104	5,792	113
Travel Agents and Tour Operators	44,067	5,761	114
Entertainers, Producers, and Agents	715,506	5,686	115
Janitorial and Related Services to Buildings	441,082	5,676	116
Household Appliances Stores	9,639	5,594	117
Mail, Reproduction, Commercial Art Services	49,724	5,463	118
Public Warehousing	3,862	5,145	119
Miscellaneous Personal Services	695,606	5,066	120
Nurseries and Garden Supply Stores	13,930	4,827	121
Vending Machine Selling	45,797	4,673	122
Boat Dealers	2,581	4,640	123
Educational Services	292,813	4,473	124
Women's Ready-to-Wear Clothing	20,019	4,328	125

APPENDIX 2, CONTINUED

THE PROFITABILITY OF SMALL BUSINESSES: NET INCOME

Category of Small Business	Number of Businesses	Average Net Income ($)	Rank According to Average Net Income
Other Transportation Services	55,228	4,291	126
Child Day Care	618,457	4,262	127
Courier or Package Delivery	182,092	4,153	128
Fabric and Needlework Stores	42,023	4,113	129
New Car Dealers	14,361	4,110	130
Catering Services	66,380	3,841	131
Computer and Software Stores	10,537	3,321	132
Family Clothing	19,325	3,183	133
Florists	50,555	2,690	134
Drinking Places	33,546	2,457	135
Stone, Clay, and Glass Products Manufacturing	21,672	2,363	136
Music and Record Stores	5,359	2,350	137
Other Amusement and Recreational Services	166,457	2,350	138
Primary Metal Industries	4,005	2,189	139
Hunting and Trapping	12,578	2,138	140
Selling Door-to-Door	922,517	2,095	141
Hobby, Toy, and Game Shops	25,936	1,223	142
Used Merchandise and Antiques Stores	103,373	1,162	143
Parking, Except Valet	6,047	902	144
Rooming Houses and Boardinghouses	11,862	678	145
Gift, Novelty, and Souvenir Shops	105,035	8[1]	146
Catalog or Mail Order	45,355	-614	147
Animal Services	72,664	-669	148
Videotape Rental	10,403	-926	149
Camps and Camping Parks	14,107	-1,498	150
Oil and Gas Extraction	113,034	-1,664	151
Livestock Breeding	26,188	-4,619	152
Luggage and Leather Goods Stores	1,428	-20,109	153

[1] Before rounding off, the average net income was $7.70.

APPENDIX 3

THE PROFITABILITY OF SMALL BUSINESSES:
RETURN ON RECEIPTS

Category of Small Business	Number of Businesses	Average Return on Receipts	Rank According to Average Return on Receipts
Physicians' Offices	192,236	.55492	1
Management Services	111,893	.54740	2
Consulting Services	591,665	.54726	3
Ministers and Chaplains	212,939	.54477	4
Registered and Practical Nurses	114,516	.51622	5
Counseling, Except Health Practitioners	75,876	.50972	6
Other Medical and Health Services	295,462	.47898	7
Legal Services	318,005	.46806	8
Real Estate Agents and Brokers	686,323	.46122	9
Mail, Reproduction, Commercial Art Services	49,724	.45689	10
Insurance Services	93,095	.45481	11
Accounting, Auditing, Bookkeeping Services	393,993	.44036	12
Engineering Services	86,090	.43897	13
Insurance Agents or Brokers	294,680	.42459	14
Utilities (Dumps, Snowplowing, Road Cleaning)	7,147	.40255	15
Real Estate Property Managers	93,776	.39831	16
Medical and Dental Laboratories	19,427	.39497	17
Child Day Care	618,457	.39072	18
Barbershops	94,308	.38319	19
Dentists' Offices	91,998	.37505	20
Surveying Services	15,598	.36955	21
Podiatrists' Offices	6,296	.36014	22
Educational Services	292,813	.35771	23
Chiropractors' Offices	31,285	.35659	24
Entertainers, Producers, and Agents	715,506	.34772	25

APPENDIX 3, CONTINUED

THE PROFITABILITY OF SMALL BUSINESSES: RETURN ON RECEIPTS

Category of Small Business	Number of Businesses	Average Return on Receipts	Rank According to Average Return on Receipts
Other Business Services	1,084,937	.34418	26
Painting and Paper Hanging	214,214	.34139	27
Janitorial and Related Services to Buildings	441,082	.32807	28
Beauty Shops	449,286	.31866	29
Primary Metal Industries	4,005	.31565	30
Motion Picture and Video Production	54,643	.31290	31
Miscellaneous Personal Services	695,606	.30071	32
Computer and Data-Processing Services	48,898	.29740	33
Carpentering and Flooring	478,025	.27811	34
Textile Mill Products Manufacturing	5,668	.27356	35
Architectural Services	70,786	.27070	36
Commercial Fishing	78,244	.26737	37
Electrical Equipment Manufacturing	20,873	.26087	38
Advertising, Except Direct Mail	86,337	.25881	39
Operators and Lessors of Buildings	16,372	.25808	40
Taxicabs	98,145	.25609	41
Optometrists' Offices	12,810	.25592	42
Electrical Work	119,468	.24852	43
Veterinary Services	20,635	.24434	44
Air Transportation	11,132	.24081	45
Other Equipment Repair	263,441	.23334	46
Communications Services	33,637	.23014	47
Courier or Package Delivery	182,092	.22738	48
Photographic Studios	91,058	.22433	49
Bus and Limousine Transportation	9,777	.21294	50

APPENDIX 3, CONTINUED

THE PROFITABILITY OF SMALL BUSINESSES:
RETURN ON RECEIPTS

Category of Small Business	Number of Businesses	Average Return on Receipts	Rank According to Average Return on Receipts
Credit Institutions and Mortgage Bankers	27,309	.21062	51
Leather and Leather Products Manufacturing	3,619	.20615	52
Professional Sports and Racing	104,807	.19587	53
Machinery Manufacturing, Except Electric	32,967	.19269	54
Highway Passenger Transportation	21,637	.18982	55
Masonry, Dry Wall, Stone, and Tile	190,962	.18734	56
Miscellaneous Specialty Trade Contractors	485,845	.18406	57
Hunting and Trapping	12,578	.18377	58
Funeral Services	9,272	.18258	59
Horticulture, Gardening, and Landscaping	241,480	.18130	60
Other Cleaning Services	68,121	.17510	61
Nursing and Personal-Care Facilities	48,026	.17402	62
Fabric and Needlework Stores	42,023	.17227	63
Roofing, Siding, and Sheet Metal	102,409	.16728	64
Electrical Repair	43,663	.16161	65
Home Furnishings and Equipment Stores	49,272	.15511	66
TV, Audio, and Electronics Stores	16,239	.15450	67
Men's and Boys' Clothing	2,417	.15444	68
Coin-Operated Laundries and Dry Cleaning	15,920	.15314	69
Lumber and Building Materials Stores	16,066	.15244	70
Other Manufacturing Industries	92,717	.14556	71
Catering Services	66,380	.14549	72
Plumbing, Heating, and Air-Conditioning	154,779	.14483	73
Printing and Publishing	36,786	.14354	74
Wholesale Durable Goods	212,735	.14017	75

APPENDIX 3, CONTINUED

THE PROFITABILITY OF SMALL BUSINESSES:
RETURN ON RECEIPTS

Category of Small Business	Number of Businesses	Average Return on Receipts	Rank According to Average Return on Receipts
Furniture and Fixtures Manufacturing	31,772	.13915	76
Fabricated Metal Products Manufacturing	29,319	.13756	77
Trucking, Local and Long-Distance	419,433	.13747	78
Subdividers and Developers	14,451	.12909	79
Automotive Repairs	138,276	.12886	80
Selling Door-to-Door	922,517	.12808	81
Automotive Service, No Repair	168,094	.12559	82
Water Transportation	4,700	.12501	83
General Building Contractor	383,626	.11944	84
Other Transportation Services	55,228	.11658	85
Camera and Photo Supply Stores	3,197	.11545	86
Equipment Rental	44,061	.11514	87
Wholesale Nondurable Goods	163,843	.11114	88
Vending Machine Selling	45,797	.11057	89
Stationery Stores	7,699	.11046	90
Quarrying and Nonmetallic Mineral Mining	4,315	.10832	91
Lumber and Wood Products Manufacturing	38,416	.10262	92
Automotive Rental	17,803	.10188	93
Jewelry Stores	32,444	.10003	94
Shoe Stores	5,875	.09830	95
Other Financial Services	151,731	.09699	96
Brokers and Dealers of Securities	20,838	.09679	97
Concrete Work	44,023	.09662	98
Other Heavy Construction	47,443	.09568	99
Farm Labor and Management Services	42,161	.09544	100

APPENDIX 3, CONTINUED

THE PROFITABILITY OF SMALL BUSINESSES:
RETURN ON RECEIPTS

Category of Small Business	Number of Businesses	Average Return on Receipts	Rank According to Average Return on Receipts
Forestry, Except Logging	55,733	.09152	101
Other Apparel and Accessories Stores	41,709	.08922	102
Apparel, Other Textile Products Manufacturing	23,213	.08860	103
Paper and Allied Products Manufacturing	1,476	.08380	104
Stone, Clay, and Glass Products Manufacturing	21,672	.08290	105
Other Amusement and Recreational Services	166,457	.08266	106
Automotive Parts and Accessories Stores	33,627	.08190	107
Highway and Street Construction	7,799	.07664	108
Drugstores	11,213	.07537	109
Building Materials Dealers	45,661	.07456	110
Travel Agents and Tour Operators	44,067	.07321	111
Miscellaneous Food Stores	42,649	.07036	112
Miscellaneous Automotive Dealers	21,305	.06932	113
Commodity Contracts Brokers	9,060	.06625	114
Food and Beverage Production	20,104	.06467	115
Eating Places	146,470	.06222	116
Variety Stores	27,061	.05887	117
Public Warehousing	3,862	.05855	118
Hotels and Motels	30,411	.05711	119
Bookstores	10,338	.05552	120
Women's Ready-to-Wear Clothing	20,019	.05340	121
Paint, Glass, and Wallpaper Stores	1,682	.05219	122
Mobile Home Dealers	5,038	.04789	123
Furniture Stores	20,622	.04475	124
Fuel Oil Dealers	3,573	.04378	125

APPENDIX 3, CONTINUED

THE PROFITABILITY OF SMALL BUSINESSES:
RETURN ON RECEIPTS

Category of Small Business	Number of Businesses	Average Return on Receipts	Rank According to Average Return on Receipts
Sporting Goods and Bicycle Shops	32,607	.04344	126
Grocery Stores	65,192	.04216	127
Liquor Stores	20,012	.04178	128
Household Appliances Stores	9,639	.04056	129
Florists	50,555	.04037	130
Family Clothing	19,325	.03592	131
Nurseries and Garden Supply Stores	13,930	.03359	132
Parking, Except Valet	6,047	.03331	133
Used Merchandise and Antiques Stores	103,373	.03306	134
Computer and Software Stores	10,537	.03285	135
Music and Record Stores	5,359	.03280	136
Hardware Stores	8,945	.03214	137
Drinking Places	33,546	.02896	138
Used Car Dealers	56,845	.02341	139
Hobby, Toy, and Game Shops	25,936	.02291	140
New Car Dealers	14,361	.02284	141
Gasoline Service Stations	37,767	.01907	142
Rooming Houses and Boardinghouses	11,862	.01443	143
Investment Advisers and Services	2,246	.01424	144
Boat Dealers	2,581	.01052	145
Gift, Novelty, and Souvenir Shops	105,035	.00023	146
Videotape Rental	10,403	-.01123	147
Animal Services	72,664	-.01686	148
Catalog or Mail Order	45,355	-.02255	149
Camps and Camping Parks	14,107	-.03363	150
Oil and Gas Extraction	113,034	-.04113	151
Luggage and Leather Goods Stores	1,428	-.18082	152
Livestock Breeding	26,188	-.20669	153

APPENDIX 4

THE PROFITABILITY OF SMALL BUSINESSES:
THE PROPORTION OF PROFITABLE BUSINESSES

Category of Small Business	Number of Businesses	Proportion of Profitable Businesses	Rank According to Proportion of Profitable Businesses
Leather and Leather Products Manufacturing	3,619	100.0000	1.5
Primary Metal Industries	4,005	100.0000	1.5
Paper and Allied Products Manufacturing	1,476	99.7970	3
Surveying Services	15,598	99.7440	4
Camera and Photo Supply Stores	3,197	99.0620	5
Water Transportation	4,700	98.4890	6
Bus and Limousine Transportation	9,777	98.4250	7
Optometrists' Offices	12,810	97.6030	8
Men's and Boys' Clothing	2,417	95.9870	9
Highway Passenger Transportation	21,637	95.6370	10
Fuel Oil Dealers	3,573	94.9620	11
Dentists' Offices	91,998	94.1100	12
Textile Mill Products Manufacturing	5,668	93.8780	13
Funeral Services	9,272	93.7990	14
Painting and Paper Hanging	214,214	93.7880	15
Drugstores	11,213	92.2860	16
Carpentering and Flooring	478,025	90.7980	17
Barbershops	94,308	90.4970	18
Registered and Practical Nurses	114,516	90.3660	19
Shoe Stores	5,875	89.9910	20
Masonry, Dry Wall, Stone, and Tile	190,962	89.8220	21
TV, Audio, and Electronics Stores	16,239	89.0820	22
Taxicabs	98,145	89.0740	23
Lumber and Building Materials Stores	16,066	89.0200	24
Janitorial and Related Services to Buildings	441,082	88.8580	25

APPENDIX 4, CONTINUED

THE PROFITABILITY OF SMALL BUSINESSES:
THE PROPORTION OF PROFITBLE BUSINESSES

Category of Small Business	Number of Businesses	Proportion of Profitable Businesses	Rank According to Proportion of Profitable Businesses
Management Services	111,893	87.7540	26
Physicians' Offices	192,236	87.6120	27
Grocery Stores	65,192	87.5980	28
Ministers and Chaplains	212,939	87.2250	29
Roofing, Siding, and Sheet Metal	102,409	87.1900	30
Liquor Stores	20,012	86.9830	31
Architectural Services	70,786	86.9140	32
Child Day Care	618,457	86.4650	33
Real Estate Property Managers	93,776	86.0850	34
Beauty Shops	449,286	85.9260	35
Other Equipment Repair	263,441	85.6340	36
Machinery Manufacturing, Except Electric	32,967	84.9090	37
Mail, Reproduction, Commercial Art Services	49,724	84.8790	38
General Building Contractor	383,626	84.7940	39
Highway and Street Construction	7,799	84.6260	40
Accounting, Auditing, Bookkeeping Services	393,993	84.6230	41
Miscellaneous Specialty Trade Contractors	485,845	84.3160	42
Chiropractors' Offices	31,285	83.9350	43
Other Cleaning Services	68,121	83.6480	44
Counseling, Except Health Practitioners	75,876	83.1750	45
Medical and Dental Laboratories	19,427	82.9000	46
Other Medical and Health Services	295,462	82.6830	47
Legal Services	318,005	82.5910	48
Family Clothing	19,325	81.8730	49
Horticulture, Gardening, and Landscaping	241,480	81.6010	50

APPENDIX 4, CONTINUED

THE PROFITABILITY OF SMALL BUSINESSES:
THE PROPORTION OF PROFITABLE BUSINESSES

Category of Small Business	Number of Businesses	Proportion of Profitable Businesses	Rank According to Proportion of Profitable Businesses
Plumbing, Heating, and Air-Conditioning	154,779	81.0240	51
Advertising, Except Direct Mail	86,337	80.7540	52
Automotive Rental	17,803	80.2560	53
Parking, Except Valet	6,047	80.0890	54
Electrical Work	119,468	80.0357	55
Jewelry Stores	32,444	79.7528	56
Trucking, Local and Long-Distance	419,433	79.6447	57
Educational Services	292,813	79.3684	58
Furniture Stores	20,622	79.2794	59
Automotive Service, No Repair	168,094	78.8071	60
Electrical Repair	43,663	78.4577	61
Coin-Operated Laundries and Dry Cleaning	15,920	77.7952	62
Home Furnishings and Equipment Stores	49,272	77.4273	63
Commercial Fishing	78,244	77.3465	64
Automotive Repairs	138,276	77.0524	65
Automotive Parts and Accessories Stores	33,627	76.8906	66
Farm Labor and Management Services	42,161	76.8886	67
Printing and Publishing	36,786	76.8472	68
Insurance Agents or Brokers	294,680	76.8186	69
Computer and Data-Processing Services	48,898	76.7127	70
Miscellaneous Personal Services	695,606	76.4853	71
Consulting Services	591,665	76.0369	72
Real Estate Agents and Brokers	686,323	75.7930	73
Courier or Package Delivery	182,092	75.5278	74
Fabricated Metal Products Manufacturing	29,319	75.4630	75

APPENDIX 4, CONTINUED

THE PROFITABILITY OF SMALL BUSINESSES:
THE PROPORTION OF PROFITABLE BUSINESSES

Category of Small Business	Number of Businesses	Proportion of Profitable Businesses	Rank According to Proportion of Profitable Businesses
Podiatrists' Offices	6,296	75.2382	76
Credit Institutions and Mortgage Bankers	27,309	75.1547	77
Air Transportation	11,132	75.0719	78
Catering Services	66,380	74.9443	79
Concrete Work	44,023	74.9381	80
Wholesale Durable Goods	212,735	74.4743	81
Public Warehousing	3,862	74.4174	82
Veterinary Services	20,635	74.3543	83
Other Business Services	1,084,937	73.9024	84
Household Appliances Stores	9,639	73.8977	85
Engineering Services	86,090	73.7472	86
Insurance Services	93,095	73.4798	87
Luggage and Leather Goods Stores	1,428	72.9692	88
Variety Stores	27,061	72.5583	89
Computer and Software Stores	10,537	72.4305	90
Other Transportation Services	55,228	72.1011	91
Camps and Camping Parks	14,107	71.9359	92
Nursing and Personal-Care Facilities	48,026	71.6258	93
Forestry, Except Logging	55,733	71.4334	94
Gasoline Service Stations	37,767	70.8211	95
Building Materials Dealers	45,661	70.7803	96
Electrical Equipment Manufacturing	20,873	70.2726	97
Wholesale Nondurable Goods	163,843	70.2325	98
Mobile Home Dealers	5,038	69.9682	99
Other Manufacturing Industries	92,717	69.1340	100

APPENDIX 4, CONTINUED

THE PROFITABILITY OF SMALL BUSINESSES:
THE PROPORTION OF PROFITABLE BUSINESSES

Category of Small Business	Number of Businesses	Proportion of Profitable Businesses	Rank According to Proportion of Profitable Businesses
Miscellaneous Food Stores	42,649	68.9395	101
Fabric and Needlework Stores	42,023	68.3435	102
Miscellaneous Automotive Dealers	21,305	67.6836	103
Hardware Stores	8,945	67.6803	104
Used Car Dealers	56,845	67.6084	105
Other Amusement and Recreational Services	166,457	67.1182	106
Other Financial Services	151,731	67.0766	107
Brokers and Dealers of Securities	20,838	66.9978	108
Travel Agents and Tour Operators	44,067	65.7499	109
Other Heavy Construction	47,443	65.7273	110
Communications Services	33,637	63.8255	111
Other Apparel and Accessories Stores	41,709	63.7728	112
Eating Places	146,470	63.2123	113
Photographic Studios	91,058	63.1938	114
New Car Dealers	14,361	62.6210	115
Stone, Clay, and Glass Products Manufacturing	21,672	62.1908	116
Hotels and Motels	30,411	61.1719	117
Apparel, Other Textile Products Manufacturing	23,213	61.0649	118
Entertainers, Producers, and Agents	715,506	60.9124	119
Quarrying and Nonmetallic Mineral Mining	4,315	59.6987	120
Subdividers and Developers	14,451	59.6360	121
Motion Picture and Video Production	54,643	59.2830	122
Nurseries and Garden Supply Stores	13,930	59.2032	123
Videotape Rental	10,403	59.1560	124
Furniture and Fixtures Manufacturing	31,772	57.7301	125

APPENDIX 4, CONTINUED

THE PROFITABILITY OF SMALL BUSINESSES:
THE PROPORTION OF PROFITABLE BUSINESSES

Category of Small Business	Number of Businesses	Proportion of Profitable Businesses	Rank According to Proportion of Profitable Businesses
Commodity Contracts Brokers	9,060	56.9978	126
Rooming Houses and Boardinghouses	11,862	55.8085	127
Sporting Goods and Bicycle Shops	32,607	53.8841	128
Operators and Lessors of Buildings	16,372	52.7303	129
Hunting and Trapping	12,578	51.5821	130
Animal Services	72,664	51.2166	131
Professional Sports and Racing	104,807	51.0891	132
Drinking Places	33,546	50.7870	133
Oil and Gas Extraction	113,034	50.4317	134
Florists	50,555	50.0544	135
Equipment Rental	44,061	49.4519	136
Selling Door-to-Door	922,517	49.1484	137
Investment Advisers and Services	2,246	48.8869	138
Music and Record Stores	5,359	47.2476	139
Stationery Stores	7,699	46.7463	140
Lumber and Wood Products Manufacturing	38,416	46.3349	141
Hobby, Toy, and Game Shops	25,936	46.1752	142
Boat Dealers	2,581	46.0674	143
Food and Beverage Production	20,104	45.1403	144
Utilities (Dumps, Snowplowing, Road Cleaning)	7,147	43.7526	145
Used Merchandise and Antiques Stores	103,373	43.7019	146
Gift, Novelty, and Souvenir Shops	105,035	41.2729	147
Women's Ready-to-Wear Clothing	20,019	41.1609	148
Bookstores	10,338	40.4624	149
Vending Machine Selling	45,797	37.2426	150
Livestock Breeding	26,188	25.4888	151
Catalog or Mail Order	45,355	18.4213	152
Paint, Glass, and Wallpaper Stores	1,682	11.4150	153

APPENDIX 5

THE PROFITABILITY OF SMALL BUSINESSES:
NET INCOME FOR BUSINESSES WITH NET INCOME

Category of Small Business	Number of Businesses	Average Net Income ($)	Rank According to Average Net Income
Dentists' Offices	86,579	105,112	1
Physicians' Offices	168,422	90,706	2
Paint, Glass, and Wallpaper Stores	192	88,375	3
Podiatrists' Offices	4,737	64,956	4
Investment Advisers and Services	1,098	62,221	5
Veterinary Services	15,343	61,776	6
Commodity Contracts Brokers	5,164	61,481	7
Brokers and Dealers of Securities	13,961	57,719	8
Chiropractors' Offices	26,259	55,057	9
Legal Services	262,643	49,541	10
Optometrists' Offices	12,503	48,204	11
Stationery Stores	3,599	43,706	12
Subdividers and Developers	8,618	39,673	13
Insurance Agents or Brokers	226,369	37,388	14
Operators and Lessors of Buildings	8,633	32,828	15
Other Financial Services	101,776	31,584	16
Real Estate Agents and Brokers	520,185	31,017	17
Drugstores	10,348	30,675	18
Engineering Services	63,489	30,496	19
Consulting Services	449,884	30,094	20
Lumber and Building Materials Stores	14,302	29,805	21
Boat Dealers	1,189	29,633	22
Machinery Manufacturing, Except Electric	27,992	29,558	23
Medical and Dental Laboratories	16,105	27,635	24
Mobile Home Dealers	3,525	27,169	25

APPENDIX 5, CONTINUED

THE PROFITABILITY OF SMALL BUSINESSES:
NET INCOME FOR BUSINESSES WITH NET INCOME

Category of Small Business	Number of Businesses	Average Net Income ($)	Rank According to Average Net Income
Funeral Services	8,697	26,066	26
Building Materials Dealers	32,319	25,634	27
Bookstores	4,183	25,507	28
Quarrying and Nonmetallic Mineral Mining	2,576	25,333	29
Equipment Rental	21,789	24,895	30
Fabricated Metal Products Manufacturing	22,125	24,888	31
Architectural Services	61,523	24,665	32
Paper and Allied Products Manufacturing	1,473	24,566	33
Hardware Stores	6,054	24,436	34
Electrical Equipment Manufacturing	14,668	24,378	35
Gasoline Service Stations	26,747	23,834	36
Shoe Stores	5,287	23,489	37
Hotels and Motels	18,603	23,451	38
Wholesale Durable Goods	158,433	22,821	39
Real Estate Property Managers	80,727	22,530	40
Utilities (Dumps, Snowplowing, Road Cleaning)	3,127	22,415	41
Furniture and Fixtures Manufacturing	18,342	21,443	42
Eating Places	92,587	21,101	43
Men's and Boys' Clothing	2,320	21,081	44
Miscellaneous Automotive Dealers	14,420	20,802	45
Professional Sports and Racing	53,545	20,286	46
Forestry, Except Logging	39,812	20,062	47
Miscellaneous Food Stores	29,402	19,602	48
Electrical Work	95,617	19,329	49
Fuel Oil Dealers	3,393	18,973	50

APPENDIX 5, CONTINUED

THE PROFITABILITY OF SMALL BUSINESSES:
NET INCOME FOR BUSINESSES WITH NET INCOME

Category of Small Business	Number of Businesses	Average Net Income ($)	Rank According to Average Net Income
Advertising, Except Direct Mail	69,721	18,856	51
Women's Ready-to-Wear Clothing	8,240	18,847	52
Vending Machine Selling	17,056	18,817	53
Automotive Parts and Accessories Stores	25,856	18,687	54
Motion Picture and Video Production	32,394	18,537	55
Printing and Publishing	28,269	18,279	56
Textile Mill Products Manufacturing	5,321	18,103	57
Wholesale Nondurable Goods	115,071	17,874	58
Food and Beverage Production	9,075	17,840	59
TV, Audio, and Electronics Stores	14,466	17,721	60
Lumber and Wood Products Manufacturing	17,800	17,481	61
Concrete Work	32,990	17,310	62
Nurseries and Garden Supply Stores	8,247	17,160	63
Other Medical and Health Services	244,298	17,156	64
Sporting Goods and Bicycle Shops	17,570	17,067	65
Insurance Services	68,406	17,038	66
Surveying Services	15,558	17,034	67
Grocery Stores	57,107	17,025	68
Used Car Dealers	38,432	16,916	69
Other Business Services	801,794	16,770	70
Trucking, Local and Long-Distance	334,056	16,566	71
General Building Contractor	325,292	16,374	72
Photographic Studios	57,543	15,925	73
Drinking Places	17,037	15,873	74
Home Furnishings and Equipment Stores	38,150	15,766	75

APPENDIX 5, CONTINUED

THE PROFITABILITY OF SMALL BUSINESSES:
NET INCOME FOR BUSINESSES WITH NET INCOME

Category of Small Business	Number of Businesses	Average Net Income ($)	Rank According to Average Net Income
Apparel, Other Textile Products Manufacturing	14,175	15,416	76
Jewelry Stores	25,875	15,133	77
Plumbing, Heating, and Air-Conditioning	125,408	14,979	78
Communications Services	21,469	14,698	79
Automotive Repairs	106,545	14,542	80
Luggage and Leather Goods Stores	1,042	14,529	81
Water Transportation	4,629	14,426	82
Furniture Stores	16,349	14,418	83
Other Heavy Construction	31,183	14,409	84
Other Apparel and Accessories Stores	26,599	14,359	85
Credit Institutions and Mortgage Bankers	20,524	14,312	86
Registered and Practical Nurses	103,483	14,310	87
Accounting, Auditing, Bookkeeping Services	333,407	14,194	88
Coin-Operated Laundries and Dry Cleaning	12,385	14,169	89
Other Manufacturing Industries	64,099	14,140	90
Air Transportation	8,357	14,106	91
Highway and Street Construction	6,600	14,013	92
Masonry, Dry Wall, Stone, and Tile	171,525	14,005	93
Carpentering and Flooring	434,037	13,938	94
Catalog or Mail Order	8,355	13,599	95
Other Cleaning Services	56,982	13,549	96
Automotive Service, No Repair	132,470	13,465	97
Roofing, Siding, and Sheet Metal	89,290	13,344	98
Management Services	98,191	13,296	99
Barbershops	85,346	13,172	100

APPENDIX 5, CONTINUED

THE PROFITABILITY OF SMALL BUSINESSES:
NET INCOME FOR BUSINESSES WITH NET INCOME

Category of Small Business	Number of Businesses	Average Net Income ($)	Rank According to Average Net Income
Nursing and Personal-Care Facilities	34,399	13,065	101
Liquor Stores	17,407	12,841	102
Miscellaneous Specialty Trade Contractors	409,644	12,685	103
Variety Stores	19,635	12,641	104
Painting and Paper Hanging	200,907	12,418	105
Camera and Photo Supply Stores	3,167	12,330	106
New Car Dealers	8,993	12,237	107
Entertainers, Producers, and Agents	435,832	12,214	108
Oil and Gas Extraction	57,005	12,142	109
Household Appliances Stores	7,123	12,051	110
Public Warehousing	2,874	11,582	111
Automotive Rental	14,288	11,370	112
Travel Agents and Tour Operators	28,974	11,274	113
Music and Record Stores	2,532	11,185	114
Electrical Repair	34,257	10,841	115
Other Equipment Repair	225,594	10,740	116
Commercial Fishing	60,519	10,719	117
Computer and Data-Processing Services	37,511	10,718	118
Rooming Houses and Boardinghouses	6,620	10,615	119
Counseling, Except Health Practitioners	63,110	10,323	120
Florists	25,305	10,097	121
Animal Services	37,216	10,092	122
Other Transportation Services	39,820	10,075	123
Beauty Shops	386,053	9,675	124
Farm Labor and Management Services	32,417	9,430	125

APPENDIX 5, CONTINUED

THE PROFITABILITY OF SMALL BUSINESSES:
NET INCOME FOR BUSINESSES WITH NET INCOME

Category of Small Business	Number of Businesses	Average Net Income ($)	Rank According to Average Net Income
Bus and Limousine Transportation	9,623	9,391	126
Hunting and Trapping	6,488	9,235	127
Videotape Rental	6,154	9,036	128
Horticulture, Gardening, and Landscaping	197,051	9,021	129
Livestock Breeding	6,675	8,835	130
Used Merchandise and Antiques Stores	45,176	8,422	131
Family Clothing	15,822	8,340	132
Computer and Software Stores	7,632	8,237	133
Ministers and Chaplains	185,737	8,049	134
Camps and Camping Parks	10,148	7,929	135
Fabric and Needlework Stores	28,720	7,858	136
Taxicabs	87,422	7,710	137
Miscellaneous Personal Services	532,036	7,469	138
Selling Door-to-Door	453,402	7,369	139
Gift, Novelty, and Souvenir Shops	43,351	7,256	140
Stone, Clay, and Glass Products Manufacturing	13,478	7,240	141
Hobby, Toy, and Game Shops	11,976	7,207	142
Janitorial and Related Services to Buildings	391,938	7,013	143
Highway Passenger Transportation	20,693	6,998	144
Other Amusement and Recreational Services	111,723	6,877	145
Catering Services	49,748	6,855	146
Leather and Leather Products Manufacturing	3,619	6,855	147
Mail, Reproduction, Commercial Art Services	42,205	6,639	148
Educational Services	232,401	6,591	149
Courier or Package Delivery	137,530	6,337	150
Child Day Care	534,746	5,199	151
Parking, Except Valet	4,843	2,454	152
Primary Metal Industries	4,005	2,188	153

APPENDIX 6

THE PROFITABILITY OF SMALL BUSINESSES:
RETURN ON RECEIPTS FOR BUSINESSES WITH NET INCOME

Category of Small Business	Number of Businesses	Average Return on Receipts	Rank According to Average Return on Receipts
Management Services	98,191	.64161	1
Consulting Services	449,884	.62536	2
Ministers and Chaplains	185,737	.59785	3
Counseling, Except Health Practitioners	63,110	.57790	4
Physicians' Offices	168,422	.57595	5
Other Medical and Health Services	244,298	.54192	6
Registered and Practical Nurses	103,483	.54117	7
Entertainers, Producers, and Agents	435,832	.53156	8
Insurance Services	68,406	.52664	9
Real Estate Agents and Brokers	520,185	.51766	10
Hunting and Trapping	6,488	.49321	11
Legal Services	262,643	.48941	12
Engineering Services	63,489	.48733	13
Insurance Agents or Brokers	226,369	.48141	14
Educational Services	232,401	.47844	15
Mail, Reproduction, Commercial Art Services	42,205	.47590	16
Air Transportation	8,357	.47565	17
Accounting, Auditing, Bookkeeping Services	333,407	.47176	18
Real Estate Property Managers	80,727	.45820	19
Child Day Care	534,746	.45610	20
Professional Sports and Racing	53,545	.43319	21
Motion Picture and Video Production	32,394	.42814	22
Operators and Lessors of Buildings	8,633	.42703	23
Utilities (Dumps, Snowplowing, Road Cleaning)	3,127	.42674	24
Other Business Services	801,794	.41852	25

APPENDIX 6, CONTINUED

THE PROFITABILITY OF SMALL BUSINESSES:
RETURN ON RECEIPTS FOR BUSINESSES WITH NET INCOME

Category of Small Business	Number of Businesses	Average Return on Receipts	Rank According to Average Return on Receipts
Medical and Dental Laboratories	16,105	.41619	26
Barbershops	85,346	.39859	27
Janitorial and Related Services to Buildings	391,938	.39771	28
Miscellaneous Personal Services	532,036	.39005	29
Chiropractors' Offices	26,259	.38962	30
Dentists' Offices	86,579	.38110	31
Beauty Shops	386,053	.37681	32
Surveying Services	15,558	.36959	33
Podiatrists' Offices	4,737	.36676	34
Painting and Paper Hanging	200,907	.35396	35
Commercial Fishing	60,519	.35165	36
Computer and Data-Processing Services	37,511	.33016	37
Subdividers and Developers	8,618	.32381	38
Advertising, Except Direct Mail	69,721	.32148	39
Communications Services	21,469	.31759	40
Primary Metal Industries	4,005	.31565	41
Taxicabs	87,422	.31407	42
Photographic Studios	57,543	.30403	43
Carpentering and Flooring	434,037	.30209	44
Courier or Package Delivery	137,530	.29734	45
Equipment Rental	21,789	.29672	46
Architectural Services	61,523	.29582	47
Electrical Equipment Manufacturing	14,668	.29326	48
Selling Door-to-Door	453,402	.28514	49
Camps and Camping Parks	10,148	.28445	50

APPENDIX 6, CONTINUED

THE PROFITABILITY OF SMALL BUSINESSES:
RETURN ON RECEIPTS FOR BUSINESSES WITH NET INCOME

Category of Small Business	Number of Businesses	Average Return on Receipts	Rank According to Average Return on Receipts
Electrical Work	95,617	.28279	51
Textile Mill Products Manufacturing	5,321	.27504	52
Other Equipment Repair	225,594	.27494	53
Veterinary Services	15,343	.27169	54
Coin-Operated Laundries and Dry Cleaning	12,385	.26737	55
Optometrists' Offices	12,503	.26496	56
Fabric and Needlework Stores	28,720	.25544	57
Catering Services	49,748	.25470	58
Nursing and Personal-Care Facilities	34,399	.24503	59
Electrical Repair	34,257	.24149	60
Oil and Gas Extraction	57,005	.23667	61
Other Transportation Services	39,820	.22969	62
Bus and Limousine Transportation	9,623	.22562	63
Machinery Manufacturing, Except Electric	27,992	.22277	64
Miscellaneous Specialty Trade Contractors	409,644	.22117	65
Horticulture, Gardening, and Landscaping	197,051	.22089	66
Other Amusement and Recreational Services	111,723	.22042	67
Highway Passenger Transportation	20,693	.21113	68
Funeral Services	8,697	.20992	69
Leather and Leather Products Manufacturing	3,619	.20615	70
Livestock Breeding	6,675	.20308	71
Other Cleaning Services	56,982	.20226	72
Masonry, Dry Wall, Stone, and Tile	171,525	.20216	73
Trucking, Local and Long-Distance	334,056	.19686	74
Men's and Boys' Clothing	2,320	.19652	75

APPENDIX 6, CONTINUED

THE PROFITABILITY OF SMALL BUSINESSES:
RETURN ON RECEIPTS FOR BUSINESSES WITH NET INCOME

Category of Small Business	Number of Businesses	Average Return on Receipts	Rank According to Average Return on Receipts
Water Transportation	4,629	.19357	76
Other Manufacturing Industries	64,099	.19224	77
Fabricated Metal Products Manufacturing	22,125	.19070	78
Automotive Rental	14,288	.18735	79
Roofing, Siding, and Sheet Metal	89,290	.18610	80
Stone, Clay, and Glass Products Manufacturing	13,478	.18506	81
Commodity Contracts Brokers	5,164	.18462	82
Vending Machine Selling	17,056	.18382	83
Other Financial Services	101,776	.18234	84
Wholesale Durable Goods	158,433	.18016	85
TV, Audio, and Electronics Stores	14,466	.17839	86
Plumbing, Heating, and Air-Conditioning	125,408	.17584	87
Credit Institutions and Mortgage Bankers	20,524	.17566	88
Automotive Service, No Repair	132,470	.17506	89
Home Furnishings and Equipment Stores	38,150	.17366	90
Brokers and Dealers of Securities	13,961	.17176	91
Lumber and Building Materials Stores	14,302	.17071	92
Rooming Houses and Boardinghouses	6,620	.17046	93
Animal Services	37,216	.17045	94
Hotels and Motels	18,603	.17042	95
Printing and Publishing	28,269	.16847	96
Furniture and Fixtures Manufacturing	18,342	.16836	97
Bookstores	4,183	.16181	98
Investment Advisers and Services	1,098	.15789	99
Automotive Repairs	106,545	.15629	100

APPENDIX 6, CONTINUED

THE PROFITABILITY OF SMALL BUSINESSES:
RETURN ON RECEIPTS FOR BUSINESSES WITH NET INCOME

Category of Small Business	Number of Businesses	Average Return on Receipts	Rank According to Average Return on Receipts
Other Heavy Construction	31,183	.14946	101
Concrete Work	32,990	.14878	102
General Building Contractor	325,292	.14814	103
Public Warehousing	2,874	.14741	104
Other Apparel and Accessories Stores	26,599	.14739	105
Lumber and Wood Products Manufacturing	17,800	.14717	106
Quarrying and Nonmetallic Mineral Mining	2,576	.14511	107
Camera and Photo Supply Stores	3,167	.14267	108
Stationery Stores	3,599	.14156	109
Drinking Places	17,037	.14002	110
Wholesale Nondurable Goods	115,071	.13833	111
Farm Labor and Management Services	32,417	.13749	112
Used Merchandise and Antiques Stores	45,176	.13397	113
Forestry, Except Logging	39,812	.13327	114
Catalog or Mail Order	8,355	.12827	115
Apparel, Other Textile Products Manufacturing	14,175	.12292	116
Food and Beverage Production	9,075	.11964	117
Gift, Novelty, and Souvenir Shops	43,351	.11869	118
Building Materials Dealers	32,319	.11739	119
Women's Ready-to-Wear Clothing	8,240	.11540	120
Shoe Stores	5,287	.11277	121
Jewelry Stores	25,875	.11087	122
Travel Agents and Tour Operators	28,974	.11069	123
Parking, Except Valet	4,843	.10861	124
Automotive Parts and Accessories Stores	25,856	.10614	125

APPENDIX 6, CONTINUED

THE PROFITABILITY OF SMALL BUSINESSES:
RETURN ON RECEIPTS FOR BUSINESSES WITH NET INCOME

Category of Small Business	Number of Businesses	Average Return on Receipts	Rank According to Average Return on Receipts
Florists	25,305	.10440	126
Miscellaneous Automotive Dealers	14,420	.10271	127
Miscellaneous Food Stores	29,402	.09966	128
Hardware Stores	6,054	.09943	129
Hobby, Toy, and Game Shops	11,976	.09852	130
Eating Places	92,587	.09839	131
Nurseries and Garden Supply Stores	8,247	.09728	132
Luggage and Leather Goods Stores	1,042	.09529	133
Highway and Street Construction	6,600	.09329	134
Music and Record Stores	2,532	.09141	135
Variety Stores	19,635	.09028	136
Drugstores	10,348	.08823	137
Family Clothing	15,822	.08535	138
Sporting Goods and Bicycle Shops	17,570	.08388	139
Paper and Allied Products Manufacturing	1,473	.08381	140
Furniture Stores	16,349	.07909	141
Videotape Rental	6,154	.07908	142
Computer and Software Stores	7,632	.07806	143
Paint, Glass, and Wallpaper Stores	192	.07403	144
Household Appliances Stores	7,123	.07392	145
Mobile Home Dealers	3,525	.06897	146
Boat Dealers	1,189	.05866	147
Grocery Stores	57,107	.05226	148
Liquor Stores	17,407	.05161	149
Fuel Oil Dealers	3,393	.05113	150
Used Car Dealers	38,432	.05062	151
New Car Dealers	8,993	.04942	152
Gasoline Service Stations	26,747	.03146	153

AUTHOR'S NOTE

In the course of my research I have met and interviewed many fascinating people who personify "The Millionaire Next Door" and "Millionaire Women Next Door," and define "The Millionaire Mind." Some of their stories are told in my books and journal articles. Hopefully, they enlighten and inspire readers who wish to increase their economic productivity and achieve millionaire status. If you have a story to tell or advice to share, perhaps for inclusion in one of my future books, please write to me at the address below.

Dr. Thomas J. Stanley
Wealthworks, Inc.
P.O. Box 680203
Marietta, GA 30068-0004

INDEX